Kerouac's Crooked Road

Kerouac's Crooked Road

Development of a Fiction

TIM HUNT

1981
Archon Books

Library of Congress Cataloging in Publication Data

Hunt, Tim, 1949–
  Kerouac's crooked road.

  Bibliography: p.
  Includes index.
  1. Kerouac, John, 1922–1969. On the road. I. Title.
PS3521.E7350534   813'.54   80-26271
ISBN 0-208-01871-9

© Tim Hunt 1981

First published 1981 as an Archon Book,
an imprint of The Shoe String Press, Inc.,
Hamden, Connecticut 06514

To John Clellon Holmes
it is fitting that the "Great Rememberer"
should have had this great friend

True and sincere traveling is no pastime, but it is as serious
as the grave, or any part of the human journey, and it requires
a long probation to be broken into it. I do not speak of those
that travel sitting, the sedentary travellers whose legs hang
dangling the while, mere idle symbols of the fact, any more
than when we speak of sitting hens we mean those that sit
standing, but I mean those to whom travelling is life for the
legs, and death too, at last. The traveller must be born again on
the road. . . .

Henry David Thoreau, in "Thursday,"
A Week on the Concord & Merrimac

It is much easier to find fault with a writer by reference to
former notions and experience than to sit down and read him,
recollecting his purpose, connecting one feeling with another,
and judging of his words and phrases . . . .

S. T. Coleridge, "Lecture IX," in
Shakespearean Criticism, vol. 1

Table of Contents

Acknowledgments

As the dedication suggests, I owe a great debt to John Clellon Holmes. He graciously allowed me to study his correspondence with Kerouac and was more than generous with his encouragement and advice. Kerouac was indeed fortunate to have such a friend, and I hope that someday soon John's own work, the novels published and those to come, attract the wider readership it deserves.

I would also like to thank Professors Jonathan Bishop and R. H. Elias of Cornell University for being tolerant when tolerance was needed and demanding when that was needed, and Professor Edward Lueders of the University of Utah for being the senior colleague that every junior member hopes to find when he attempts to assume a place in the academy. I am grateful to these gentlemen for putting preconception aside and believing in the worth of this project and my own eventual competence to complete it.

Finally, I would like to note the more usual but equally critical debts incurred in a project of this sort. David Farmer and the Humanities Research Center of the University of Texas, Mr. Kenneth Lohf of the Baker Library of Columbia University, Mr. Elbert Lenrow, and Mr. Allen Ginsberg kindly allowed me access to material for this study. My wife Merrill did her best with the language of each draft and with my recalcitrance. The study is surely more readable for her efforts, and she above all should not be blamed for the faults that remain. I would also like to thank Bud Bynack of the University of California, Berkeley. His suggestions for restructuring the study were thoughtful and most welcome. I hope this final version meets with his approval. I was also fortunate to have the encouragement and advice of Don Bialostosky of the University of Washington. His help with an early draft came at the time help was most needed. Finally, I would like to note that my research for this study was aided by two travel grants, one from the Graduate School of Cornell University and the other from the faculty research fund of the University of Utah.

A Note on Texts and Sources

The material used to prepare this study is delineated clearly in the text and notes, but a few matters deserve further comment. The manuscripts of the various *On the Roads* are held by the Kerouac estate and were not available to me. My construction of the development of *On the Road* is based on Kerouac's correspondence and his 1948–49 work journal. These materials contain excerpts of the book and extended descriptions of its various phases. These materials have been supplemented by the recollections of John Clellon Holmes. Through the period that Kerouac was working on *On the Road*, Holmes was probably closer to Kerouac's work than anyone else. Both he and Kerouac were young novelists trying to find their voice and to establish themselves, and they often discussed and examined each other's work.

There is, at the least, some difference in emphasis between myself and Kerouac's biographers about the relationship between the published *On the Road* and *Visions of Cody*. I think it is quite clear that *Visions of Cody* was originally titled *On the Road*, that it was written after what is now published as *On the Road*, and that *Visions of Cody* was meant to replace *On the Road*. Readers must judge for themselves, of course, but those who would like to examine the textual history of *On the Road* and *Visions of Cody* might look at my dissertation, "Off the Road: Jack Kerouac's Literary Maturation," submitted to Cornell University for my doctorate in 1975. It is available from University Microfilms. Unfortunately, the whole matter cannot be presented as fully and precisely as one would like. The Kerouac estate refuses either to allow anyone access to Kerouac's papers or to allow anyone to quote from the large body of material held in library research collections. Kerouac's reputation as a serious and accomplished writer can only be enhanced when this material is finally available. In the interim, I have done my best to characterize and paraphrase the material that is available as accurately as possible.

Finally, I would like to point out that what criticism there is of Kerouac's work is collected and readily available in two volumes: Scott Donaldson's critical edition of *On the Road* published by The Viking Press in 1979; and Thomas Parkinson's anthology, *A Casebook on the Beat*, published by Thomas Y. Crowell Company in 1961. One essay of note, though, is not available in either of these volumes. George Dardess's "The Logic of Spontaneity: A Reconsideration of Kerouac's Spontaneous Prose Method," *Boundary 2* 3 (1975), was written after Parkinson's volume and falls outside the scope of Donaldson's edition. Parts of my discussion of Spontaneous Prose are parallel to Dardess's. The basic points of my discussion were developed in my doctoral dissertation which predates Dardess's essay, though it was not available to him just as his piece was not available to me at that time. In writing the chapter on *Visions of Cody* for this study, I found it simpler to develop my reading from my own terms rather than to recast that segment of it in Dardess's terms. Readers interested in the implications of

Kerouac's style and method will want to refer to Dardess's piece as well as to Warren Tallman's "Kerouac's Sound," which appears in both the critical *On the Road* and *A Casebook on the Beat*.

Introduction

Jack Kerouac is hardly a neglected writer. His novels are in print. There are now three biographies. One can find rock song odes to "Kerouac," and Hollywood will soon issue its first portrayal. But what all this interest points to is Kerouac's ambiguous status. Were Kerouac a truly popular writer, there would be no film and no songs. The readers of a best-selling writer like Arthur Hailey do not care to know the details of his personal life. Were Kerouac actually taken seriously as a writer, there would be some kind of serious discussion of Kerouac's writing instead of all this interest in the athlete-hobo-artist. As things stand now, the criticism one can find typically treats Kerouac only symptomatically by looking at his work as an example of one social trend or another. There is no denying that Kerouac was a colorful and compelling individual, but as John Clellon Holmes, novelist and friend of Kerouac, asserts, the fascination with Kerouac the figure has left Kerouac "heir" to the same "neglect" that once befell Melville as a "'writer of boys' sea stories!'" and Whitman as the "author of 'O Captain, My

Captain.'"[1] The public infatuation with Kerouac has yet to subside enough for us to reach the situation we now have with F. Scott Fitzgerald where some are free to enjoy Fitzgerald's rather unfortunate life and others to consider the work. It may be true that the cult of Fitzgerald would have died out were he not also a good writer, but the works would still be read had Fitzgerald led the dullest of lives and survived to ninety.

This study, then, begins from the premise that Kerouac's writing is neglected even though he himself is not, and it attempts to look carefully at two key texts: *On the Road*, the basis of whatever reputation Kerouac currently has, and *Visions of Cody*, which I take to be the ultimate basis of Kerouac's claims as a writer. Several matters complicate a study of these two works. First, *On the Road* is a book that almost everyone assumes they know whether they have read it or not. The controversy over it and the so-called Beat Generation in 1957 and the year or two following fixed the image of Kerouac as a kind of literary James Dean and fixed most readers' attitudes toward the book as well. Typically *On the Road* is seen as naive autobiography, controversial best-seller of little merit, or as "inspired" testament, a harbinger of a new confessional literature free of past constraints on form and subject matter.[2] These three approaches actually share a similar sense of the novel. They begin from the story that the book was the product of only three weeks of impetuous work in the spring of 1951 and see this as proof of the book's transparency. Those who view *On the Road* as naive autobiography identify Kerouac with the narrator Sal Paradise, conclude that the book reports events without reflection, and reduce it to the mores of a particular bohemia. The second group deals with the book as a pop culture artifact. Oddly, the third group also treats *On the Road* as subliterary. By elevating the book to the status of testament for a new generation, these readers in effect claim that the book is a product of a communal consciousness and insist that the book advocates a way of life. All three senses of the book rule out the possibility that Kerouac might have been dealing with his material critically or in a spirit of literary exploration. These views must simply be ignored. A significant study could be done of the reasons for the distortions of *On the Road* by its proponents and opponents, but that would deflect attention from the text itself which is a much more conventional, skillful, and literarily significant work than is commonly assumed.

On the Road complicates a fresh reading of Kerouac in another way as well. The book is widely assumed to be Kerouac's best piece of work and his most representative, but this is not the case. *On the Road* does reflect concerns that were part of Kerouac's writing throughout his life, but it was written before Kerouac had established either the voice or approach to structure that characterizes most of his work and certainly all of his best work. *On the Road*, in spite of its very substantial achievement, is Kerouac's last apprentice work. *Visions of Cody* is his first mature text and the paradigmatic text for his career. The status of *Visions of Cody* is indicated by the manuscript history of *On the Road*. From 1948 to 1952, Kerouac worked on his Road book. In that time, the book went through five primary versions. What was published in 1957 by Viking Press as *On the Road* was the fourth version. *Visions of Cody* was the fifth and final version of *On the Road* and the book that Kerouac always maintained was his masterpiece even though it would not be published in its entirety until after his death.

To date, Kerouac's biographers and critics have not wanted to credit either *On the Road*'s conventional nature or *Visions of Cody*'s centrality. But the dimension of Kerouac's achievement and the nature of it will remain obscured until these two works are understood more clearly on their own terms and in relation to each other. It is as if, to extend Holmes's comment, we insisted on passing over *Moby-Dick* to pay homage to *Typee*. Whether or not linking

Kerouac to Melville is entirely justified. Melville's true relevance for the 1850s goes beyond the temporary fascination with the man who lived with the cannibals, and Kerouac's true relevance for the 1950s goes beyond the contemporary fascination for the man who found himself labeled "King of the Beatniks." Critics and literary historians have by and large not noticed what Kerouac's fellow writers, particularly poets such as Robert Creeley and Robert Duncan, have been aware of for years: that is, that Kerouac's work in books like *Visions of Cody, Doctor Sax,* and *Desolation Angels* is of a piece with the vital experiments in the American arts in the years 1945–55. Hopefully, the time has come when Kerouac's writing can be approached as part of the general interest in those years in composition by "field," as a prose equivalent to Action Painting and Projective Verse.

Chapter One
An American Education

In spite of its reputation, *On the Road* is best understood as
a skillfully managed traditional novel. Both the manuscript
history and the text itself make it clear that Kerouac's most
famous book is a good deal more challenging and intricate,
if less innovative, than has been generally believed. Even
though the particular version that led to *On the Road* as
published was drafted in about three weeks of typing onto a
continuous roll of paper, at that point Kerouac had been
working on versions of the book for two and a half years,
and he viewed the work that has become known as the
"scroll" as an experiment to discover the direction his book
should take. He hoped that drafting a version at high speed
would enable him to clarify his feelings about his materials
so that he could proceed to a final version of the novel.
Kerouac spent months revising and reworking the results of
his experiment. By the time *On the Road* was finally
published in 1957, he had reworked the book several more
times, as well.

Kerouac's later claims that he did not revise are not accurate reflections of his practice or even his theory. He revised carefully both *On the Road* and most of the novels that followed it. In a letter to Allen Ginsberg in May 1952, Kerouac talks about *Visions of Cody*, the text that follows what is now *On the Road*, and complains that, even though he is sure the book is a major achievement, he may be forced to dare a publisher to issue it. Kerouac seemingly then contradicts himself. He first insists that he will not allow anyone to edit the book and then talks about how hard he has been laboring with his revisions of the book.[1] It is clear from this letter that what Kerouac opposes is having others cut material out of his manuscript. He is not opposed to craft with language. Even Kerouac's "Essentials of Spontaneous Prose," published in 1958 and a primary source for the notion that Kerouac refused to revise, indicates that his primary concern was that the conscious critical mind might censor the richness of the imagination. Kerouac insisted on the writer's obligation to explore the entire range of experience whether currently fashionable or not. At least when he wrote *On the Road* and *Visions of Cody*, Kerouac saw no contradiction in refusing an editor the right to cut material from the novel and his own "slaving over revisions" prior to submission.

On the Road's traditional nature is also suggested by its relationship to *Visions of Cody*. In letters in 1952 and his introductory note to *Excerpts from Visions of Cody* in 1960, Kerouac characterized the structure of *On the Road* as "horizontal" and *Visions of Cody* as "vertical."[2] For Kerouac, vertical structure or "wild form" derives from the experimental impulse of sketching codified in "Essentials of Spontaneous Prose." Horizontal structure is his term for the more traditional approach that organizes a novel by means of plot. Until Kerouac had completed what is now *On the Road*, he blamed his dissatisfactions with his work on his failure to use the resources of fiction skillfully enough. Only after he had attained the degree of mastery evident in *On the Road* could he decide that his material and concerns required him to dispense with fictional conventions as he understood them.

Kerouac's reputation has certainly encouraged readers to deal with *On the Road* superficially, but it is also important to recognize that some aspects of the novel are temptingly easy to oversimplify. The book's narrator, Sal Paradise, is seemingly too enthusiastic and naive. The four transcontinental trips that make up the book's action seem to blur together. And the book's echoing of earlier American texts seems accidental or reductive. A careful examination of *On the Road*, though, shows that Kerouac deliberately exploits the naiveté of his narrator, organizes the four trips as distinct stages in the narrator's growth, and carefully borrows classic American motifs to measure the novel's incidents and characters.

As a narrator, Sal Paradise is alternately self-conscious about his reader and oblivious to him. He oscillates between enthusiasm and despair in a way that has contributed to the general impression of his shallowness.

> I first met Dean not long after my wife and I split up. I had just gotten over a serious illness that I won't bother to talk about, except that it had something to do with the miserably weary split-up and my feeling that everything was dead. With the coming of Dean Moriarity began that part of my life you could call my life on the road. Before that I'd often dreamed of going West to see the country, always vaguely planning and never taking off. Dean is the perfect guy for the road because he actually was born on the road, when his parents were passing through Salt Lake City in 1926, in a jalopy, on their way to Los Angeles.[3]

In this, the book's opening passage, Sal goes out of his way to bring his illness up and then withholds the details. When he talks about himself, Sal is diffident and awkward but, when he deals with Dean, Sal's enthusiasm sweeps all else before it. He describes Dean as

bobbing his head . . . like a young boxer to instructions . . . throwing a thousand "Yesses" and "That's rights" . . . thin-hipped, blue-eyed with a real Oklahoma accent—a sideburned hero of the snowy West. (OR, 4–5)

This passage is as fluid and direct as the other is stacatto and self-conscious. Participles kick the details ahead, and, when credibility strains at Sal's extreme attention to detail, the banal "Oklahoma accent," the meaningless "real," and the inflated "hero of the snowy West" reestablish the impression of an artless speaker.

Earlier versions of *On the Road* demonstrate Kerouac's interest in narrators whose naiveté has thematic purposes. In his notes for the second version, the character Smitty who will be the hero's "Boswell" is to be too saintly for this world, and Kerouac likens him to Pip and Sancho Panza. In the third version, *Pic*, the full name of the narrator and hero, Pictorial Review, suggests his childlike directness, and in *On the Road* as in *Pic*, Sal's full name, Salvatore Paradise, calls attention to a Candide-like nature. Sal overlooks whatever might threaten his faith that the world will willingly conform to his wants. At one point in the book, Sal's willful blindness makes him and his name the butt of another character's joke. When Sal arrives in New Orleans to visit his mentor Bull Lee, Lee's wife Jane asks Sal,

"Isn't that a fire or something over there?"
We both looked toward the sun.
"You mean the sun?"
"Of course I don't mean the sun—I heard sirens that way. Don't you know a peculiar glow?" It was toward

New Orleans; the clouds were strange.
"I don't see anything," I said.
Jane snuffed down her nose. "Same old Paradise."
(OR, 142)

Jane Lee's notion that Sal often fails to see what is going on reveals the danger of relying too heavily on his representation of what takes place in the novel. It also suggests the danger of assuming too simple an identity between Kerouac and his narrator.

If Sal and Kerouac are interchangeable, as some have claimed, Kerouac is at least aware of and mocking certain limitations in his way of seeing the world. Kerouac's letters and journal make clear that he adapts his experiences to serve his thematic ends. He omits or modifies events that would undercut the reader's impression of Sal's naiveté. In fictionalizing his relationship with Cassady's first wife, Kerouac avoids talking about his affair with her in New York in order to maintain the contrast between Dean's sexual aggressiveness and Sal's courtly, bumbling shyness. The principle behind Kerouac's adaptation of his personality and experiences is indicated by a quotation from Henry Murray's edition of Melville's *Pierre*. In March 1951, just before drafting *On the Road*, Kerouac read Murray's introduction and underlined "Melville was not writing autobiography in the usual sense, but, from first to last, the biography of his self-image."[4] Kerouac also is writing a "biography of his self-image." Autobiography in the "usual sense" is unreflexive and anecdotal. This is certainly what is meant when *On the Road* is criticized as being superficially autobiographical. But biography is reflexive and interpretive. Details of the life are selected and arranged according to some principle of illustration. In *On the Road*, Sal is certainly an image of Kerouac but an image which Kerouac uses to measure his own growth and to explore his interaction with his cultural heritage.

5

Significantly, Kerouac makes Sal aware of his limited understanding of what takes place in the novel. By distinguishing between the time of the book's action and the time of its telling, Kerouac distinguishes between Sal the character who never sees anything and Sal the narrator who is aware of his earlier naiveté.

> First reports of [Dean] came to me through Chad King, who'd shown me a few letters from him written in a New Mexico reform school. I was tremendously interested in the letters because they so naively and sweetly asked Chad to teach him all about Nietzsche and all the wonderful intellectual things that Chad knew. At one point Carlo and I talked about the letters and wondered if we would ever meet the strange Dean Moriarity. This is all far back, when Dean was not the way he is today, when he was a young jailkid shrouded in mystery. (OR, 3–4)

For the earlier Sal who participates in the novel's action, there *is* something sweet and naive in the "young jailkid" which is matched by Sal's own initial naiveté. Yet the Sal who narrates is no longer so naive. He is thinking back and knows that he and Dean have both changed. Carol Gottlieb Vopat in her essay "Jack Kerouac's *On the Road:* A Reevaluation" was perhaps the first to note Sal's doubleness.

> Kerouac equips his narrator with a double vision, enabling Sal to comment on the people and events of the novel as he saw them when they happened, and as he views them now that they are over, a sadder-but-wiser hindsight which acts as a check upon his naive, undiscriminating exuberances. . . .[5]

Vopat is right that Sal's "hindsight" undercuts his earlier "exuberances," but she fails to recognize that Kerouac and

his narrator, though wary of Sal's earlier foolishness, are unwilling to dismiss it for fear that that might mean dismissing
the vitality that went with it.

It is, in fact, the tension between the competing claims of
"hindsight" and "exuberances" that controls *On the Road.*
Kerouac is careful to point out Sal's "hindsight," and it
often reveals Sal's initial lack of understanding. But Sal also
recognizes in his earlier self a positive sense of "mystery," an
engagement with things, that he has lost and would like to
recover. Sal is willing to recognize his earlier limitations but
avoids condeming them in order not to dismiss the positive
along with the negative. Sal's ambivalent tolerance of his
earlier self can be seen in his description of his two days of
"Frisco kicks" with Dean before the two are to leave for
New York. A former poolroom buddy of Dean's, Roy
Johnson, has been elected chauffeur.

> Roy was now living in Frisco, working as a clerk and
> married to a pretty little blonde called Dorothy. Dean
> confided that her nose was too long—this was his big
> point of contention about her, for some strange reason
> —but her nose wasn't too long after all. (OR, 191)

Dorothy Johnson resents her husband's loyalty to Dean, and
Dean figuratively expresses his annoyance at her meddling.
Sal, though, is absurdly literal about the whole affair and
insists on missing the point. The effect is similar to Twain's
use of Huck's dogged literalness for satiric effect in scenes
like the "House Beautiful." Twain manages to suggest a
critical perspective beyond Huck's understanding, while at
the same time savoring Huck's delight in the sensual details
of the physical world. Twain through Huck evokes simultaneously the pretensions of a family that keeps a clock that
chimes with no relationship to time and the immediacy of a
child's delight in the chiming. Like Twain, Kerouac wants
to imply the limitations of the character's view without

being forced to dismiss the immediacy of that view. Kerouac wants to be able to express the value in feeling wonder at a "young jailkid," the value in seeing freshly, if imperfectly, from a perspective that temporarily precedes society's categories, without being trapped by the limitations of that wonder.

The example of Huck does not by itself explain the way Sal functions in the book. The "hindsight" that Vopat notes, though it still allows for effects similar to Twain's, is itself quite different from what is found in *Huck Finn*. In *On the Road*, it is necessary to deal not only with Kerouac's strategies for revealing Sal, but also with Sal's strategies for revealing his earlier self. This situation is reminiscent of *The Great Gatsby*, where it is necessary to consider both Fitzgerald's sense of his narrator Nick Carraway and Nick's hindsight of his earlier self. There is no way of knowing whether Kerouac drew on Fitzgerald's classic, but the parallels between it and *On the Road* are useful, and Kerouac was familiar with the book. Holmes recalls that *The Great Gatsby* experienced "a second revival" in early 1951 and circulated among the writers of his and Kerouac's set. Kerouac, in fact, seems to have known *The Great Gatsby* as early as 1948. In the last section of *The Town and the City*, Kerouac describes a peeling advertisement across the back of the building that overlooks the basement apartment of the hero's family. The advertisement, for a headache remedy whose name is now obscured, portrays a man holding his head in "despair." Kerouac develops the advertisement as an emblem for the red brick world of the inner city into which the hero's family has been forced by the social upheavals of World War II. Kerouac uses the emblem to preside over the death of the hero's father in much the same way that the eyeless glasses of Dr. T. J. Eckleburg's billboard preside over the valley of ashes and the blindness of the characters in *The Great Gatsby*. There are also touches that suggest *The Great Gatsby* in *Visions of Cody*.

8

In that book, Kerouac attributes to the adolescent Cody Pomeray a regimen of study similar to the one that Jay Gatz had copied onto the flyleaf of a Hopalong Cassidy novel. Also, the name Cody itself recalls not only Buffalo Bill Cody, the prototypical pop western figure, but also Dan Cody, the nouveau riche westerner who befriends Gatsby.

Both *On the Road* and *The Great Gatsby* are dominated by heroes whose story is presented by a middle-class and college-educated narrator who seems relatively objective but also rather bland. Most readers could describe either Jay Gatsby or Dean Moriarity in detail. They are self-made men of tremendous magnetism who seem almost mythically American. At the same time, though, most readers could find little to say about Nick and Sal even though the first third of each book deals almost exclusively with their actions and not those of the two heroes. In each book, the narrator is initiated into a realm of experience that he has previously managed to ignore. The cautious Nick must recognize and finally acknowledge the "corrupt" Gatsby whose "incorruptible dream" in some sense redeems him and reveals to Nick his own callowness. Likewise, the optimistic Sal must eventually claim the seemingly inexhaustible Moriarity as a brother, and, in doing so, experience Moriarity's "burdensome" extremes of ecstasy and despair and recognize his own shallowness.

With *The Great Gatsby*, the disparity between the seeming centrality of Gatsby and the actual centrality of Nick has led to the recognition that the book is primarily about Nick's attempt to understand the implications of Gatsby and the implications of a society that could produce a Gatsby. Nick does not present Gatsby's story; rather, he meditates on it and undergoes through that meditation the dramatic development that Gatsby (as distinct from Gatz) cannot undergo without losing his mythic status. In this sense, *The Great Gatsby* is a novel of education centered on Nick's growth as he studies his past. In this same sense, *On the*

Road is a novel of education but with an important difference that clarifies the limitations of Vopat's observation about Sal's "sadder-but-wiser hindsight." In *The Great Gatsby*, Nick's growth is almost entirely after the fact, after the novel's action has run its course. As a character in the action, he is static. As a narrator, he is dynamic. Sal is dynamic as both a character and a narrator, and, in effect, this makes *On the Road* a novel of two educations. As a character, Sal can be likened to a somewhat older Huck Finn. He learns, often painfully, from his encounters with the world, and his naiveté is his strength and weakness, what impels him to explore his American "inheritance" and what he must outgrow if he is to survive this "inheritance." As a narrator, Sal looks back on an earlier self seemingly irrevocably lost and tries, as he says at one point, to "figure the losses and the gain." The interplay between these two processes of education is precisely the conflict between the inner world of the child and the outer world of the adult that Kerouac defined to Ginsberg in 1948 when first starting *On the Road*. This conflict as Kerouac experienced it was inherently unresolvable. The richness and intensity of the naive sense of the child inevitably collide with the demands of the outside world, but the realistic view of the adult is emotionally sterile and inevitably awakens a sense of nostalgia for what had to be abandoned.

As a character, Sal is often naive; as a narrator, he is often nostalgic. But *On the Road* is not controlled by either the character's or the narrator's point of view. Kerouac juxtaposes these two perspectives so that they reveal and modify each other. *On the Road* admits the appeal of naiveté and nostalgia, and the interplay between Sal's two educations is an attempt to understand the perspective of adult and child in a comprehensive and fruitful manner. Those who use the story of the April scroll as a license for driving through the book at high speed are apt to miss this doubleness of voice and miss as well the book's richness and structural coherence. Even though the four trips that make up *On the Road* seem initially to be random and picaresque, recognizing the interplay between Sal's perspective as a character and as a narrator reveals that each is a distinct stage in Sal's two educations.

Part one of *On the Road* is an extended confrontation between the "sadder-but-wiser" hindsight of the narrator Sal and his earlier "exuberances." In this first section, Sal as a character is most naive and open to ridicule. Throughout his trip west, Sal's fantasies about himself, Dean, and the road bring him into conflict with a world unconcerned with his fantasies, and Sal looks back on his trip of rude awakenings with a mixture of tolerance and embarassment. Sal's reasons for crossing the country underscore his optimistic shallowness. After his initial encounter with Dean, Sal decides to explore the West and the road for himself in order to become what he imagines Dean to be, a "sideburned hero of the snowy West." Sal certainly hopes to escape the weary oversophistication of his New York circle and his own depression over recent illness and a failed marriage. Sal's springtime pilgrimage, it should be noted, begins not with adolescent enthusiasm but with adult despair. Sal is not encountering adult realities for the first time. His naiveté as a character stems from the faith that Dean awakens in the redemptiveness of America. Like the hero of the second version of *On the Road*, Sal decides that he has failed to realize his "inheritance" and that the West is the appropriate place to search for it.

In part one, Sal is the college boy on a lark. He plays at being Dean in much the same way that Tom Sawyer plays at being Huck Finn. Sal, like Tom, can always count on his aunt to bail him out. Like Huck, Dean relies on himself. He has no aunt, and his alcoholic father is probably dead. Kerouac seems aware of this parallel between the family

11

situations of Sal and Dean and of Tom and Huck. In fictionalizing his own situation, Kerouac changes his mother
into an aunt, and in part two as Sal and Dean travel west
together, they pick up a series of hitchhikers who each earn
their rides by claiming they have an aunt at their destination who will contribute gas money. The aunts all turn out
to be fictitious, and Dean finally complains, "Everybody
has an aunt!" Everybody has one, that is, except Dean, who
must rely on his own resources, primarily his cunning, to
keep the gas tank full and everyone in motion. Sal, as it
turns out, is not the only "Tom Sawyer" in the book who
substitutes an aunt for a mother.[6]

Setting off, Sal is convinced that the world will serve him
if he only shows up and gives it the chance. "Somewhere
along the line I knew there'd be girls, visions, everything;
somewhere along the line the pearl would be handed to me"
(OR, 11). "Filled with dreams" and confidence, Sal chooses
to hitchhike Route 6 to Denver because it makes such a
straight red line on the map. When Route 6 turns out to be a
minor highway with little traffic and he is drenched in a
thunderstorm, Sal must retrace the little distance he has
covered "in a bus with a delegation of school teachers" (OR,
13). As Sal in his role of narrator says,

> It was my dream that screwed up, the stupid hearth-
> side idea that is would be wonderful to follow one
> great red line across America instead of trying various
> roads and routes. (OR, 13)

Dean's world and the reality of the road is not governed by
the aesthetics of maps, and America will not turn out to be a
single reality but a series of conflicting realities.

In spite of the fiascoes, much in the trip is positive to Sal.
He is a great tourist, and the Mississippi River, his first truck
driver, his first cowboy, and the vistas of the range all trigger descriptive epiphanies.

And here for the first time in my life I saw my beloved Mississippi River, dry in the summer haze, low water, with its big rank smell that smells like the raw body of America itself because it washes it up. (OR, 15)

But even the tourist sights are not always up to his expectations.

We arrived at Council Bluffs at dawn; I looked out. All winter I'd been reading of the great wagon parties that held council there before hitting the Oregon and Sante Fe trails; and of course now it was only cute suburban cottages of one damn kind and another, all laid out in the dismal gray dawn. (OR, 19)

And in Cheyenne, instead of the old West of his imagination, he finds the old West as imagined by the chamber of commerce of the new West, the West of "Wild West Week" where

fat businessmen in boots and ten-gallon hats, with their hefty wives in cowgirl attire, bustled and whooped on the wooden sidewalks. . . . I was amazed, and at the same time I felt it was ridiculous: in my first shot at the West I was seeing to what absurd devices it had fallen to keep its proud tradition. (OR, 33)

Initially as he travels, Sal alone is inconvenienced by his mistakes and illusions. Impatient with hitchhiking, he wastes money on bus rides. At the Wild West Week, he throws away his money buying drinks for a hitchhiking buddy and trying to seduce a farm girl only to wind up the next morning in the bus station alone, hung over, and broke. But as Sal moves westward, his mistakes increasingly have serious consequences for people he is with. In California, Sal moves into a shack with his bohemian, merchant seaman buddy Remi Boncoeur and Boncoeur's shrewish girl friend. Sal becomes embroiled in their domestic quarrels and their schemes for getting rich. Boncoeur puts Sal to work writing a film script to make his girl a star and the three of them rich. When that fails, the triangle begins to disintegrate, and at a dinner party Sal insults Boncoeur's stepfather even though he knows it is important to Boncoeur to impress the gentleman. Sal humiliates Boncoeur needlessly and must move on.

In the fiasco with Boncoeur's stepfather, Sal is only partly at fault. In his affair with the Mexican girl Terry that follows, though, he is wholly to blame. The guilt for meddling in someone else's world is his alone, and he is forced to recognize that his actions affect others. When Sal spots Terry on the evening bus to LA, he is "so lonely, so sad, so quivering, so broken, so beat" that he manages to get up "the courage necessary to approach a strange girl" (OR, 81). What follows is a pastiche of Sal's fantasies of Dean and of half-remembered movie images. Sal's language becomes an imitation of Dean's so that "it was mutely and beautifully and purely decided that when I got my hotel room in LA she would be beside me" (OR, 82). Sal makes their arrival in LA real to himself by equating it with a Hollywood fantasy. "The bus arrived in Hollywood. In the dirty dawn, like the dawn when Joel McCrea met Veronica Lake in a diner in the picture *Sullivan's Travels*, she slept in my lap" (OR, 82). The reference to *Sullivan's Travels*, though seemingly random, is actually quite suggestive. The hero of the movie is a director of cartoons who flees Hollywood and takes to the road to find out what life is *really* like, only to find it more violent and dangerous than his romanticized image. By a twist of plot and amnesia, the director becomes first a hobo and then a prison inmate before his chance rescue. Back in Hollywood, he decides to return to making cartoons and lighten the load of the poor by entertaining them. The character Sal is interested only in the meeting between two cinema lovers, but it seems likely that Kerouac, and prob-

ably the narrator Sal as well, are aware of the more suggestive parallel between the film director's dangerous fantasies
about life on the road and Sal's fantasies.

The references to *Sullivan's Travels* comments ironically
on Sal's affair with Terry. Throughout the encounter, the
narrator juxtaposes his earlier fantasies with the details that
undercut them and reveal their reality. When Sal and Terry
hit Los Angeles, Sal worries that she may be a "tramp" setting him up for a mugging. Confused by his nervousness,
Terry in turn assumes that Sal must be a pimp rather that
the "nice college boy" she originally took him to be. The affair is consummated, but sorrowfully at best. When the two
get to Terry's home town in the San Joaquin Valley, Sal-the-
college-boy approaches the episode as a pastoral interlude of
sex in William Saroyan's sun-warmed valley. After Terry
collects her little boy from her family, Sal sets to work picking cotton only to find that without the help of Terry and
her little boy, he is incapable of picking enough to support
them. Gradually Sal is forced to recognize that while he
wants simply "experience," Terry wants and deserves a
father for her son. Finally Sal has no choice but to wire his
aunt for bus fare and leave, and the guilt he feels shows that
even the optimistic Sal cannot completely ignore the
demystifying force of Dean's world with its painful under-
side of poverty and rootlessness.

Episodes like the affair with Terry reveal the somber un-
dercurrent beneath the often comic surface of *On the Road*.
By the time Sal is ready to return to New York in the fall
("everybody goes home in October" just as "everybody" takes
a trip in the spring), the spring dreams that had led him west
have given way to the sense of isolation and mortality that
turns the trip into a nightmare. In Los Angeles, Sal first
claims the rejected movie script he had written for Boncoeur.
He then has four hours before his bus to Pittsburgh.

First I bought a loaf of bread and salami and made
myself ten sandwiches to cross the country on. I had a

dollar left. I sat on the low cement wall in back of a Hollywood parking lot and made the sandwiches. As I labored at this absurd task, great Kleig lights of a Hollywood premiere stabbed the sky, that humming West Coast sky. All around me were the noises of the crazy gold-coast city. And this was my last night in Hollywood, and I was spreading mustard on my lap in the back of a parking lot john. (OR, 102)

Through the passage, the word *Hollywood* is repeated almost as a dirge, and the description is organized as a series of movie shots. The figure in the foreground is juxtaposed against the panoramic night, kleig lights, and excitement of the premiere. Then the camera pans in to emphasize the mustard-stained Sal, his rejected script an emblem of his collapsed fantasies.

When Sal reaches Pittsburgh, he is "wearier than [he has] been for years," and has a dime in his pocket and 365 miles left to hitchhike to his aunt's house in New Jersey. Outside Harrisburg he meets "the Ghost of the Susquehanna . . . a shriveled little old man with a paper satchel who claimed he was headed for 'Canady' (OR, 103). Sal first sees him as a "semi-respectable walking hobo" and follows when the Ghost claims he can lead Sal to a bridge that will shorten the trip. As the Ghost maintains a hypnotic stream of disconnected details of past handouts, Sal gradually realizes the little man's insanity, abandons him, and flags down a ride only to find he has been travelling west not east, back to the world of the road and not toward home. For Sal, the encounter with the Ghost becomes an experience of terror, a vision of hell faintly reminiscent of "The Try-Works" in *Moby-Dick* in its colors and sense of inversion.

We were bums together. We walked seven miles along the mournful Susquehanna. It is a terrifying river. It has bushy cliffs on both sides that lean like hairy ghosts

over the unknown waters. Inky night covers all. Sometimes from the railyards across the river rises a great
red locomotive flare that illuminates the horrid cliffs.
(OR, 104)

The perpetual disappointment of missed rides, aimless
wanderings, and isolation is not an escape across the bridge
into a land of free meals and free lodging but a shortcut to
insanity and death.

I thought all of the wilderness of America was in the
West till the Ghost of the Susquehanna showed me different. No there is a wilderness in the East. (OR, 105)

There is also wilderness in the self, society, and history, and
the discovery drives Sal to despair.

That night in Harrisburg I had to sleep in the railroad station on a bench; at dawn the station masters
threw me out. Isn't it true that you start your life a
sweet child believing in everything under your father's
roof? Then comes the day of the Laodiceans, when you
know you are wretched and miserable and poor and
blind and naked with the visage of a gruesome grieving
ghost you go shuddering through nightmare life. I
stumbled haggardly out of the station; I had no more
control. All I could see of the morning was a whiteness
like the whiteness of the tombs. (OR, 105)

Sal's vision of "whiteness" echoes the famous passage in
Moby-Dick and epitomizes his new awareness of death and
loss. He can no longer play Tom Sawyer but must, when he
reaches home, "lay [his] head down and figure the losses
and figure the gain that . . . was in there somewhere too"
(OR, 106–7).
    The encounter with the Ghost is an indictment of Sal's

reasons for travelling west. In imitating Dean, Sal in effect parodies what is perhaps the archetypal American tale: he flees the constrictions of the East hoping to find freedom and regeneration in the West. But Sal's vision of the West is childish and superficial. He refuses to recognize the possibility that his actions may involve cost to himself or others much as, in the final section of *Huck Finn*, Tom Sawyer refuses to recognize the dangers and immorality of playing at freeing the already freed slave Jim. Tom's belief in the inviolability of the child's world is so strong that he can refuse to recognize the wound from an adult bullet. As Sal Travels west, he is convinced he can make it on his own and that the world will shape itself to his "dream." By the time he encounters the Ghost on his return, Sal has begun to see the consequences of this attitude. Sal, like Tom Sawyer presumably an orphan, discovers his need for direction only to find that there is no one to provide it. When Sal turns to the Ghost as a surrogate father, the Ghost can offer him only loss, isolation, and death. The Ghost awakens Sal to his need for the father that he, in his childish confidence, has not even seemed to miss, but the Ghost is as unable to be a father to Sal as Sal was to Terry's little boy. The Ghost reveals to Sal that the father is as lost as the son and that each son must confront his own inadequacy and mortality, must become his own father.

Understanding the Ghost, we can see the importance of chapter 4 of part one, where Sal hitches "the greatest ride in my life." Although this scene is one of the novel's most comic, it prefigures Sal's grim return in the fall. Sal's ride is with "two young farmers from Minnesota" who haul farm machinery on their flat bed truck from Los Angeles to the Midwest and then pick up whoever they pass on their return. On the truck Sal finds, in addition to the two drivers, "two young farmer boys," "two young city boys," "Mississippi Gene and his charge" (a "tall blond kid . . . running away from something"), and "a tall slim fellow

who had a sneaky look" called Montana Slim. With the
exception of Slim and Sal, everyone on the truck is paired.
Three pairs are innocuous; they suggest the pattern but contribute little else. Mississippi Gene, his charge, and Montana Slim, though, are of interest, and Sal's failure to
understand the contrast between Gene's and Slim's
responses to being on the road is the crux of the episode.

Gene is patient and soft-spoken. He accepts what comes
his way and makes the best of it. When Sal asks about his
charge, Gene explains,

> "He got into some kind of trouble back in Mississippi,
> so I offered to help him out. Boy's never been out on his
> own. I take care of him best as I can, he's only a child."
> Although Gene was white there was something of the
> wise and tired old Negro in him. . . . (OR, 28)

There is perhaps as well something of Twain's Jim in
Mississippi Gene. Gene has not sought his comrade but accepts him and offers what support he can. Slim, on the
other hand, is "all insinuation," a loner who feels no com-
punction about using people. Slim boasts that he always
knows where to get money, and when Sal asks him to explain, Slim replies, "'Anywhere. You can always folly a
man down an alley, can't you?'" (OR, 26).

Kerouac carefully contrasts Gene and Slim.

> Gene was taking care of [his charge], of his moods and
> his fears. I wondered where the hell they would go and
> what they would do. They had no cigarettes. I
> squandered my pack on them, I loved them so. They
> were grateful and gracious. They never asked, I kept
> offering. Montana Slim had his own but never passed
> the pack. (OR, 30)

In spite of the contrast between Gene and Slim, Sal declines

19

Gene's invitation to go to Ogden with him and aligns himself with Slim, who drinks up Sal's money and leaves him flat in the Cheyenne bus station. Sal is not yet ready to accept Gene's example. He intuitively recognizes that Gene's ease and gentleness are a result of how little he demands from the world, but Sal is too optimistic and too sure of his own self-reliance to accept Gene as a guide or to accept Gene's gentle fatalism. Sal is still convinced that "the pearl" will be "handed" to him, and cannot deal with Gene's well-intentioned question about where he is going. When Gene sings what Sal takes to be "'the prettiest song,'" Sal offers, "'I hope you get where you're going, and be happy when you do.'"

Sal does not understand that Gene is always wherever he is going and, because he is without goals, able to respond calmly to whatever comes his way. Gene's reply, "'I always make out and move along one way or another'" (OR, 32), is finally too stark and simple for Sal, and so he hops off the truck to follow the more exciting but destructive Slim, a comrade who requires no allegiance and offers none in return. Sal's search for excitement and fear of responsibility make him unable to share in the relationship of comrades. He is neither Jim nor Huck, Gene nor his charge; he is the orphan Tom not yet recognizing his own poverty and illusions. Unable to share in Gene's world, Sal makes inevitable the collapse at the end of his trip in October. Sal does not understand Gene or Slim anymore than he later understands the Ghost, but these three figures reveal that the Indian Territory is no longer, if it ever was, an option. One can give up like Gene, turn sly and predatory like Slim, or, like the Ghost, escape into insanity. Sal rejects all three options, but all are relevant to his fantasy of America and the West.

Throughout part one, Sal is essentially alone, and the experiences of his trip teach him the implications of his solitariness and the inadequacy of his fantasies. Early in part one, Sal finds himself halfway West. Ahead is the "Promised Land" of Denver and "the greater vision of San Francisco." Behind is the college world of his past, of which Sal is reminded when he hitches a ride with two University of Iowa students who "talk of exams." The students drop Sal in Des Moines, where he takes a room in "a gloomy old Plains inn of a hotel by the locomotive roundhouse." There,

> I woke up as the sun was reddening; and that was the one distinct time in my life, the strangest moment of all, when I didn't know who I was—I was far away from home, haunted and tired with travel, in a cheap hotel room I'd never seen, hearing the hiss of steam outside, and the creak of the old wood of the hotel, and footsteps upstairs, and all the sad sounds, and I looked at the cracked high ceiling and really didn't know who I was for about fifteen strange seconds. I wasn't scared; I was just somebody else, some stranger, and my whole life was a haunted life, the life of a ghost. I was halfway across America, at the dividing line between the East of my youth and the West of my future, and maybe that's why it happened right there and then, that strange red afternoon. (OR, 17)

Sal, here, recognizes his need to go forward and establish a new identity but does not recognize the cost that will be involved. In America, the future is always in the West and a source of hope. In its attainment, the future, in becoming present, ceases to be West, ceases to be a matter of place, and necessarily involves admitting failure.

The themes established in part one—the search for identity, the relationship between comrades, the problem of the father, and the belief in the West—intersect for Sal in the figure of Dean and the three trips Dean and Sal take in parts

21

two, three, and four. Unlike Gene, Slim, and the Ghost, Dean is a Huck Finn not yet defeated, an active figure willing to attempt to create his freedom, and from the beginning of their trips together, Sal looks to Dean as a brother. Unlike the "intellectuals" of Sal's crowd, Dean

> reminded me of some long-lost brother; the sight of his suffering bony face with the long sideburns, and his straining muscular sweating neck made me remember my boyhood in those dye-dumps and swim-holes and riversides of Paterson and the Passaic. (OR, 10)

And Dean is consistently searching for his hobo father, a search that Sal makes in part his own in aligning himself with Dean.

> At dusk I walked. I felt like a speck on the surface of the sad red earth. I passed the Windsor Hotel, where Dean Moriarity had lived with his father in the depression thirties and as of yore I looked everywhere for the sad and fabled tinsmith of my mind. Either you find someone who looks like your father in places like Montana or you look for a friend's father where he is no more. (OR, 180)

But most basically, Sal responds to Dean's amazing energy, his seemingly limitless vitality which contrasts sharply with Sal's own lethargy at the beginning of the book. Sal admires Dean's freedom from social constraint, his success with women, and his ability to ignore social patterns. Dean is a "natural" and Sal sees in that a traditional American ethos more fundamental than any Protestant work ethic. Dean is Whitman's (and R. W. B. Lewis's) "American Adam." His "dirty workclothes" have that fit earned "from the Natural Tailor of Natural Joy" (OR, 10). Dean is a "cowboy" and evokes in Sal a nostalgia for the frontier and escape from adult responsibilities. And, finally, Dean projects an aura of "knowing time" that Sal comes to feel might offer a way beyond the despair of his encounter with the Ghost of the Susquehanna.

Even though the plot action from part two on makes *On the Road* seem more Dean's than Sal's story, it is Sal's stake in the action that structures the book and gives it coherence. If this is forgotten, the trips do blur together. But each one is a distinct stage in Sal's understanding of the images associated with Dean. Viewed from Sal's perspective, each trip shows a common pattern. Sal begins by breaking out of an established routine or order in search of kicks and the knowledge of time. He then proceeds through a series of road experiences that end in vision, exhaustion, and a return to the established order. Sal flees the order of his aunt's home, enters the disorder of the road, and returns at the end of each trip to figure his losses and gains. As early as 1949 in the second version, Kerouac thought of *On the Road* as a quest or pilgrimage, and Sal, not Dean, is the one who reaches the moment of vision on each trip. Dean, at times the guide, at times the goal, at times the obstacle, gives Sal a focus for his search and gives the book much of its energy, but Dean does not grow in the way Sal does. His trips end in a defeat quite different from Sal's partial defeat of losses and gains. Dean leaves his wives and children for the disorder of the road only to settle with a new woman and new children, creating an increasingly oppressive "order" of domestic and economic obligations.

In one way, part two, Sal's initial trip with Dean, resembles part one. The optimistic Paradise is still being disabused of his illusions. No longer confident in his self-sufficiency, he is still infatuated with a romanticized image of Dean and must learn firsthand the cost of Dean's ecstasy. Sal must also experience for himself the callous way Dean often uses the people close to him. Sal admits near the end of the section, "I lost faith in [Dean] that year" (OR, 177). But there is also a new dimension to Sal in part two. For the first time he thinks of his travelling explicitly and consciously as a "quest."

> I only went along for the ride, and to see what else Dean was going to do, and finally, also, knowing Dean would go back to Camille in Frisco, I wanted to have an affair with Marylou. (OR, 129)

Kerouac here points out that Sal's notion of questing is inadequate and that his motives in travelling are still mixed, but Sal is not longer the college boy on a lark. He is Dean's disciple, and Dean is "a monk peering into the manuscripts of the snow." When Sal resorts to religious language in part one, it reveals his shallowness and lack of self-control. He talks of the Hudson's "mysterious source," the "Promised Land" of Denver, and laments at one point having compromised "the purity of his trip," but Sal's experience of the Hudson is being stranded in a thunderstorm, Denver is a series of missed connections, and the trip's purity was compromised from the beginning. When Sal goes to the Central City opera in part one, it is no accident that he sees *Fidelio* and that the tenor is named "D'Annunzio or some such thing." But Sal, for all of his excitement at the opera, is basically unaffected. He is primarily interested in playing out drunken Hemingway fantasies with his friend Roland Major. At one point, Sal pauses to say,

> The night was getting more and more frantic. I wished Dean and Carlo were there—then I realized they'd be out of place and unhappy. They were like the man with the dungeon stone and the gloom, rising from the underground, the sordid hipsters of America, a new beat generation that I was slowly joining. (OR, 54)

The "dungeon stone" image refers to a scene from the opera,

and the reference is ironic. As Sal finds out later, Dean and Carlo have been in Central City that night, and Sal has been, figuratively, blind to the fact. Sal may, in retrospect, realize that his wandering education is already leading him to be a subterranean seeker, but at the time of the trip to Central City, Sal is frightened by the intense, though erratic, self-exploration of Dean and Carlo. Just before the Central City episode, Sal watches them through one all-night manic session and wants no part of it. Sal may sing "Ah me, what gloom!" in imitation of D'Annunzio, but he is playing a role and knows it:

> I wondered what the Spirit of the Mountain was thinking, and looked up and saw jackpines in the moon, and saw ghosts of old miners, and wondered about it. In the whole eastern dark wall of the Divide this night there was silence and the whisper of the wind, except in the ravine where we roared; and on the other side of the Divide was the great Western Slope, and the big plateau that went to Steamboat Springs, and dropped, and led you to the western Colorado desert and the Utah desert; all in darkness now as we fumed and screamed in our mountain nook, mad drunken Americans in the mighty land. We were on the roof of America and all we could do was yell, I guess—across the night, eastward over the Plains, where somewhere an old man with white hair was probably walking toward us with the Word, and would arrive any minute and make us silent. (OR, 55)

Sal's shallow and childish version of the American past traps him into aligning himself with the facileness of the new West's "Old West Week" in order not to confront the problematic heritage of the actual old West. Sal aligns himself with the spirit of boosterism and shuts out the spirit of a Whitman, avoiding in the process the demands of a visionary past and avoiding, as well, having to recognize society's and history's betrayal of that past. The Ghost of the Susquehanna is neither Whitman nor the "old man . . . with the Word," but Sal's intense response to the Ghost reveals, in any case, the gloom and silence (that is, lack of language to "figure the losses and the gain") that comes from confronting the reality and extent of the American "wilderness."

The different character of part two is suggested early in the trip by the encounter with the Jewish bum Hyman Solomon. Dean and Sal find Solomon in "the Virginia wilderness" and carry him with them to the town of Testament. The conjunction of "Solomon," "wilderness," and "Testament" is not accidental. Solomon is

> a ragged, bespectacled mad type, walking along reading a paperback muddy book he'd found in a culvert by the road . . . We asked him what he was reading. He didn't know. He didn't bother to look at the title page. He was only looking at the words, as though he had found the real Torah where it belonged, in the wilderness. (OR, 137)

For Solomon to find the "real Torah" in the wilderness is, appropriately, both American and biblical. However, in Testament, Solomon promises to "'hustle up a few dollars'" and continue with Sal and Dean, but he simply disappears.

> Solomon never showed up so we roared out of Testament. "Now you see, Sal, God does exist, because we keep getting hung-up with this town, no matter what we try to do, and you'll notice the strange Biblical name of it, and that strange Biblical character who made us stop here once more, and all things tied together all over like rain connecting everybody the world over by chain touch . . . " Dean rattled on like this; he was overjoyed and exuberant. He and I sud-

denly saw the whole country like an oyster for us to
open; and the pearl was there, the pearl was there.
(OR, 137–38)

Dean's and, through Dean, Sal's response to Solomon mixes
religious fervor and American opportunism. Sal is no longer
convinced that "the pearl [will] be handed to [him]"
(OR,10). But he and Dean are still convinced that "the
pearl" exists. They see the world as their "oyster." In spite of
this juxtaposition, Sal, both at the time of the action and
retrospectively, is convinced of the legitimacy of Dean's
"Mysticism." Early in the trip, Sal notes that Dean is "out of
his mind with real belief," and Dean rambles on about
"God," "time," and his ability to transcend the troubles of
his life. Sal concludes,

> There was nothing clear about the things he said, but
> what he meant to say was somehow made pure and
> clear. He used the word "pure" a great deal; I had
> never dreamed Dean would become a mystic. These
> were the first days of his mysticism, which would lead
> to the strange, ragged W.C. Fields saintliness of his
> later days. (OR, 121)

Although Dean communicates his faith in the "rain connecting everybody" through the force of his enthusiasm, his
religious impulse has no shape or definition and, as a result,
even though Sal and Dean *are* following "the white line in
the holy road," they are wandering and lack a map. The
naive American, Dean is out to make it on his own, sure
that "God does exist," untroubled by the fact that the "real
Torah" is unread or that God's prophet is a fool who
wanders off and abandons them.

Solomon is an avatar of the Ghost of the Susquehanna,
revealing Sal's and Dean's lack of any testament other than
perhaps that all-American book, the landscape which Sal

reads with descriptive fervor:

> we leaned and looked at the great brown father of
> waters rolling down from mid-America like the torrent
> of broken souls—bearing Montana logs and Dakota
> muds and Iowa vales and things that had drowned in
> Three Forks, where the secret began in ice. (OR, 141)

Sal and Dean are not playing at being "on the road," as
Sal was in part one. They are serious about "leaving confusions and nonsense behind and performing [their] one and
noble function of the time," which is to "*move*" (OR, 133).
Yet, however real the faith and energy, Sal and Dean are
not so much searching for vision as they are attempting to
avoid certain realities of their lives, and this escapist energy
at the center of their travels dooms the trip.

The escapist nature of the trip is apparent to Sal's and
Dean's friends. Early in part two, Sal's girlfriend Lucille
notices Sal's behavior when he is with Dean.

> When Lucille saw me with Dean and Marylou her face
> darkened—she sensed the madness they put in me.
> "I don't like you when you're with them."
> "Ah, it's all right, it's just kicks. We only live once.
> We're having a good time."
> "No, it's sad and I don't like it." (OR, 125)

And Carlo Marx, now settled in New York after "a terrible
period" of visions and introspection, confronts Sal and Dean
several times in a reversal of the Denver situation in part
one.

> Carlo watched this silly madness with slitted eyes.
> Finally he slapped his knee and said, "I have an an-
> nouncement to make."
> "Yes? Yes?"

"What is the meaning of this voyage to New York? What kind of sordid business are you on now? I mean, man, whither goest thou, America, in thy shiny car in the night?"

"Whither goest thou?" echoed Dean with his mouth open. We sat and didn't know what to say; there was nothing to talk about any more. The only thing to do was go. (OR, 119)

Even Bull Lee, "a teacher" from whom they've all learned, is "curious to know the reason for this trip." He gets no more answer than Carlo. Carlo and Bull can only warn that the maniacal energy sustaining Dean must eventually run out. Carlo pronounces,

"The days of wrath are yet to come. The balloon won't sustain you much longer. And not only that, but it's an abstract balloon. You'll all go flying to the West Coast and come staggering back in search of your stone."

In those days Carlo had developed a tone of voice which he hoped sounded like what he called The Voice of the Rock; the whole idea was to stun people into the realization of the rock. (OR, 130)

"The rock" Dean and Sal try to avoid dealing with is at least in part the mystery of evil and death. Leaving New Orleans after the visit with Bull Lee, Sal and Dean lose their way in a swamp.

We were surrounded by a great forest of viny trees in which we could almost hear the slither of a million copperheads. The only thing we could see was the red ampere button on the Hudson dashboard. Marylou squealed with fright. We began laughing maniac laughs to scare her. We were scared too. We wanted to get out of this mansion of the snake, this mireful droop-

ing dark, and zoom on back to familiar American
ground and cowtowns. There was a smell of oil and
dead water in the air. This was a manuscript of the
night we could't read. (OR, 158)

The one landscape "manuscript" that Sal and Dean cannot
read is the one that would force them to deal with the
reality of darkness. They can attempt to trivialize evil by
imitating a Hollywood thriller, but they cannot confront it
without admitting its reality which would, in effect, burst
"the balloon" and reveal the emptiness of the encounter in
Testament. Sal and Dean are running from the superficial
banalities of modern America but are equipped only with a
superficial idealism and the complete faith in self that
perhaps has led to what they would escape. Sal and Dean
insist that "the golden land's ahead" (OR, 135), and that
faith is based on their ability to ignore or forget the "smell of
oil and dead water."

Sal's sense of death is tied to his dream of the "Shrouded
Traveler."

Just about that time a strange thing began to haunt
me. It was this: I had forgotten something. There was
a decision that I was about to make before Dean
showed up, and now it was driven clear out of my
mind but still hung on the tip of my mind's tongue . . .
It had to do somewhat with the Shrouded Traveler.
Carlo Marx and I once sat down together . . . and I
told him a dream I had about a strange Arabian figure
that was pursuing me across the desert; that I tried to
avoid; that finally overtook me before I reached the
Protective City . . . I proposed it was myself, wearing
a shroud. That wasn't it. Something, someone, some
spirit was pursuing all of us across the desert of life and
was bound to catch us before we reached heaven.
Naturally, now that I look back on it, this is only

death: death will overtake us before heaven. The one
thing that we yearn for in our living days, that makes
us sigh and groan and undergo sweet nauseas of all
kinds, is the remembrance of some lost bliss that was
probably experienced in the womb and can only be
reproduced (though we hate to admit it) in death. But
who wants to die? In the rush of events I keep thinking
about this in the back of my mind. I told it to Dean and
he instantly recognized it as the mere simple longing
for pure death; and because we're all of us never in life
again, he, rightly, would have nothing to do with it,
and I agreed with him then. (OR, 124)

Sal interprets his dream correctly, but his response is problematic. Dean's arrival prevents Sal from coming to terms
with his own death, and this leaves Sal haunted and pur-
sued. The fact is, Sal and Dean do want to die just as they
want to live and Sal's interpretation avoids recognizing this
conflict. Dean's strategy is to ignore and avoid the recognition of death if at all possible, and this is his advice to Sal.
The concluding phrase shows that Sal agreed with Dean at
the time but leaves open the possibility that Sal is less sure
about the matter retrospectively.

Neither Sal nor Dean is able to be as blasé about their
own death as their companion Ed Dunkel, who tells Sal,

"Last night I walked clear down to Times Square and
just as I arrived I suddenly realized I was a ghost—it
was my ghost walking on the sidewalk." He said these
things to me without comment, nodding his head emphatically. Ten hours later, in the midst of someone
else's conversation, Ed said, "Yep, it was my ghost
walking on the sidewalk." (OR, 130)

By refusing to see their "ghost," Sal and Dean become their
own pursuers. At two points, Sal, Dean, and those in the car

are described as a "band of Arabs," and at times Dean himself is described as an "Angel of terror" (OR, 237), "a burning shuddering frightful angel . . . pursuing me like the shrouded traveler" (OR, 259). The doubleness of Dean's motivation is suggested by his response to women:

> I could hear Dean, blissful and blabbering and frantically rocking. Only a guy who's spent five years in jail can go to such maniacal helpless extremes; beseeching at the portals of the soft source, mad with a completely physical realization of the origins of life-bliss; blindly seeking to return the way he came. This is the result of years looking at sexy pictures behind bars; looking at the legs and breasts of women in popular magazines; evaluating the hardness of the steel halls and the softness of the woman who is not there. Prison is where you promise yourself the right to live. Dean had never seen his mother's face. Every new girl, every new wife, every new child was an addition to his bleak impoverishment . . . Dean had every right to die the sweet deaths of complete love of his Marylou. (OR, 132)

In his passion, Dean both affirms and denies. His involvement with Marylou demonstrates his intense experiences of the world but also his lack of perspective. Blind to everything but the moment, Dean experiences the world, even in the confused demands he makes on it, with visionary intensity, but his blindness also sets in motion the social forces, the increasingly complicated series of marriages, divorces, and children that constrict his ability to experience the moment. In New York, Sal and Dean spend an evening with Rollo Greb whose "excitement," like Dean's, "blew out of his eyes in stabs of fiendish light" (OR, 127). Dean tells Sal,

"That Rollo Greb is the greatest, most wonderful of

all. That's what I was trying to tell you—that's what I want to be. I want to be like him. He's never hung-up . . . he knows time . . . You see, if you go like him all the time you'll finally get it."

"Get what?"

"IT! IT! I'll tell you—now no time, we have no time now." (OR, 127)

Dean seems to be too busy to notice the irony, as Sal does retrospectively, of having "no time" in the middle of "knowing time."

Almost inevitably, the intense self-absorption of Dean leads to his own exhaustion and the exhaustion of those with him. As Sal notes at the end of the visit to Bull Lee, "Conman Dean was antagonizing people away from him by degrees" (OR, 155), and even Sal is antagonized when Dean abandons him in San Francisco. Dean is so intensely into his own world, as Sal discovers, that no one else's world exists. And in San Francisco, not only is Sal abandoned by Dean but his affair with Marylou turns into a fiasco. Rather than manipulating the jealousies of Marylou and Dean for his ends, Sal becomes the pawn of Dean and Marylou in their conflict. Instead of the masterful and adult lover, Sal is reduced to the level of miscreant child, doubly abandoned and "out of" his "mind with hunger and bitterness." As in part one, exhaustion and failure lead to a vision of death. In his despair, Sal imagines a woman to be his "strange Dickensian mother." She begs him to "go" on his "knees and pray for deliverance" for his "sins and scoundrel's acts," and her plea leads Sal to remember an earlier vision of his father. These two visions of parentage give way immediately to "the point of ecstasy":

I walked around, picking butts from the street. I passed a fish-'n-chips joint on Market Street, and suddenly the woman in there gave me a terrified look as I

33

passed; she was the proprietess, she apparently thought I was coming in there with a gun to hold up the joint. I walked on a few feet. It suddenly occurred to me this was my mother of about two hundred years ago in England, and that I was her footpad son, returning from gaol to haunt her honest labors in the hashery. I stopped, frozen with ecstasy on the sidewalk. I looked down Market Street. I didn't know whether it was that or Canal Street in New Orleans: it led to water, ambiguous, universal water, just as 42nd Street, New York, leads to water, and you never know where you are. I thought of Ed Dunkel's ghost on times square. I was delirious. I wanted to go back and leer at my strange Dickensian mother in the joint. I tingled all over from head to foot. It seemed I had a whole host of memories leading back to 1750 in England and that I was in San Francisco now only in another life and in another body . . . for just a moment I had reached the point of ecstasy that I always wanted to reach, which was the complete step across chronological time into timeless shadows, and wonderment in the bleakness of the mortal realm, and the sensation of death kicking at my heels to move on, with a phantom dogging its own heels, and myself hurrying to a plank where all the angels dove off and flew into the holy void of uncreated emptiness, the potent and inconceivable radiancies shining in bright Mind Essence, innumerable lotus-lands falling open in the magic mothswarm of heaven . . . I realized that I had died and been reborn numberless times but just didn't remember especially because the transitions from life to death and back to life are so ghostly easy, a magical action . . . I realized it was only because of the stability of the intrinsic Mind that these ripples of birth and death took place, like the action of wind on a sheet of pure, serene, mirror-like water. I felt sweet, swinging bliss

> . . . I thought I was going to die . . . But I didn't
> die. . . . (OR, 172–73)

Death no longer evokes so deep a terror for Sal as it did in part one; he sees it in a larger context of birth and rebirth. He describes literally an experience of "ecstasy," of moving beyond physical limits, and the effect is strangely calming and reassuring. By moving outside of himself, Sal is able to feel less threatened by his own eventual death and also for the first time to feel a degree of empathy for others. Sal may be wrong about the details behind the "terrified look" of the proprietess, but he is intensely aware of her response nonetheless and is willing to try to imagine her situation.

The gain in perspective evident in Sal's vision at the end of part two controls part three. More at ease with his own mortality, more aware of the emotional life of others, and more able to admit his own isolation, Sal begins to act purposefully, instead of drifting as in part one or taking his direction from someone else as in part two. Instead of simply responding to Dean's invitation to travel, as in part two, Sal now sets out for Denver where he is "thinking of settling down." Sal sees himself becoming "a patriarch" in "Middle America." He sees himself, that is, halfway between the isolation of the West and the stultification of the East, but in Denver Sal has no idea of how to become "a patriarch." He finds that his friends have all left Denver, and ends up a day laborer.

> At lilac evening I walked with every muscle aching among the lights of 27th and Welton in the Denver colored section, wishing I were a Negro, feeling that the best the white world had offered was not enough ecstasy for me, not enough life, joy, kicks, darkness, music, not enough night. I stopped at a little shack

where a man sold hot red chili in paper containers; I bought some and ate it, strolling in the dark mysterious streets. I wished I were a Denver Mexican, or even a poor overworked Jap, anything but what I was so drearily, a "white man" disillusioned. All my life I'd had white ambitions; that was why I'd abandoned a good woman like Terry in the San Joaquin Valley. . . . (OR, 180) ⟨⟨⟨

Some have attacked Sal's condescension, but Sal, though "disillusioned," has yet to find anything to replace his original values. He mistrusts his original middle-class, success-oriented perspective, but it still shapes his view of the world. Sal's nostalgia reflects his sense of his own problems and not necessarily Kerouac's solution to these problems.

Coming on a neighborhood softball game, Sal laments,

Never in my life as an athlete had I ever permitted myself to perform like this in front of families and girl friends and kids of the neighborhood, at night, under lights; always it had been college, big-time, sober-faced; no boyish, human joy like this. Now it was too late. Near me sat an old Negro who apparently watched the games every night. Next to him was an old white bum; then a Mexican family, then some girls, some boys—all humanity, the lot. Oh, the sadness of the lights that night! The young pitcher looked just like Dean. A pretty blonde in the seats looked just like Marylou. It was the Denver Night; all I did was die. (OR, 181)

The one entry that Sal has into this world is Dean, and Sal is so lonely that he flees west to him in San Francisco. At first glance, this suggests the escapism of parts one and two, but the trip that follows is of a different sort altogether. For one thing, Sal and Dean now travel east instead of west. Not only do they travel in the direction associated in the book with family, society, and history, but their ultimate destination, though never reached, is Italy, the Old World. More importantly, Sal's sense of his relationship to Dean is radically different. Dean is no longer a fantasy figure or a rival to be studied and bested. Dean is now a comrade. When Sal finds Dean near "idiocy" and his wife throws them out, Sal responds unexpectedly by assuming responsibility for Dean. Sal becomes, in a sense, Mississippi Gene and Dean "his charge," and part three explores Sal's and Dean's attempt to make a go of this relationship which, for the first time, involves Sal as the active partner.

The relationship between Sal and Dean is metaphorically a marriage. Unlike the situation with Mississippi Gene and his "charge," Sal and Dean choose to enter into an alliance. Sal proposes and Dean accepts:

> —"Come to New York with me; I've got the money." I looked at him; my eyes were watering with embarrassment and tears. . . It was probably the pivotal point in our friendship. . . . Something clicked in both of us. He became extremely joyful and said everything was settled. (OR, 189–90)

The description that follows this "pivotal point" suggests how much is at stake for Sal and Dean. As they stand on the sidewalk after settling their affairs, a Greek wedding party files out of the tenement next door:

> We gaped at these ancient people who were having a wedding party for one of their daughters, probably the thousandth in an unbroken dark generation of smiling in the sun. . . . Dean and I might have been in Cyprus. . . .
> "Well," said Dean in a very shy and sweet voice, "shall we go?" (OR, 190)

The description of the wedding party echoes Sal's description of the Denver world he has just left. It also reflects Sal's notion of marriage in which being absorbed into the context of the extended nuclear family takes precedence over the actual relationship between husband and wife. At the beginning of part two, Sal tells Dean and Marylou,

> "I want to marry a girl . . . so I can rest my soul with her til we both get old. This can't go on all the time— all this franticness and jumping around. We've got to go someplace, find something."
> "Ah now, man," said Dean, "I've been digging you for years about the *home* and marriage and all those fine wonderful things about your soul." (OR, 116)

And at the end of part one, Sal describes how Dean

> spent afternoons talking to my aunt as she worked on a great rag rug woven of all the clothes in my family for years, which was now finished and spread on my bedroom floor, as complex and as rich as the passage of time itself. . . (OR, 107)

These passages link with Sal's desire at the beginning of part three to be a "patriarch." Sal's sense of marriage is a response to isolation and his dread of death. By becoming a "patriarch," by submerging himself into the cyclical pattern of generation succeeding generation, Sal seems to see his own individual death subsumed into and overcome by the ongoing process of the family.

It is worth noting that these images of "generation" are primarily associated with the "old world." Lucille and Sal's aunt are both Italian, and Sal presents them as stereotypical first generation immigrants. Similarly, the Greek wedding party makes Sal feel as if he and Dean are in Cypress. These images suggest that Sal's nostalgia for an Old World peasant order may actually be the impulse behind his romanticized version of Denver slum life, but Sal's actual choice of a partner, Dean, represents the New World at its most anarchistic and individualistic. For this reason, if no other, Dean's "marriage" to Sal is fated to end in divorce, as are all his other marriages. The disintegration of the relationship, though, defines for Sal a basic dichotomy. He can respond to his vision of death by accepting "marriage," by believing in the purposefulness of death in the cyclical, Old World pattern; or he can respond by becoming an "American" like Dean, by taking his isolation, his individuality, as an opportunity to ignore death by ignoring time and social pattern. He can try to overcome death by living as if outside time and society, cultivating the moment and torturing the senses to attain the "timeless" through temporary vision and ecstasy. The problem with the first response is that it is likely to result in the shallowness and social constriction that Sal flees in the book's beginning. The problem with the second, as Dean knows and as Sal discovers in part three, is that it leads to exhaustion and quite probably an early death.

In part three by assuming resonsibility for Dean, Sal comes to understand the cost of Dean's attempt to "know time." Before leaving San Francisco for the East, Sal must watch the friends of Dean's wife confront him with the social consequences of his freedom and irresponsibility. Galatea, Dunkel's wife, reminds Dean of his children and his obligations. Not surprisingly, she "looks like the daughter of the Greeks with the sunny camera" (OR, 192). Dean's response is silence. He stands as if "tremendous revelations were pouring into him. . . . He was BEAT—the root, the soul of Beatific" (OR, 195). When Dean leaves the apartment to wait for the others to make up their minds "about time," Sal sees him

> alone in the doorway, digging the street. Bitterness, recriminations, advice, morality, sadness—everything

> was behind him, and ahead of him was the ragged and
> ecstatic joy of pure being. (OR, 195)

Sal is beginning to realize that Dean is the victim or
scapegoat as much as the "con man" or manipulator.

Sal is also realizing that Dean is at least partly aware of
the cost of his attempt to have "IT," to "know time." That
last night in Frisco, Dean, Sal, Galatea and the rest of the
crew find a sax player who has "IT," and the next day Dean
tries to explain to Sal.

> "Now, man, that alto man last night had IT—he held
> it once he found it; I've never seen a guy who could
> hold so long." I wanted to know what "IT" meant.
> "Ah well"—Dean laughed—"now you're asking me
> impon-de-rables—ahem! Here's a guy and everybody's
> there, right? Up to him to put down what's on
> everybody's mind. He starts the first chorus, then lines
> up his ideas, people, yeah, yeah, but get it, and then he
> rises to his fate and has to blow equal to it. All of a sud-
> den somewhere in the middle of a chorus he *gets
> it*—everybody looks up and knows; they listen; he picks
> it up and carries. Time stops. He's filling empty space
> with the substance of our lives, confessions of his
> bellybottom strain, remembrance of ideas, rehashes of
> old blowing. He has to blow across bridges and come
> back and do it with such infinite feeling soul-
> exploratory for the tune of the moment that everybody
> knows it's not the tune that counts but IT—" Dean
> could go no further; he was sweating telling about it.
> (OR, 206)

Logically, the alto man's performance is a series of contradictions. He releases his audience from their oppression
by celebrating it. He escapes time by being preternaturally
aware of it. He crosses the bridge of the tune as if it were the

Ghost of the Susquehanna's bridge beyond death by willing himself to recognize the temporary and doomed quality of his gesture. The alto man wills himself to create in the face of his despair at recognizing his own inevitable decline and inability to create. He escapes by accepting momentarily that there is no escape.

Dean's sense of the alto's relationship to his audience is also important. The alto suffers not only to attain his own fleeting moments of ecstasy but in order to renew his audience by creating a momentary experience of community among them based, paradoxically, on each one's recognition of his own isolation. And this sense of community has nothing to do with the Old World community of hierarchy where one inevitably has a role and place. This community is a Whitmanesque community of undifferentiated equals. Each member is isolated but still free to attain on his own the highest pitch of vision, and thereby recognize his similarity to the other isolates and experience a belonging beyond space, time, or social role. It is the community of "Crossing Brooklyn Ferry" which Whitman imagines among those who have crossed, are crossing, and will cross, a community more complete than any offered by the Old World and yet a community that exists at best momentarily, and then primarily in the imagination.

As Sal comes to realize in part three, Dean serves the same function for their circle as the alto player for his. Sal sees Dean as a scapegoat figure, "the Saint of the lot" (OR, 193), "the HOLY GOOF" (OR, 194), and as they ride east in a travel bureau car swapping the megalomaniacal fantasies of childhood, both Sal and Dean get "IT."

At one point the driver said, "For God's sakes, you're rocking the boat back there." Actually we were; the car was swaying as Dean and I both swayed to the rhythm and the IT of our final excited joy in talking and living to the blank tranced end of all innumerable

41

riotous angelic particulars that had been lurking in our souls all our lives.

"Oh, man! man! man!" moaned Dean. "And it's not even the beginning of it—and now here we are at last going together, we've never gone east together, Sal, think of it, we'll dig Denver together and see what everybody's doing although that matters little to us, the point being that we know what IT is and we know TIME and we know that everything is really FINE." Then he whispered, clutching my sleeve, sweating, "Now you just dig them in front. They have worries, they're thinking about where to sleep tonight, how much money for gas, the weather, how they'll get there—and all the time they'll get there anyway, you see. But they need to worry and betray time with urgencies false and otherwise, purely anxious and whiny, their souls really won't be at peace unless they can latch on to an established and proven worry. . . ." (OR, 208)

But as it turns out, Sal and Dean are also apt to "betray time." Even that least constraining of all possible "marriages," the idealized marriage of male comrades, inevitably involves a confrontation with aging and the ultimate constraint of death.

In Denver, Dean advises Sal to take care of himself physically "'because you're getting a little older now'" and eventually there will be the "'years of misery in your old age . . . when you sit in parks'" (OR, 212). Although Dean means well, Sal lashes out, and Dean retreats in tears. When Dean returns, Sal tells him bitterly, "'You don't die enough to cry.'" Dean, too, confronted with the Denver scenes and memories of his barren childhood, turns bitter. His search for kicks loses its joyous quality. "All the bitterness and madness of his entire Denver life was blasting out of his system like daggers. His face was red and sweaty and mean" (OR, 221).

Once Sal and Dean get back on the road, though, Dean recovers his equilibrium.

> It was remarkable how Dean could go mad and then suddenly continue with his soul—which I think is wrapped up in a fast car, a coast to reach, and a woman at the end of the road—calmly and sanely as though nothing had happened. "I get like that every time in Denver now—I can't make that town any more. Gookly, gooky, Dean's a spooky. Zoom!" (OR, 230)

The ecstasy and community of "IT" are at best temporary states and thrive perhaps only at moments of transition or outside the normal social order. Like Huck and Jim on the raft or Whitman on the ferry, Sal and Dean in the car pass through the world but are not forced (at least temporarily) to be of it. They are free to respond to the landscape as it "unreels, with dreamlike rapidity," just as Huck and Jim muse on the stars and Whitman on the "fluttering pennants" along the shore. But the inevitable result of being on the road is exhaustion. As Huck and Jim know always in the backs of their minds, the river ends. Even the car cannot escape, finally, the presence of the outside world. As Dean drives on after Denver, he again goes mad and becomes for Sal an "Angel of Terror." By the time the two comrades reach New York, they are so consumed by their travels that they

> walk all over Long Island, but there was no more land, just the Atlantic Ocean, and we could only go so far. We clasped hands and agreed to be friends forever. (OR, 246)

Five days later when Sal introduces Dean to a woman at a

party, she is so infatuated with the image of Dean as a "cowboy" that she becomes his wife and eventually the mother of Dean's fourth child.

> With one illegitimate child in the West somewhere, Dean then had four little ones and not a cent, and was all troubles and ecstasy and speed as ever. So we didn't go to Italy. (OR, 247)

Dean the "cowboy" can no more go to Europe than he can bring order to his domestic affairs.

Dean's liaison with a third wife is in effect a double betrayal, a double failure. It is a betrayal of his comradely marriage with Sal, and a betrayal of the freedom of action and movement that goes with "IT." Sal's response to this and the failure to make it to Italy is surprisingly mild and understated. Perhaps this is in part because Sal has come to recognize the inherent mismatch between his nostalgia for an Old World order of pastoral stability and his desire to participate in Dean's anarchistic, New World search for moments of individual ecstasy. But the experience of travelling with Dean as his "brother" and participating fully in the life of the road has also led Sal to question the desirability of "IT." This is in part because of the chaos, isolation, and exhaustion necessary to attain "IT," but it is also because of the nature of "IT" itself.

The ambiguity of "IT" shows up as Sal and Dean make their way from Denver to Chicago. At first, the car functions much as Huck's and Jim's raft. The comrades regain their equilibrium after the chaos of Denver. Like Huck and Jim, Sal and Dean muse on the landscape and reminisce, but then a glimpse of some bums by a fire reminds Dean of his missing wino father. He turns first morose and then demonic. For Sal, and perhaps Dean as well, "all that old road of the past" is soon "unreeling dizzily as if the cup of life had been overturned and everything gone mad. My eyes

44

An American Education

ached in nightmare day." (OR, 234). The openness and hypersensitivity that leads to the joy of "IT" also leaves one vulnerable and open to a sense of horror. As Dean's driving becomes increasingly wild, Sal crawls into the back seat.

> I got down on the floor and closed my eyes and tried to go to sleep. As a seaman I used to think of the waves rushing beneath the shell of the ship and the bottomless deeps thereunder—now I could feel the road some twenty inches beneath me, unfurling and flying and hissing at incredible speeds across the groaning continent with that mad Ahab at the wheel. When I closed my eyes all I could see was the road unwinding into me. When I opened them I saw flashing shadows of trees vibrating on the floor of the car. There was no escaping it. I resigned myself to all. (OR, 234)

Sal, like Ishmael, has signed on for the cruise and must see it through whether or not a mad captain holds the wheel. The reference to Dean as Ahab is more than a mere tag. In chapter 60 of *Moby-Dick*, "The Line," Melville describes the unfurling whale line in the same terms that Sal uses to describe the flying and hissing road. For Melville, the hissing "halter" that surrounds whalers as they work is a conceit for the way people live surrounded by, yet usually oblivious to, death. It is hardly necessary to catch this echo of Melville to catch Sal's sense of fear, but this and other parallels to *Huck Finn* and *Moby-Dick* (consider such things as the marriage of Dean and Sal, Ishmael and Queequeg, and the comradeship of Mississippi Gene and his charge, Huck and Jim) underscore that it is finally a question for the narrator and reader whether Dean is Huck or Ahab, whether the car is the raft or the *Pequod*. Is Dean the "Holy Goof," a saint who knows time, or is he a destructive and revenging "angel" who pursues Sal to destroy him? Is it monomania to step out of society or is it an experience of grace in nature? Is

45

the American past with its emphasis on vision, individuality, freedom, and movement, a life-giving or life-denying
heritage? Is the road salvation or damnation? These questions are not easily answered, as regards either Dean or the
American tradition. Certainly Melville understood the
potential for inverting Emerson's optimistic transcendentalism, understood how easily the emphasis on an idealistic
universe and individualism could open one to both the
beatific view from the masthead and the damning look into
the try works. And Twain also had some sense of the lone-
some deathlike sounds a boy is apt to hear when alone, or
the arrogant but compelling power of a Colonel Sherburn
that went hand in hand with the beauty of the river and the
exhilaration of lighting out. In his recent book *Mystery
Train*, Greil Marcus is writing about rock and roll politics,
but his comments help explain the doubleness of Dean's
example and the doubleness of "IT":

> one of America's secrets is that the dreams of Huck and
> Ahab are not always very far apart. Both of them em-
> body an impulse to freedom, an escape from restraints
> and authority that sometimes seems like the only really
> American story there is. That one figure is passive and
> benign, the other aggressive and in the end malignant;
> the one full of humor and regret, and the other cold
> and determined never to look back; the one as unsure
> of his own authority as he is of anyone else's, the other
> felling authority only to replace it with his own—all
> this hides the common bond between the two
> characters, and suggests how strong would be a figure
> who could put the two together. For all that is dif-
> ferent about Ahab and Huck Finn, they are two
> American heroes who say, yes, they will go to hell if
> they have to: they will go as far as anyone can.[8]

Like the two previous sections, part three ends with a vision of death that summarizes the lessons Sal learns from the road and Dean, and the vision that closes the third trip shows how clearly Sal is aware of the duality of "IT." By the time Sal and Dean reach Detroit, they are as "ragged and dirty as if [they] had lived off locust" (OR, 243), and must wait a day before pushing on to New York. They decide to spend the night in a skid row movie house.

> If you sifted all Detroit in a wire basket the beater solid core of dregs couldn't be better gathered. The picture was Singing Cowboy Eddie Dean and his gallant white horse Bloop, that was number one; number two double-feature film was George Raft, Sidney Greenstreet, and Peter Lorre in a picture about Istanbul. We saw both of these things six times each during the night. We saw them waking, we heard them sleeping, we sensed them dreaming, we were permeated completely with the strange Gray Myth of the West and the weird dark Myth of the East when morning came. All my actions since than have been dictated automatically to my subconscious by this horrible osmotic experience. I heard big Greenstreet sneer a hundred times; I heard Peter Lorre make his sinister come-on; I was with George Raft in his paranoiac fears; I rode and sang with Eddie Dean and shot up the rustlers innumerable times. People slugged out of bottles and turned around and looked everywhere in the dark theatre for something to do, somebody to talk to. In the head everybody was guiltily quiet, nobody talked. In the gray dawn that puffed ghostlike about the windows of the theatre and hugged its eaves I was sleeping with my head on the wooden arm of a seat as six attendants of the theatre converged with their night's total of swept-up rubbish and created a huge dusty pile that reached to my nose as I snored head down—till they almost swept me away too. This was reported to me by Dean,

who was watching from ten seats behind. All the cigarette butts, the bottles, the matchbooks, the come and the gone were swept up in this pile. Had they taken me with it, Dean would never have seen me again. He would have had to roam the entire coast to coast before he found me embryonically convoluted among the rubbishes of my life, and the life of everybody concerned and not concerned. What would I have said to him from my rubbish womb? "Don't bother me, man, I'm happy where I am." (OR, 244–45)

Most simply this passage suggests that Sal has given up. he is buried in "the rubbishes" of his life. Metaphorically, his past is dead. He is perhaps haunted, but there is no indication that he has the volition to act to change his situation. He is no longer "disillusioned"; he is simply illusionless, neither happy nor unhappy, simply exhausted and apathetic. Sal is also buried among "the rubbishes" of his culture which have been so much a part of his experiments with the road. The scene in the movie house suggests the extent to which the economy functions by discarding at least some people. Sal, here, is far removed from the fantasies of success that barred him from Terry. And the movies themselves amount to a kind of cultural rubbish: the lowest example of a popular medium that has picked up, simplified, and debased imaginative patterns critical to the culture's awareness of itself. As such, the two movies that are etched into Sal's "subconscious" parody the double experience of "IT," the double experience of the car as the raft and the Pequod.

In a letter to John Holmes of 24 June 1949, Kerouac writes about the people of the Colorado foothills who belong to no social class. These people do not read newspapers but make a social and imaginative reality out of Tex Ritter and Gene Autry movies. They allude to the movie figures in the same way Eastern intellectuals allude to literary ones.[9] Here, almost two years before *On the Road* and the trip portrayed in part three, the "Gray Myth of the West" is unambiguously positive. It represents a democratic classless ideal and evokes a time when goals were clear and morality as simple as white hats and black hats. By the time of *On the Road,* though, Kerouac has come to see the "Gray Myth" as facile and superficial in spite of its appeal. This indictment has obvious implications for an understanding of Sal's and Kerouac's attitude toward Dean at this point, since several factors connect Dean to the "Gray Myth of the West." Sal introduces Dean to the woman who becomes his third wife as a "cowboy," and Sal first thought of Dean as a "young Gene Autry . . . a sideburned hero of the snowy West" (OR, 5). There is also the partial overlap between "Eddie Dean" and "Dean Moriarity." Even without these indicators, it is obvious that Dean initiates Sal's interest in the "West" and to some degree symbolizes it for him, but the sarcasm Sal directs at the western movie reveals the extent to which he has come to realize that Dean's absolute faith in the self-sufficiency of the individual is more complicated and volatile than anything admitted to in the adolescent and optimistic fantasies that typically pass for America.

The connection of "the weird dark Myth of the East" to the "Gray Myth of the West" may at first seem unclear, but the inevitable counterpart of a myth of absolute goodness and life is a myth of absolute evil and death. If Emerson's transcendentalism is one side of the coin, Poe's nightmare of the Arabesque is the other. If one side of the Hollywood imagination is the western, Busby Berkely musicals, and the romantic comedy, the other side is the film noir, the horror film, and the uncompromising aggression of a gangster film like *Little Caesar.* As the example of Poe and stories like "Ligeia" suggest, there is an American tradition of evoking fantasies of evil with Arabian and Middle Eastern imagery.

Even in *Moby-Dick*, Ahab's monomania is fueled and given its particular tinge by the figure of the fire worshipping Parsee "devil" Fedallah. Certainly, Sal experiences the "Myth of the East" as a counterpoint to the "Myth of the West," and this myth is also linked to Dean through the dream of the Shrouded Traveler and the book's earlier Arabian imagery. In effect, the two films link with and reinforce even as they burlesque motifs that have run through the entire book. In addition, they show Sal for the first time aware of how each of these myths or ways of looking at the world are simultaneously part of his "sub-conscious," and this amounts to a recognition, though perhaps not articulated by the character Sal, that Dean can be both "Saint" and "Angel of Terror," that Sal himself may be both searching for life and running toward death to escape life, that one's cultural heritage is perhaps based on a kind of simultaneous schizophrenia and amnesia. This implicit recognition of his own dualistic nature and the dualistic nature of experience is what gives Sal the sense of being buried in the "rubbishes of [his] life," but Sal's seeming acceptance of his discovery is what prepares him to move on toward some further confrontation with, some final attempt to understand, the mystery of death. And it is this acceptance that justifies the image of rebirth suggested by the words "womb" and "embryonically."

Sal's discovery of the dualistic nature of things is itself a dualistic matter. On the one hand, the character Sal is discovering the way good and evil, positive and negative, life and death, east and west interpenetrate and make his experience of the world inherently ambiguous. But at the same time that the character Sal is recognizing this, the narrator Sal, as he reflects on and expresses his own experiences, is coming to recognize a second duality between the world as it exists for others—that is, the world as it is by agreed social convention or verifiable measurement—and the world as it exists in the imagination. This double perspective helps explain the tone of Sal's description of the Detroit movie house. For the character experiencing the movies in his exhaustion following his epic ride and disorienting brush with the positive and negative facets of "IT," the movies are indeed a sinister and even mythic experience of the interpenetration of good and evil. Sal, though, looking back and trying to interpret and give form to his experiences, is aware of both the intensity of the experience and the shallow, ephemeral nature of the actual stimulus. The movies are Hollywood pap, but they are experienced with an intensity that suggests something much more profound because of the imagination's power to transform what it encounters. Sal may, looking back, satirize the movies themselves, but he recognizes the validity of his imaginative reception of the "Myth of the West" and the "Myth of the East." The imaginative reality of the individual does not deny the social reality of the group, nor does the reality, the realism, of the group deny the imagination's ability to perceive and create. Rather, they interact just as the competing myths interact. The point, as Sal is coming to recognize, is not to subjugate one to the other, not to deny the romantic experience of the self for the naturalistic experience of the group or vice versa, but to understand the way these different modes interrelate.

Sal's attempt retrospectively to order the competing realities of imagination and social world explains in part the pervasiveness of references to earlier American texts. Ahab and Huck offer Sal a yardstick for measuring his own experiences against earlier cultural models. It is as if Sal is able to give significance to his experiences only as he is able to relate them to the cultural patterns evoked in these earlier texts. The question of the car as raft or *Pequod* is not for Sal as narrator or Kerouac a matter of literary play but a matter of substance, a question of the first order. The typically American patterns of *On the Road* have, of course, long been recognized.[10] Dean embodies the conflict between the autonomous, visionary isolation of the adolescent and the constricting but sustaining social world of the adult. Dean is Huck Finn a few years older and refusing to give in to the fact that there is no more "Indian Territory." He is Gatsby living as if he can control time. And *On the Road* is typically American in the way it opposes fluidity and form, ecstasy and reason, individual and society, East and West, frontier past and urban present. But this Americanness has not usually been taken as a point in the book's favor. When Leslie Fiedler complains that Kerouac's "transparent, not-quite-fictional representations of himself and his friends emulate Huck Finn when they, at best capture the spirit of Tom Sawyer and, at worst, Becky Thatcher," he seems not to notice that Kerouac is aware of this.

Kerouac's sense of earlier American texts is more complex and serious than Fiedler recognizes. Kerouac uses the allusions and parallels to classic American texts along with such obviously iconographic images as cowboys and hobos to define the substance of Sal's education. For Sal, understanding Dean is also a matter of confronting the culture and the images that have shaped Dean since these underlie Sal's fascination with him. Sal is not fascinated with cowboys, the West, and travelling because of Dean; he is fascinated with Dean because Dean crystalizes Sal's recognition of these images. Dean reminds Sal of his romantic American heritage and does so at precisely the moment when Sal's allegiance to that other stereotypical American pattern, the middle-class faith in education, marriage, and success has left him "feeling that everything was dead" (OR, 3). Dean motivates Sal to explore his heritage, and this means grappling not only with the real world of Cheyenne's Wild West Week but with the symbolic landscape of East, West, and Mississippi, and the imaginative past of Huck, Ahab, and frontier; and this enables Kerouac to use these images and patterns to measure the progress of Sal's education.

Each trip and section of *On the Road* is characterized by

a distinct attitude on Sal's part toward his cultural heritage. In part one, Sal's sense of America, Dean, and the West is a nostalgic fantasy of adolescent adventure that assumes life can be reduced to a matter of fences to be whitewashed, and that someone else will always be there to ply the brush. It may be a bit strong to equate this fantasy with Becky Thatcher as Fiedler does, but the limitations of Sal's view are obvious, first to the reader and, finally, even to Sal. Fantasies about red lines on maps and the greatest ride or greatest laugh reinvigorate Sal from his initial despair at the opening of the book, but they finally obscure reality. They provide escape but offer no growth. They offer Sal an approach to the solitary world of hitchhiking but offer no guidance for the more complex and social situations that he encounters in the later stages of the trip.

In part one, Sal's shallow use of cultural myths obscures reality and leads ultimately to the insanity of the Ghost of the Susquehanna. In part two, Sal attempts to do without cultural models altogether. In effect, he blames the failure of the first trip on his use of cultural models rather than his shallow understanding of them. In part two Sal and Dean have no map; their "testament" is an unread paperback found by the side of the road. Ironically, Sal, in trying to ignore his cultural heritage, fulfills it even more slavishly in his second trip than his first. Nothing is more American than Sal's programmatic dismissal of precedent and his faith that immediate experience indulged in for its own sake will yield meaning.

If parts one and two show Sal discovering the liabilities of individualism, part three shows him searching for an alternative to it. Figuratively, the comradely marriage of Sal and Dean echoes such pairings as Natty and Chingachgook, Ishmael and Queequeg, and Huck and Jim. Like their precursers, Sal and Dean search for a compromise between the isolation of the individual and the entrapment of society and family. Their failure to create a timeless society of two comes as no surprise. Their own characters are perhaps too erratic for a lengthy relationship and, even were this not the case, rivers end, ships sink, and the westward creep of civilization, Christianity, and old age separate even the most mythic of pairs. It is unclear whether Sal realizes at the time of the trip the Americanness of his pact with Dean or the questions it implies, but he certainly recognizes these matters retrospectively. As he narrates the trip, Sal actually discovers and defines its ambiguous nature through his recognition of such analogues for Dean and the car as Huck and the raft and Ahab and the *Pequod*. These analogues cannot solve Sal's experiences for him, but they allow him to define what is at stake and are Sal's means for grappling with the ambiguities of his American journey. While Sal assumed in part one that the ambiguities were not there and in part two that the heritage was not there, in part three he is aware of both the compelling nature of cultural heritage and the conflicts within such a heritage. He is aware of his compulsion to discover an individuality and freedom, yet aware also that this attempt opens him to the conflict between the shallow innocence of the "Gray Myth of the West" and the corruption of the "weird dark Myth of the East." Sal may still, as Fiedler suggests, be more of a Tom Sawyer than a Huck Finn, but if so, he is Tom Sawyer in the process of becoming Nick Carraway. Like Nick, Sal must mediate between East and West and between the sanctity of the imagination and the corruption of history.

Like Nick, Sal must distinguish between the symbolic truth of the hero as he exists for the imagination, and the much more indeterminate reality of the hero as he exists in the actual world. In part three, Sal begins to recognize that the imagination is a fundamental tool for interpreting experience. It allows a coherence and depth not possible in the real world. For Sal, the car is raft, *Pequod*, and simply a car being driven into a wreck. Sal's recognition of the car's symbolic possibilities is not an attempt to escape the experience but to interpret it through images that suggest a truth the stiuation itself can only partly contain. In this sense, the failure of the comradely alliance of Sal and Dean comes not from choosing inappropriate roles, but from their inability to distinguish between the imaginative truth of the timeless partnership of comrades and the time-bound relationship of actual friends. As Sal becomes increasingly clear in part four about the relationship between the life one lives imaginatively and the life one lives in society, he attains, finally, the seemingly contradictory but liberating recognition that Dean is both "God" and a "rat," both the mythic avatar of the free and independent American and the victim of his society and his own personal excesses. He begins to understand that his recognition of the myths of East and West is a discovery of the necessity of the imagination, as well as a discovery of the competing principles of good and evil.

Initially in part four, Sal is simply marking time, waiting for something to indicate the direction he should take. As with the earlier sections, his lethargy is disrupted by spring and the urge to travel. Also as before, Sal's decision to travel is in part an attempt to avoid issues and in part an attempt to respond to them. When he goes to say good-bye to Dean before heading for Denver, Sal is reminded of Dean's essential westernness. Dean "the cowboy" is out of place in crowded parties and looks "more like himself huddling in the cold . . . rain on empty Madison Avenue" (OR, 251). Space and isolation are integral to the "Myth of the West." As Dean later tells Sal, the inscriptions on the toilet walls in the East and West are

> entirely different; in the East they make cracks and corny jokes and obvious references, scatological bits of data and drawings; in the West they just write their

names, Red O'Hara, Blufftown Montana, came by
here, date, real solemn, like, say, Ed Dunkel, the
reason being the enormous loneliness that differs just a
shade and cu[n]t hair as you move across the Mississippi." (OR, 267)

To travel west means Sal must confront again his loneliness
and lack of identity. Yet to stay amounts to giving up. The
image of Dean on Madison Avenue also evokes the way urban life has encroached on the heritage of open space. Social
relationships and urban sprawl leave Dean no "Indian Territory," and Sal realizes that Dean's recognition of this or
something like it has left him at least temporarily defeated.
As Dean admits,

"I've decided to leave everything out of my hands.
You've seen me try and break my ass to make it and *you*
know that it doesn't matter and we know time—how
to slow it up and walk and dig and just old-fashioned
spade kicks, what other kicks are there? *We* know."
(OR, 251–52)

Dean's abdication from decision reminds Sal that his own
refusal to "decide" is in effect a decision. Sal claims to agree
when Dean looks to their future and says,

"You see, man, you get older and troubles pile up.
Someday you and me'll be coming down an alley
together at sundown and looking in the cans to see."
"You mean we'll end up old bums?"
"Why not, man? Of course we will if we want to,
and all that. There's no harm in ending that way. You
spend a whole life of non-interference with the wishes
of others. . . ." (OR, 251)

But Dean's fatalism is of a piece with Mississippi Gene's and is something Sal cannot yet accept. When he sees Dean "the following Sunday," Sal admits, "'All I hope, Dean, is someday we'll be able to live on the same street with our families and get to be a couple of oldtimers together'" (OR, 254). And Dean responds by showing Sal a snapshot of his ex-wife in San Francisco and their new child.

> He took out a snapshot of Camille in Frisco with the new baby girl. The shadow of a man crossed the child on the sunny pavement, two long trouser legs in the sadness. "Who's that?"
> "That's only Ed Dunkel. He came back to Galatea, they're gone to Denver now. They spent a day taking pictures." (OR, 254)

Sal notes Dunkel's "compassion," but at least in part it is Sal's remembrance of Dunkel's "ghost" and other ghosts that shapes his next comments:

> I realized these were all the snapshots which our children would look at someday with wonder, thinking their parents had lived smooth, well-ordered, stabilized-within-the-photo lives and got up in the morning to walk proudly on the sidewalks of life, never dreaming the raggedy madness and riot of our actual lives, our actual night, the hell of it, the senseless nightmare road. All or it inside endless and beginningless emptiness. . . . Dean walked off in the long red dusk. Locomotives smoked and reeled above him. His shadow followed him, it aped his walk and thoughts and very being. . . . All the time he came closer to the concrete corner of the railroad overpass. He made one last signal. I waved back. Suddenly he bent to his life and walked quickly out of sight. I gaped into the bleakness of my own days. I had an awful long way to go too. (OR, 254)

Sal as yet can accept neither the compromises that might lead to the security of being an "oldtimer" nor the cost that comes with the freedom of remaining alone. When Sal sets out the "following midnight," he sings, "Home in Missoula / Home in Truckee, / Home in Opelousas, / Ain't no home for me. / Home in old Medora, / Home in Wounded Knee, / Home in Ogallala, / Home I'll never be" (OR, 255). Even though the West still lures Sal, it offers him no home, and yet, since the East itself is no home either, Sal prefers to travel rather than sit tight.

Like the earlier trips, the fourth one begins with Sal, unable to deal with his obsessions, wandering off to escape for a time the pressures that build up when he stays in one place. But this time, Sal is free of the illusion that the trip will resolve anything. He does not assume that he will find "the pearl" nor does he intend to found a patriarchy. He's travelling because he "can't stand the suggestions of the land that come blowing over the river." In Denver, Sal has a "wonderful time." He finds that "the whole world" opens for him because he has "no dreams." Because he has no dreams, Sal is able and willing to see clearly what he encounters. Things are no longer the greatest or most fantastic. He is willing to enjoy what comes his way without justifying himself through hyperbole.

Sal's realistic acceptance is typified by his dealings with Henry Glass, whom Sal meets on the bus to Denver. Glass, a "curly-haired kid of twenty," has just gotten out of jail, and Sal agrees to chaperone him as far as his brother's in Denver.

> His ticket was bought by the feds, his destination the parole. Here was a young kid like Dean had been; his blood boiled too much for him to bear; his nose opened up; but no native strange saintliness to save him from the iron fate. (OR, 257)

Sal in no way romanticizes Glass even though superficially
he is of a type with Dean. Glass is ultimately pathetic and
vicious, and Sal perceives the difference between Glass and
Dean even though Sal's buddies in Denver from his college
days do not. "They loved Henry and bought him beers"
(OR, 257). They patronize Henry as they once patronized
Dean. In contrast to his college buddies, Sal does not use
Glass. Rather, almost as Mississippi Gene might, he lends a
hand seemingly without expecting anything in return or
without attempting to prolong the encounter. But there is
an important difference between Gene's tolerance and Sal's.
Gene's seems based on a belief that certain questions cannot
be answered and Sal's, judging from his encounter with
Dean before leaving New York, on a temporary decision not
to ask certain questions. His clarity about Glass in effect
presents Sal with a problem. He is able to distinguish Glass
from Dean because he has "no dreams," and yet what
redeems Dean and distinguishes him from Glass is Dean's
ability to dream, his imaginative vitality, his "strange
saintliness." Sal's dreamlessness allows him to see others as
they are; yet what makes other people humanly important
to him are their dreams. And finally, Sal's dreamlessness
makes his own life temporarily tolerable; and yet dreams
are necessary if an alternative is to be found to the simple
fatalism of Mississippi Gene.

Not surprisingly, it is Dean who ends Sal's passivity. Sal
has planned a trip to Mexico, and Dean buys a car to join
him and do the driving. In Mexico, Dean intends to get a
quickie divorce from his third wife in order to rejoin his second wife and most recent child. Sal reacts almost apocalyp-
tically to the news that Dean is on the way and imagines a
figure of mythic proportions.

> Suddenly I had a vision of Dean, a burning shuddering
> frightful Angel, palpitating toward me across the road,

approaching like a cloud, with enormous speed, pursuing me like the Shrouded Traveler on the plain, bearing down on me. I saw his huge face over the plains with the mad, bony purpose and the gleaming eyes; I saw his wings; I saw his old jalopy chariot with thousands of sparking flames shooting out from it; I saw the path it burned over the road; it even made its own road and went over the corn, through cities, destroying bridges, drying rivers. It came like wrath to the West. I knew Dean had gone mad again. There was no chance to send money to either wife if he took all his savings out of the bank and bought a car. Everything was up, the jig and all. Behind him charred ruins smoked. He rushed westward over the groaning and awful continent again, and soon he would arrive. (OR, 259)

Yet Sal is also aware that this vision does not coincide with the Dean others perceive.

He [Dean] stood and performed before Shephard, Tim, Babe, and myself, who all sat side by side in kitchen chairs along the wall. . . . Then Dean suddenly grew quiet and sat in a kitchen chair between Stan and me and stared straight ahead with rocky doglike wonder and paid no attention to anybody. He simply disappeared for a moment to gather up more energy. If you touched him he would sway like a boulder suspended on a pebble on the precipice of a cliff. He might come crashing down or just sway rocklike. Then the boulder exploded into a flower and his face lit up with a lovely smile and he looked around like a man waking up. . . . He had no idea of the impression he was making and cared less. People were now beginning to look at Dean with maternal and paternal affection glowing in their faces. He was finally an Angel, as

I always knew he would become; but like any Angel he still had rages and furies, and that night . . . Dean became frantically and demonically and seraphically drunk. (OR, 262–63)

Sal sees Dean's mythic dimensions, both "demonic" and "seraphic," Dean's social dimension, and something of the extent to which Dean does and does not understand the interaction of the two. Sal sees Dean as he exists in time, suffering and as hung up as any character in the book, and Dean as he exists out of time, rising to his role and opening the possibilities of vision. Sal perceives and accepts Dean much as he perceives and accepts Henry Glass. But Dean is so compelling that Sal cannot, as he could with Glass, maintain his distance or equanimity, and Dean's arrival changes the trip to Mexico from a matter of casual sight-seeing into yet another quest. In setting out one final time with Dean, Sal puts himself in a situation where he must give in to vision and dream again.

Sal and Dean approach their journey to Mexico as if it will finally resolve the conflict between East and West. It is an attempt to get beyond the American patterns that have controlled the first three trips. At the end of part three, Sal admits that his repeated east-west crossings have made him feel "as though I were a traveling salesman—raggedy travelings, bad stock, rotten beans in the bottom of my bag of tricks, nobody buying" (OR, 245). But the new trip will be

the most fabulous of all. It was no longer east-west, but magic *south*. We saw a vision of the entire Western Hemisphere rockribbing clear down to Tierra del Fuego and us flying down the curve of the world into other tropics and other worlds. "Man, this will finally take us to IT!" said Dean with definite faith. (OR, 265–66)

In fact, Sal feels the trip will be so "fabulous" that he can not "imagine" it. Nevertheless, it is clear that Sal and Dean approach it as an escape from their Americanness. "'Ah,' sighed Dean, 'the end of Texas, the end of America, we don't know no more'" (OR, 273). And while Laredo is "the bottom and dregs of America where all the heavy villains sink, where disoriented people have to go to be near a specific elsewhere they can slip into unnoticed" (OR, 274), when Sal and Dean look across into Mexico, they do so

> with wonder. To our amazement, it looked exactly like Mexico. . . . We were longing to rush right up there and get lost in those mysterious Spanish streets. It was only Nuevo Laredo but it looked like Holy Lhasa to us. (OR, 274)

And once they are in Mexico, Sal comments,

> Behind us lay the whole of America and everything Dean and I had previously known about life, and life on the road. We had finally found the magic land at the end of the road and we never dreamed the extent of the magic. (OR, 276)

The magic and the holiness Sal and Dean perceive in Mexico comes from the same source. They see Mexico as primitive. Its people live in a manner so old and fundamental that they are before history and timeless. To Sal, it is "the golden world that Jesus came from" (OR, 300), and "these vast and Biblical areas of the world" are

> the places where we would finally learn ourselves among the Fellahin Indians of the world, the essential strain of the basic primitive, wailing humanity that stretches in a belt around the equatorial belly of the world. . . . These people were unmistakably Indians

and were not at all like the Pedros and Panchos of silly
civilized Amerian lore . . . they were great, grave Indians and they were the source of mankind and the
fathers of it. . . . As essential as rocks in the desert are
they in the desert of "history." . . . For when destruction comes to the world of "history" and the Apoca-
lypse of the Fellahin returns once more as so many
times before, people will still stare with the same eyes
from the caves of Mexico as well as from the caves of
Bali, where it all began and where Adam was suckled
and taught to know. (OR, 280–81)

In spite of the ambiguities of Adam's lesson in knowledge, to
Sal and Dean the Mexican "Fellahin" is a positive figure. He
is free from the dialectic of "East" and "West." He is neither
restricted or oppressed by his society, nor is he isolated in his
freedom. And his sense of the magical promises to heal the
split between the reality of dream and the reality of Western
culture.

According to Dean, even the Mexican border guards are
"lazy and tender" and "n[o]t like officials at all" (OR, 274),
and, as Dean eyes the girls they pass, he tells Sal,

"Oh, man, I want to stop and twiddle thumbs with the
little darlings," cried Dean, "but notice the old lady or
the old man is always somewhere around—in the back
usually, sometimes a hundred yards, gathering twigs
and wood or tending animals. They're never alone.
Nobody's ever alone in this country. While you've been
sleeping I've been digging this road and this country,
and if I could only tell you all the thoughts I've had
man!" He was sweating. His eyes were red-streaked
and mad and also subdued and tender—he had found
people like himself. (OR, 279–80)

However, these people are only partly like Dean, and the

conflict Sal senses in Dean's eyes prefigures the failure of the trip. The Fellahin peasants suggest the source of Dean's energy and authenticity which is, in effect, preverbal just as the Fellahin precedes history, but the Fellahin peasants exemplify the primal in a calm and simple way that Dean, for all his atavism, can not. Dean belongs to a society which is historical and anything but primitive, and Dean's confused motivation for traveling to Mexico suggests the extent of his problem. He is both questing for some final and absolute version of "IT" and trying to resolve his tangled legal and social obligations, and Dean can no more separate his social life from his religious life than he can accept a marriage or do without one. Dean and Sal can recognize their source in the primitive but can no more return to it than Sal could return to childhood in part one.

Even could Sal and Dean become Fellahin, the world of the Fellahin also turns out to have its sorrows. In the "sun-baked town of Gregoria," Sal and Dean meet Victor, a Mexican "kid," who procures "'ma-ree-gwana'" and women for them. At first as Sal and Dean smoke "a tremendous Corona cigar of tea" with Victor and his brothers, they seem to be realizing their dream and entering the community of the Fellahin and the world of magic.

> It seemed the car was surrounded by brothers, for another one appeared on Dean's side. Then the strangest thing happened. Everybody became so high that usual formalities were dispensed with and the things of immediate interest were concentrated on, and now it was the strangeness of Americans and Mexicans blasting together on the desert and, more than that, the strangeness of seeing in close proximity the faces and pores of skin and calluses of fingers and general abashed cheekbones of another world. (OR, 283)

And as Victor and Dean try to talk without a common language, Sal experiences the entire encounter as an ecstatic vision.

> For a mad moment I thought Dean was understanding everything he said by sheer wild insight and sudden revelatory genius inconceivably inspired by his glowing happiness. In that moment, too, he looked so exactly like Franklin Delano Roosevelt—some delusion in my flaming eyes and floating brain—that I drew up in my seat and gasped with amazement. In myriad pricklings of heavenly radiation I had to struggle to see Dean's figure and he looked like God. I was so high I had to lean my head back on the seat; the bouncing of the car sent shivers of ecstasy through me. The mere thought of looking out the window at Mexico—which was now something else in my mind—was like recoiling from some gloriously riddled glittering treasure-box that you're afraid to look at because of your eyes, they bend inward, the riches and the treasures are too much to take all at once. I gulped. I saw streams of gold pouring through the sky and right across the tattered roof of the poor old car, right across my eyeballs and indeed right inside them. . . . For a long time I lost consciousness in my lower mind of what we were doing and only came around sometime later when I looked up from fire and silence like waking from sleep to the world, or waking from void to a dream. . . . (OR, 285)

But this ecstatic moment is quickly undercut. As Sal, Dean, and Victor look into the eyes of Victor's infant son to see "'the loveliest of souls,'" the child begins to cry.

> So great was our intensity over the child's soul that he sensed something and began a grimace which led to

> bitter tears and some unknown sorrow that we had no means to soothe because it reached too far back into innumerable mysteries and time. (OR, 286)

And then, when Victor takes them to the brothel, the visit, though performed without fear for appearances, is finally driven and frantic as much as it is orgiastic and celebratory. Even Mexican whores have their "grief," and Sal is left guilt ridden by the encounter. He has dispensed with a certain amount of American propriety only to encounter a more fundamental version of human suffering.

The visit to Gregoria suggests that the journey from Denver has involved an attempt to strip away old cultural and social identities. Sal and Dean, socially marginal even before the trip, attempt to communicate with Victor and his brothers at a level that precedes language and cultural distinctions, and in the brothel, Sal and Dean seek to become totally and only physical. They are not completely successful in either attempt, though Sal typically seems more aware of this in retrospect. After Gregoria, Sal and Dean move even farther from Denver and America both geographically and metaphorically. As they move south, night and jungle take from Sal and Dean even their awareness of themselves as human. It is not that Sal and Dean become simply physical, but, rather, they lose even the sense of their own bodies. Engulfed in the oppressive heat and insects, they merge with the jungle until

> I realized the jungle takes you over and you become it. Lying on top of the car with my face to the black sky was like lying in a closed trunk on a summer night. For the first time in my life the weather was not something that touched me, that caressed me, froze or sweated me, but became me. The atmosphere and I became the same. Soft infinitesimal showers of microscopic bugs fanned down on my face as I slept, and they were ex-

tremely pleasant and soothing. The sky was starless, utterly unseen and heavy. I could lie there all night long with my face exposed to the heavens, and it would do me no more harm than a velvet drape drawn over me. The dead bugs mingled with my blood; the live mosquitoes exchanged further portions; I began to tingle all over and to smell of the rank, hot, and rotten jungle. . . . I opened my mouth to it and drew deep breaths of jungle atmosphere. It was not air, never air, but the palpable and living emanation of trees and swamp. (OR, 294–95)

This deathlike state is the polar opposite of Sal's vision in Gregoria where he loses "consciousness" in his "lower mind," though the "infinitesimal showers of microscopic bugs" is reminiscent of the "myriad pricklings of heavenly radiation." In the first case, one escapes consciousness by transcending the body in an ecstasy of light which is beyond the physical. In the second, one escapes consciousness by descending into the body and a darkness which is even physical in its radiation.

To the extent that the Mexican pilgrimage has religious dimensions, Sal has had a perception of absolute life and absolute death. He has died out of his old social identity and been reduced through a kind of death to a primal substance and process. The movement has been from life to death, and this prepares for the final phase of the quest, a return to life and the possession of "IT" and the end of the road. But the rebirth that follows the jungle night and the arrival in Mexico City are both finally ambiguous. At dawn as roosters "crow the dawn," though there is "no sign of dawn in the skies," Sal sees "an apparition: a wild horse, white as a ghost. . .white as snow and immense and almost phosphorescent." The horse passes by Dean and the car "like a ship" and disappears into the jungle, leaving Sal to wonder, "What was this horse? What myth and ghost, what spirit?" (OR, 295–96) Sal offers no interpretation, though Dean has also "faintly" dreamed or seen the horse. The incident is one of the most puzzling in the book. One possible source of the explanation Sal fails to give may be chapter 42 of *Moby-Dick*, "The Whiteness of the Whale."

> Most famous in our Western annals and Indian traditions is . . .the White Steed of the Prairies; a magnificent milk-white charger, large-eyed. . . with the dignity of a thousand monarchs. . .the elected Xerxes of vast herds of wild horses, whose pastures in those days were only fenced by the Rocky Mountains and the Alleghanies [sic]. At their flaming head he westward trooped it like that chosen star which every evening leads on the hosts of light. The flashing cascade of his mane, the curving comet of his tail, invested him with housings more resplendent than gold and silver-beaters. . . . A most imperial and archangelical apparition of that unfallen, western world, which to the eyes of the old trappers and hunters revived the glories of those primeval times when Adam walked majestic as a god, bluff-bowed and fearless as this mighty steed. . . .in whatever aspect he presented himself, always to the bravest Indians he was the object of trembling reverence and awe.[12]

Whatever the precise import of the white horse, the dawn it announces should presumably lead to the climactic vision of "IT," and, as Sal and Dean leave the jungle, they appropriately begin to climb the mountain that leads to the high plateau and Mexico City. As they climb, Sal and Dean encounter "mountain Indians." These Indians make Victor and the people of Gregoria seem positively European by contrast. They are "short and squat and dark" and "shut off from everything else but the Pan American Highway" (OR, 297). Dean is "in awe" of these people even though he realizes that the "Highway partially civilizes" those by the road and that those in the mountains "must be even wilder and stranger." Finally, Sal and Dean stop to deal with some girls who sell "little pieces of crystal."

> Their great brown, innocent eyes looked into ours with such soulful intensity that not one of us had the slightest sexual thought about them; moreover they were very young, some of them eleven and looking almost thirty. "Look at those eyes!" breathed Dean. They were like the eyes of the Virgin Mother when she was a child. We saw in them the tender and forgiving gaze of Jesus. And they stared unflinching into ours. We rubbed our nervous blue eyes and looked again. Still they penetrated us with sorrowful and hypnotic gleam. When they talked they suddenly became frantic and almost silly. In their silence they were themselves. "They've only *recently* learned to sell these crystals, since the highway was built about ten years back—up until that time this entire nation must have been *silent*!" (OR, 298)

Dean then fishes a wristwatch out of his "old tortured American trunk" and trades it for a crystal.

> Then Dean poked in the little girl's hand for "the sweetest and purest and smallest crystal she has personally picked from the mountain for me." He found one no bigger than a berry. And he handed her the wristwatch dangling. . . . He stood among them with his ragged face to the sky, looking for the next and highest and final pass, and seemed like the prophet that had come to them. (OR, 298–99)

The action is inherently allegorical. Dean attempts to give away his awareness of time and language for the timelessness and pure silence of the mountain Indian. And yet Dean can no more give away time with his wristwatch than the girl can assume Dean's awareness of history with it. Dean's prophetic status is ultimately ambiguous. His refusal to give into history is heroic and vicious, insightful and deluded.

> They watched Dean, serious and insane at this raving wheel, with eyes of hawks. All had their hands outstretched. They had come down from the back mountains and higher places to hold forth their hands for something they thought civilization could offer, and they never dreamed the sadness and the poor broken delusion of it. They didn't know that a bomb had come that could crack all our bridges and roads and reduce them to jumbles, and we would be as poor as they someday, and stretching out our hands in the same, same way. Our broken Ford, old thirties upgoing America Ford, rattled through them and vanished in dust. (OR, 299)

Yet this is as close to an ultimate vision of "IT" as Sal and Dean are to come. Like it or not, Sal cannot put aside his past of "old thirties upgoing America" nor the awareness of history, progress, and ultimate failure that that suggests to him. At best, Sal can only recognize that Dean is both prophet and fool: prophet for the awareness of primal vitality that he evokes in his most intense gesture, and fool for his refusal to recognize more clearly the way his allegiance to impulse and energy is gradually damning him. Like Huck sitting to his waist in the Mississippi and musing with Jim, Dean stands for the rejoining of man and nature and man and man outside of society; like Ahab almost admitting his doubts to Starbuck and himself, Dean stands for the ultimate conflict between the will and all else even at the expense of its own destruction. At best, Sal can only recognize the distinction between the grandeur of Dean's symbolic truth, that which makes him seem like a "God," even if a god torn between light and dark, and the pettiness of much of his actual life. Certainly it is something like this recognition that enables Sal to accept Dean's betrayal of him in Mexico City, when their stay in "the great and final wild uninhibited Fellahin-childlike city" they "knew" they "would find at the end of the road" (OR, 302) fails to provide a final vision. In Mexico City, Sal is soon "delirious and unconscious" with dysentery, and Dean, divorce completed, within a few days feels the need "'to get back to my life'" (OR, 302) and starts back alone leaving Sal to fend for himself.

> When I got better I realized what a rat he was, but then I had to understand the impossible complexity of his life, how he had to leave me there, sick, to get on with his wives and woes. "Okay, old Dean, I'll say nothing." (OR, 303)

Dean is a "rat" and as much driven as the driver, but Sal is able to see that this does not negate the other side of the matter. Dean's intensity is the source of both his transcendence and his tendency to victimize those around him. Dean's "strange saintliness" does not negate his tendency to be a "rat," but it does redeem him from being merely a Henry Glass.

When Sal sees Dean the winter following their trip to Mexico, he realizes that Dean's doubleness is further complicated by the fact that the person most victimized by Dean is Dean himself. Having made his own way from Mexico City to New York, Sal takes up with a "girl with the pure and innocent dear eyes" that Sal claims he has "searched for and for so long" (OR, 306). When Sal writes Dean to tell makes his way to New York to drive them west. But Dean has not allowed Sal the time to save for the "jalopy panel truck" that was to haul them all to California, and Dean ends up going back as he came, alone riding in freight train cabooses with a borrowed railroad pass. The Dean that Sal sees in New York has been reduced by exhaustion and confusion and perhaps even despair to a point where he can express himself only through vague and disconnected phrases and gestures.

> He couldn't talk anymore. He hopped and laughed, he stuttered and fluttered his hands and said, "Ah—ah—you must listen to hear." We listened all ears. But he forgot what he wanted to say. "Really listen—ahem. Look. . . ." And he stared with rocky sorrow into his hands. "Can't talk no more—do you understand that it is—or might be—But listen!"(OR, 306–7)

And when Sal sees Dean off, he thinks to himself, "Old Dean's gone," which seems as much a comment on what has become of Dean as it is on his having "rounded the corner. . . and bent to it again"(OR, 309).

Dean's intensity and refusal to consider costs both redeems him and makes a shambles of his life and the lives of those close to him. And at the end of *On the Road*, Sal is left to try to make some sort of peace with his encounter with Dean, the road, America, and himself. In spite of the mawkish note introduced by Sal's sudden discovery of his one true love and the hint that "her innocent eyes" are the answer to all the failures of the book, Sal actually ends his story with a final recognition that there is probably no resolution to the conflict of "East" and "West" and that human experience is partial and a matter of conflict. At best, and Sal suggests it is enough to make life worthwhile, the imagination can place the fragments of time-bound experience within a timeless coherence that can be grasped symbolically by the imagination. The activity of the imagination does not allow escape from the sorrowful, but it allows a certain acceptance through the recognition of an absolute and the recognition that human experience itself is always a falling away from this absolute. In this sense, *On the Road* ends up being not so much "a lyrical Yea-saying outburst"[13] as an elegy for the inevitable failure that follows that "outburst."

Like that other American novel, *The Great Gatsby*, in which the narrator must make his peace with a larger-than-life, self-made hero who lives out his tawdry version of America's idealized past, *On the Road* ends with a lyric passage that evokes what has become a quintessentially American mixture of past and present, dream and nightmare, hope and nostalgia. Both passages evoke the original promise of the land. Fitzgerald dreams of "the green breast of the new world."[14] Kerouac sees the "raw land that rolls in one unbelievable huge bulge over to the West Coast." In both, a nightlike, deathlike "enchantment" competes with what seems the lost and perhaps illusory promise of America. Fitzgerald writes that Gatsby's "dream must have seemed so close. . . . He did not know that it was already behind him, somewhere back in that vast obscurity beyond the city, where the dark fields of the republic rolled on under the night." Kerouac describes "all the people dreaming in the immensity of [the land] . . . just before the coming of complete night that blesses the earth, darkens all rivers, cups the peaks and folds the final shore in, and nobody, nobody knows what's going to happen to anybody besides the forlorn rags of growing old." And both passages end by blending past and present into a timeless sense of process. In *The Great Gatsby*, "we beat on, boats against the current, borne back ceaselessly into the past." In *On the Road*, we sense the merging of the generations, of Dean and Old Dean his father. "I think of Dean Moriarity, I even think of Old Dean Moriarity the father we never found, I him that they plan "to migrate to San Francisco," Dean think of Dean Moriarity." In America, Sal learns, the child must be father to himself. This is his freedom and his ultimate burden. The father is "never found" and perhaps neither is the self.

In thinking of Dean Moriarity, Sal is clearly thinking of himself, "dreaming in the immensity" of "that raw land," and the presentness of the action in the final passage suggests that Sal will "sit on the old broken-down river pier" whenever "the sun goes down" as long as he is "in America," which, as Richard Brautigan notes, is "often only a place in the mind."[15] In this "America" that Sal discovers, the conflict of "East" and "West" finally translates into the contrast between the society of everyday life and the visionary society of one. Both are a state of isolation and suffering, but the visionary society of one, the true "West" of the "America" of the imagination, transcends and contains the actual society of the "East." The visionary America of one pays for its transcendence by its heightened awareness of its loneliness and suffering, and it is in turn rewarded by the timeless presentness visible in Sal's final vision as he looks out as "the sun goes down" and anticipates "the coming of complete night" which "blesses the earth," "folds the final shore in" and in death accomplishes the union of father and son, self and other, man and nature.

Short of "complete night," the closest possible approximation to union seems to be the community of comrades, and this too is finally more real in the timeless retrospect of the imagination and may be based on nothing more that the uneasiness of sons about the father. At the beginning of the trip to Mexico, Sal comments about himself, Dean, and Stan, a young Denverite who travels with them: "Here were the three of us—Dean looking for his father, mine dead, Stan fleeing his old one, and going off into the night together" (OR, 267). At best, the conflict with the father must simply be recognized and accepted, just as Sal must recognize and accept a phenomenon like the river that both divides and joins "East" and "West." The river, "the great brown father of waters" rolls "down from mid-America like the torrent of broken souls" (OR, 141), "washes" America's "raw body" (OR, 15), and is itself the "endless poem" (OR, 255).

The father cannot be escaped or replaced. He can only be acknowledged and that acknowledgment may partially heal and give one the recognition of the order of one's suffering, which in turn may allow one partially to recognize a kinship and from that kinship give speech to the paradoxical vision of suffering which in some way heals, as Sal attempts to do in his closing speech. At least, this is one way to understand the function of the various prophet-father figures that Sal encounters or imagines encountering throughout the book from the "old man with white hair" who is probably "walking" from "the Plains" toward Central City "with the Word" (OR, 55), to the old man who confronts Sal "one night just over Laredo border" as Sal is heading home from Mexico:

> I heard the sound of footsteps from the darkness beyond, and lo, a tall old man with flowing white hair came clomping by with a pack on his back, and when he saw me as he passed, he said, *"Go moan for man,"* and clomped on back to his dark. Did this mean that I should at last go on my pilgrimage on foot on the dark roads around America? (OR, 306)

The religious dimension of the encounter is perhaps made clearer by a letter of Kerouac's to Holmes dated 11–12 July 1950 and written from Mexico City where Kerouac describes walking home from the bullfights. He describes his remorse over the bull's death and how he contemplated walking to New York in penance. When Kerouac sees a pile of bricks lit oddly by the sun and shade, he says that he sensed that God was waiting there for him. As Kerouac stands at the bricks, he has a vision of a man who walks across the country communing with all he encounters until his death. In the letter, Kerouac refers to this figure as the saint of *On the Road*, and as in *On the Road*, this figure continually confronts those he encounters with the phrase "Whither goest thou?"[16]

And yet it is the religious import of the encounter with the old man that finally creates a problem for Kerouac and his reader at the end of the novel by raising the need for Sal to speak, not as the student he has been throughout the novel, but as the prophetic commentator Kerouac yearns to become but as yet cannot believe himself to be. The imagistic summing in the final description is formally more in keeping with the book, and yet the portentous encounters with the walking saints suggests the restlessness and confusion within the substantial achievement of the book.

Chapter Two

From Fact to Vision: The Road Book

On the Road is an important point in Kerouac's development, but in spite of its very real achievement and its popularity, *On the Road* is not a good indication of Kerouac's achievement. It suggests his concern with the American tradition, but *On the Road* was written before Kerouac had established his sense of voice. Attempts to describe Kerouac's career in terms of *On the Road* inevitably distort his practice, since such key matters as Spontaneous Prose and his allegiance to a "confessional" literature all developed after what is now known as *On the Road*. Part of the problem in understanding *On the Road*'s proper place in Kerouac's career stems from the book's manuscript history. Begun 9 November 1948, *On the Road* was three and a half years in the writing, and in that time Kerouac worked on at least five distinct versions of the book. The one ultimately published as *On the Road* in 1957 by Viking is the fourth of these versions. Kerouac's final version, now issued under the title *Visions of Cody*, was drafted after what is now called *On the Road*, and it was this book that Kerouac considered the true *On the Road*. And it is this final version of *On the Road* that defines Kerouac not only thematically but stylistically.

The manuscript history of *On the Road* is the history of Kerouac's development as a writer. It is in large part the story of Kerouac's attempt to resolve his conflicting sense of writing as a naturalistic and romantic activity, and to develop a way of writing that would simultaneously analyze the external social world and celebrate the self's ability to transcend that world imaginatively. Each stage of *On the Road*, each of its five versions, marks a new understanding for Kerouac of what he once described as his need "to tell the truth (all of it, in every conceivable mask) and yet digress from that to my lyric-alto knowing of this land . . . a deep form bringing together of two ultimate and at-present-conflicting streaks in me."[1]

Kerouac's dualistic sense of writing is already apparent in *The Town and the City*, his first book and the work that immediately precedes the long struggle to write *On the Road*. Kerouac later described *The Town and the City* as "fiction" which was "written according to what they told me at Columbia University," and he distinguished it from the work that followed, which he described as "confessions."[2] In spite of this, the book is in many ways Kerouac's most directly autobiographical. Kerouac is largely unselfconscious about why he is writing the book, and the "fictional" characters and situations more directly reveal Kerouac's sense of himself and his reasons for writing than any of the books that followed.

Most simply, *The Town and the City* suggests what John Clellon Holmes has called Kerouac's "deeply traditional nature":

> I never fully understood the hunger that was gnawing in him then, and didn't realize the extent to which the break-up of his Lowell home, the chaos of the war

years and the death of his father had left him
disrupted, anchorless; a deeply traditional nature
thrown out of kilter . . . intent on righting itself
through the creative act.[3]

In *The Town and the City*, Kerouac seems to have wanted
to recover or reaffirm some sense of stability that he
associated with the large families and Catholic
neighborhoods of his Massachusetts hometown. The Second
World War, as he understood it, had largely destroyed that
world. Kerouac's sense of uncertainty about his own present
is also probably tied to what he perceived as his own failure
since leaving the small-town world of Lowell. He entered
Columbia University on a football scholarship just as the
Second World War was beginning, and found he could
tolerate neither the regime of the practice field nor that of
the classroom. He dropped out of school and drifted
through most of the war, working occasionally as a construction worker or merchant seamen and spending the rest
of his time hanging around Columbia with, as he later
described them, "the despairists of my time."[4] When his
health broke and he wound up in a VA hospital for treatment of phlebitis, as Kerouac later represented it in the
Vanity of Duluoz, he came "to understand that the city intellectuals of the world were divorced from the folkbody
blood of the land and were just rootless fools."[5] And so
Kerouac "decided to become a writer, write a huge novel
explaining everything to everybody,"[6] including his father
who intensely disapproved of Kerouac's drifting and who
died of stomach cancer before Kerouac completed the book.
Even in this brief summary, it is possible to see how Kerouac
might be "thrown out of kilter." His transition from the
small town of his adolescence to the city of his adulthood
had been complicated by the outbreak of war, his father's
illness, and his own failure to realize his and his father's goal
of all-American glory at Columbia. It is also no wonder that

Kerouac always looked back to the thirties as a period of stability, and the war years as a period of breakdown and confusion.

In a letter written while working on *The Town and the City*, Kerouac states, "When this book is finished, which is going to be the sum and substance and crap of everything I've been thru throughout this whole goddam life, I shall be redeemed."[7] And some twenty years later in his *Paris Review* interview, Kerouac said that at the time of *The Town and the City* he "was determined to be a 'great writer' in quotes like Thomas Wolfe," whose novels had "opened my eyes to America as a subject in itself."[8] These statements imply two fundamentally different views of writing. In the first, writing is primarily a private, or at least a personal, gesture. It is self-justification. In the second, writing is public, a gesture the self makes toward the world around it. This dichotomy between writing as self-affirmation and writing as social analysis is more than a difference between the earlier and later Kerouac. It reflects the doubleness in Kerouac's attempt at "righting" himself through writing.

The impact of Wolfe on Kerouac is apparent in his use of Wolfe's *Look Homeward, Angel* as a model for *the Town and the City*. Kerouac recounts the history of the Martin clan of Galloway, Massachusetts. The novel follows the Martin parents and their eight children from the year 1935 to the end of the Second World War and the father's death. Kerouac took most of the incidents from his own experience but expanded the size of his own family, himself and his sister, to the eight Martin children in order to match the large Gant family of Wolfe's novel. In a letter a year after completing the novel, Kerouac wrote, "It's not strictly autobiographical since I used various friends and girl-friends, and my own parents, to form a large family, the Martin family."[9] Kerouac also substitutes from Wolfe an eccentric "Victorian house" for the tenement of his youth, and bases his description of the head of the Martin family on Wolfe's portrayal of Oliver Gant.

Ann Charters suggests that Kerouac made these changes in his own experience in order to follow "an American literary tradition of contrasting the innocence of the country and small town life with the destructive experience of a big city,"[10] but *The Town and the City* is more complex than this. Although Kerouac left the five parts of the novel untitled, it is relatively easy to characterize each one, and this clarifies the relationship between small town and big city. The innocent, static small town is found only in part one, the first eight of five hundred pages. Part two is the one section of the novel that actually contains the conflict between town and city, a conflict expressed in the form of an argument between two of the Martin brothers. The small-town brother, Peter, brings to New York sympathies which are out of place in the city. Francis, tutored by an older, worldly, and (Kerouac implies) homosexual gentleman, professes a brand of aesthetic cynicism that fits him for city life but cuts him off permanently from the town. Both town and city values are presented as permanent and permanently in conflict.

Part three focuses on the war, which for Kerouac was the dividing line between the town of his past and the city of his present. Much of *The Town and the City*'s best writing is in this, the longest, section of the book. Kerouac explores a changing America through vignettes of train stations, diners, and all-night vigils, and is here most purely "realistic," most purely an observer. But the war also breaks up the dichotomy that has controlled the book. In part four, the remnants of the Martin family have relocated in New York, and in this, the section dealing most purely with the city, the town-city dichotomy of the early sections of the novel has disappeared. The war has destroyed the small town of the thirties and with it the static and synchronic basis of the contrast on which the novel is ostensibly constructed. In effect, the war replaces the conflict between town and city with the contrast between past and present. Unfortunately, Kerouac seems only partly aware of the way the war shifts the terms, and in the fifth and final section of the novel, he can only oscillate between a nostalgic affirmation of the stable past and a fatalistic acceptance of the chaotic present.

In a sense, Kerouac's problem in *The Town and the City* comes from his unwillingness to admit that his sense of conflict came from something within himself as well as from a conflict between two styles of life. By locating the conflict between two symbolic locales, Kerouac does not allow himself to admit that he was attracted to the city's freedom as well as troubled by its chaos, and that he was oppressed by the town's order as well as nostalgic for its certainty. By locating his conflict and loss only in the world of town-city, Kerouac is unable to address the more intensely emotional issue of the relationship between his past and present, and without doing that his novel can neither redeem him nor control and organize the circumstances of his life.

Kerouac completed *The Town and the City* in May of 1948, and proceeded to revise it and struggle with the ending while he circulated it to publishers during the summer and early fall. By the time Kerouac put the book aside to begin *On the Road* in November 1948, he had begun to realize that his sense of conflict came as much from the way he approached his material as from the material itself. In a letter to Ginsberg, he writes that he has come to see *The Town and the City* and the years spent writing it as a delusion. Kerouac claims that he accepts this realization because he now understands that art itself is suspect, a fantasy or escape from the real world and the reality of death. Kerouac then explains that his new sense of these matters has led him to realize that he identifies the pastoral world of *The Town and the City* and of home with the perspective of the child and its creative impulse to make itself immortal by modifying the world to its own ends; and that he identifies the world of Ginsberg and Cassady, hitchhiking, and sexual relationships with the perspective of the adult and its emphasis on the outer world, the consequence of actions, and realistic limitations. In writing *The Town and the City*, Kerouac seems to feel that he has paid insufficient attention to the demands of the outer world. And so he tells Ginsberg that he will start over with his writing, taking his cue from Theodore Dreiser's work and the perspective of William Burroughs. His new work, *On the Road*, will be factualist (Kerouac to Ginsberg, 10 November 1948, GA).

Kerouac's reaction against *The Town and the City* is perhaps harsh, but having sensed a duality in his view of the world, his first response is to reject one term of the duality. *On the Road* will deal with the outside world. In beginning *On the Road*, Kerouac seems to feel it more important to control the experiences of his chaotic present that to recover and validate his past. Later Kerouac could deal with his hitchhiking experiences of the summer of 1947 as a comic education, but in 1948 he still wanted to keep this disillusioning encounter with the adult world at enough distance to interpret it.

Although the earliest two versions of *On the Road* have never been published, Kerouac's correspondence and work journal make it possible to reconstruct them and establish the pattern of growth from the "fictional" *Town and the City* to the experimental *Visions of Cody*. In spite of his dissatisfaction with *The Town and the City*, the earliest *On the Road* was apparently of a piece with it stylistically. Holmes recalls that Kerouac "began prosing [*On the Road*] more or less in the style of [*The Town and the City*]" and "completed a few 'New York' scenes (some of them very fine)."[11] And in letters and his journal, Kerouac mapped out the characters for his new book by comparing them with the characters of *The Town and the City*'s city sections. Some, like "Levinsky," modeled on Ginsberg, were to be borrowed intact. Journal references also suggest the earliest Road book relied heavily on *The Town and the City*'s New York material. The two chapters that Kerouac mentions specifically for the new book deal with a marijuana party and with Times Square.

Kerouac's need to avoid emotional involvement with his road material is signalled in the letter to Ginsberg by the references to William Burroughs and Theodore Dreiser. Burrough's friendship with and influence on Kerouac is well documented. However, 1948 predates Burrough's own work, and the reference is probably explained by a letter of Burroughs to Ginsberg dated 9 November 1948:

> Myself I am about to annunciate a new philosophy called "factualism." All arguments, all nonsensical considerations as to what people "should do" are irrelevant. Ultimately, there is only fact on all levels, and the more one argues, verbalizes, moralizes the less he will see and feel of fact. Needless to say I will not write any formal statement on the subject. Talk is incompatible with factualism. (Burroughs to Ginsberg 9 November 1948, GA)

Burroughs must have written something similar to Kerouac at about this time since Kerouac cites 9 November as the beginning of *On the Road* and the letter to Ginsberg mentioning factualism is dated 10 November. Burrough's emphasis on "only fact" and on dispensing with "nonsensical considerations" perhaps suggested to Kerouac a rationale for avoiding too much involvement in his material. Factualism minimized the need to characterize and judge.

The reference to Theodore Dreiser also clarifies Kerouac's sense of an art based on factualism. In the fall of 1948, Kerouac took a course in the modern American novel at the

New School. The course covered, among others, Dreiser, Wolfe, Sinclair Lewis, Ernest Hemingway, and Fitzgerald. For the course, Kerouac wrote an essay on Dreiser and Lewis that contrasted what Kerouac saw as Dreiser's calm, neutral, and complete reporting with Lewis's more agitated tendency to manipulate the reader's sympathy by juxtaposing the naive hopes of his characters with the actual shabbiness of their condition. To Kerouac, Dreiser and Lewis define completely different categories of artists. The angry Lewis is a reformer who, in his zeal to improve society, ignores and defies the terms of the human condition. Dreiser, though, is a stoic observer who sees the worst and still has the equanimity to describe the entire range of American experience with the serenity that Kerouac sees as typifying the factualist.[12]

For *On the Road* to be factualist, it would have to deal with the reality of the outer world on all its levels without giving in to the self-lacerating fury that Kerouac finds in Lewis or the naiveté that he found retrospectively in *The Town and the City*. Kerouac's paper suggests not simply his admiration of Dreiser's detachment but his sense that he, like Lewis, might tend to lose himself in his material.

In spite of the liberation Kerouac found in Factualism and the example of Dreiser, the energy of "childish immortality" was simply too important to Kerouac to be dropped, and Kerouac soon found himself questioning the direction he should take with *On the Road*. In his journal, he wrote:

> 32,500 words since I started on November 9 . . . . I delight in the figures, as always, because they are concrete evidence of a greater freedom in writing than I had in Town & City . . . . I hope I can go on like this from now on and write a great many good books all intertwined. Still—lately—I've had a feeling of emptiness . . . *not* boredom, just emptiness and even falseness. These are not the reverent mad feelings dur-

> ing Town & City . . . . My whole feeling and
> knowledge now is concentrated on people and not
> beyond them in the realms of "spirituality" . . . .[13]

The distancing of factualism leads to "greater freedom" and productivity, but it also leaves out "realms of 'spirituality' " and that leads to "emptiness."

Kerouac's uncertainty about factualism is evident in the history of *Doctor Sax*. As Charters has pointed out, Kerouac began *Doctor Sax* immediately after *The Town and the City* in October 1948,[14] abandoned it in his initial excitement over *On the Road* and factualism, then dabbled with it at various points during the work on *On the Road*, and completed it finally in 1952 in several months of intense work after finishing *Visions of Cody*. *Doctor Sax*'s earliest title, "A novella of Children and Evil, The Myth of the Rainy Night," its genesis as the dream later described in *On the Road*,[15] and the text as published all indicate that Kerouac associated *Doctor Sax* with the inspired world of the child; it is supernatural in contrast to the naturalistic *On the Road* (WJ, 14 December 1948). In a later journal entry, Kerouac writes that he thinks of it as a poem that bridges between *The Town and the City* and *On the Road* because he needs an idea of this sort to justify the project. Kerouac claims that *Doctor Sax* seems too crazy and slight, too much shaped by the mysical side of Ginsberg to bother completing and yet too beautiful not to finish. Kerouac talks of the piece as poetic in contrast to the quicker paced and prosy *On the Road* (WJ, 25 April 1949).

Kerouac's confused allegiance to both the supernatural and the naturalistic is apparent in his journal account of a session of his creative writing class with Brom Weber at the New School. Kerouac writes that he had taken Ginsberg to the class as a visitor and that Ginsberg set the usually dull class ablazing with four strange hours of debate about the divine, praying, and contemporary saintliness. In the middle of this, Kerouac reports that he announced to Weber that he could not pay attention to criticism of his work because his writing was an act of praying. According to the entry, Weber explained that criticism should be understood intellectually, to which Kerouac replied, in effect, that emotion, not intellect, was everything to him (WJ, 9 December 1948). In this entry, Kerouac uses the supernatural perspective of *Doctor Sax* to defend himself in the workshop where he had been submitting the naturalistic *On the Road*.

By December 1948, Kerouac apparently had stopped working on the factualist *On the Road*. The initial impetus for the book had run out partly because it did not provide "the reverent mad feelings" of *The Town and the City* (WJ, 29 November 1948). December was also given over to schoolwork and a trip to North Carolina for Christmas with his sister. This trip in turn was interrupted by the arrival of Neal Cassady from California and the series of parties and travels that took Kerouac to California and back before he settled in to finish his fall term school work in mid-February.

Neal Cassady, prototype for Dean Moriarity in *On the Road* and Cody Pomeray in *Visions of Cody*, plays a prominent role in the development of Kerouac's Road book. The example of Cassady in large part led Kerouac to travel west in the summer of 1947 and in that sense was a prod to the project itself, but in the fall of 1948 when Kerouac began *On the Road*, Kerouac had known Cassady only briefly. And Kerouac's factualist *On the Road* was largely without characters based on or incidents derived from Cassady. The six weeks from December 1948 to February 1949, which Kerouac describes in part two of *On the Road*, was Kerouac's first chance to study Cassady closely and see the road from his perspective. This experience moved Kerouac even farther from his initial intention for a Dreiserian book. In his journal, Kerouac writes that much to his surprise and almost as a miracle, Cassady's coming reinforced his allegiance to the supernatural *Doctor Sax* rather than the naturalistic *On the Road*. Furthermore, Cassady's arrival reminded Kerouac of an earlier perception that the young and homeless of America were intrinsically religiously motivated (WJ, 10 January 1949). And so, when Kerouac returned to New York in February, he first returned to *Doctor Sax* rather than *On the Road*.

Kerouac's schoolwork in February 1949 shows him attempting to resolve the dichotomy between supernatural and naturalistic writing. Kerouac's final essay for the American novel course dealt with the critical reception of Thomas Wolfe. Kerouac's journal contains an extensive gloss on this essay where he discusses the relationship of the intellectual mind and the metaphysical mind (WJ, 20–21 February 1949). For Kerouac, these are different and conflicting approaches to accounting for situations. Kerouac writes that an intellectual attempting to describe the sight of a man contemplating eternity would hastily dispense with the matter by labeling it with a convenient phrase. To Kerouac, the intellectual mind functions by labeling and then arranging, rearranging, and systematizing other labels. By contrast, the metaphysical mind, typified for Kerouac by Shakespeare, would use a different phrase, a phrase partly controlled by aesthetic considerations and for that reason not only more beautiful but more precise and usable as well. To Kerouac at the time of this entry, the result of the intellectual response was prose, and the result of the metaphysician's response was poetry, a mystical matter of the word as seen, the word as presence. Kerouac then goes on to illustrate metaphysical language in Wolfe, who Kerouac admits only intermittently attains the combination of precision and resonance that for him characterize the metaphysical response.

Kerouac's analysis of Wolfe's style is acute and shows more critical awareness than he is usually credited with.

Kerouac's concern is not only with the need for mood and texture but with accuracy and clarity as well. Clearly emotion is more important for the metaphysician, as Kerouac uses the term, than for the intellectual, but Kerouac perceives the metaphysician's need for certain checks on his use of the emotional. In the gloss on his Wolfe essay, Kerouac talks about the relative nature of meaning and the writer's need constantly to check the poetry of his language with a rigorous sense of structure. If this control of the emotional is lost, the impression on the reader will be vague and meaning will be generalized to the point of triviality. If the metaphysician fails to focus the general emotional response with the particularity of context, he will commit the same error as the intellectual by substituting a generalization for perception.

By March 1949, a month after the Wolfe essay, Kerouac was again thinking about *On the Road*. In two long journal entries from late March and early April, Kerouac outlines plans for a new version of *On the Road* that would dispense with the original factualist or naturalistic sense of the work, in favor of a metaphysical or romantic sense of it. In the entry for 25 March 1949, Kerouac states that the book would now be organized as a quest. Ray Smith, hero of the factualist version of the previous fall, would now become the narrator and be known as Smitty. It is not clear that this means Smitty would in fact speak in the first person. Rather it seems that his perspective will govern the book with the narrative managed in a limited third-person voice. Although Kerouac is vague about voice, he makes Smitty's function quite clear by comparing him to Sancho Panza, Boswell, and Pip. The hero of the new version is to be named Red Moultrie, a man of about Kerouac's age at this point, his late twenties, and one who has bounced around a bit and then finds himself in jail thinking he must (here Kerouac quotes John Bunyan) "seek an inheritance, incorruptible, undefiled, and that fadeth not away." As the reference to *Pilgrim's Progress* suggests, the Road book would now consider the spiritual mode originally associated with *Doctor Sax*.

In fact, the notion that the road material might have spiritual significance may predate the factualist conception of November 1948. In one paragraph of this new phase of journal notes, Kerouac seems to be quoting himself from an earlier notebook that he might have kept during his hitchhiking trip west in the summer of 1947. He writes that those who are beat interest him because, besides being poor and bereft of the consolation of family, they have an aura of pilgrimage and, with someone like Cassady, a mystical intensity lacking in other classes of American wanderers such as winos and hobos. Kerouac labels this entry with the date 1947, the designation California, and a note to the effect that the beat young wanderers seem a social phenomena. In any case, Kerouac's new plans for *On the Road* emphasized the internal world, the world of childish immortality, at the expense of the external world, and his excitement over the new notion of the book leads him to decide near the end of the entry to put off *Doctor Sax* until after completing *On the Road* in order to make *Doctor Sax* completely fantasy.

Much of the 25 March entry details the character of the hero Red, who is said to be an artist with his life. Kerouac describes Red as a man of experience who has a number of different skills and abilities and a wide range to his character. According to Kerouac, Red's background, logically, does not explain his spiritual stature, and Kerouac compares this aspect of Red to Melville's figure of the Confidence Man. In spite of his maturity, Red is concerned with the world of the child. He seeks to be redeemed. He has grown up in California's central valley, and he now looks to regain the richness of life which should have been his inheritance. At the opening of the novel, Red—an ex–minor league ballplayer, ex–jazz drummer, ex–London University student, ex–seaman, ex–truck driver—is spending his final night in jail where, in spite of his role as an accomplice in a robbery, he has prayed and studied the Bible while awaiting his release. Once out, Red is to linger in New York with the characters of the city sections of *The Town and the City*. Kerouac may even have hoped to rework such material as the Times Square chapter from the fall and fit it into this new opening. Then Red and Smitty, his saintly Pip who Kerouac describes as a boy whose nature is almost too naive for the real world, are to go west to join Red's other sidekick, Vern Pomeray, a figure modeled on Cassady. Kerouac seems to have planned to give Red the best of his own experiences from the hitchhiking trip of 1947 and then to flesh these out with incidents from Cassady's life.

Red's past is a romanticized version of Kerouac's own, but when Kerouac describes what will be the novel's action (that is, Red's future), he closely prefigures his portrayal of Cassady as Dean Moriarity in *On the Road*. Kerouac's description of Red travelling west after his release from jail could almost be a gloss for the scene in part three of *On the Road* where Sal notes, "how Dean could go mad and then suddenly continue with his soul—which I think is wrapped up in a fast car . . ." (OR, 230).

Kerouac's notes for the Red version of *On the Road* show a deepening sense of the symbolic possibilities of his material, but they also show his uncertainty about how to organize them into a novel. Red seeks a lost inheritance, but Kerouac seems uncertain about its nature. It may be tied to finding the father, but the notes imply that this will happen early in the book, in contrast to the long and finally futile search for Dean's father *On the Road*. At another point, inheritance is a matter of regaining lost joy. Elsewhere, it seems to be a humble spirit and endless revelation. Quests are inevitably vague as to their goal. They are searches for something, but Parzival's grail, Pilgrim's city, and Ahab's whale are each evoked concretely and are present as symbolic entities in a way that inheritance is not.

Similarly, after suggesting an opening for the novel, Kerouac largely ignores plot. He mentions that Red, Smitty, and Vern will find Red's father in Montana and then locate Vern's father in Denver before going on to California. Kerouac notes that this is an approximate sense of the quest's beginning. Kerouac then breaks away from the novel's action to discuss Red's soul. Over the course of the novel, Red's soul will pass through five stages, and Kerouac lists them by number. First, in jail and initially on the road, Red's soul will be pure. Then will come a painful apathy that Kerouac links in the entry to drugs, Vern, and the later experiences of the Road. Third will be a crisis brought on by the chance winning of a great sum of money in Butte, Montana. This crisis will at first derange Red and then trigger the fourth phase, Red's attempt to reattain his initial sanity and purity. Finally, the novel will end with Red repenting and recovering his previous joy.

Kerouac's wording of this list of Red's soul states implies only two actual incidents. Judging from references in *Doctor Sax*, the crisis in Butte would probably have taken the form of an epic pool match, and Kerouac seems to have intended to use the encounter near Harrisburg with the "Ghost of the Susquehanna," later used in both *Pic* and *On the Road*, as part of his portrayal of Red's early road purity. The states of Red's soul are nothing more than an abstraction of the history of Red Cross Knight in Spenser's *Faerie Queene*, which Kerouac was reading about this time, and the comparison with Spenser, whether Kerouac had it in mind, defines the problem. Spenser's imagination is highly dramatic. Each stage of Red Cross's journey from innocence through corruption and despair to grace is portrayed in terms of a confrontation with something or someone, but in Kerouac's journal, the dramatic is largely absent both in the above entry and in the remainder of the March and April entries. At another point in the 25 March entry, Kerouac describes what will happen when Red is in Arizona. After Red witnesses a beautiful dawn, he is troubled by the local police. Kerouac then explains that after the police leave Red simply stares into emptiness, feeling that there is nothing that gives him the right to take joy in the dawn or to be angry at the police. Kerouac closes this section of the note with the reminder to himself that this scene will introduce the theme of men and stars being intermingled. The scene as Kerouac presents it in the journal is a series of contrasts: the beauty of the desert sunrise and the pettiness of the police, Red's sense of unworthiness before nature and his resentment and possibly guilt over the police. However, the elements are connected in an interesting way only in Red's own mind; and Red can only stare off into the distance, forcing the third-person narrator or Smitty—the journal does not specify—to fill in the significance of the scene or forcing Kerouac to leave it as a tableau. Apparently Kerouac felt uneasy with simply describing a series of incidents, perhaps because it now seemed too factualistic, and as yet he had not figured out how to shift the action to the growth of the characters' perceptions and their own internal worlds.

In the notes of March and April 1949, Kerouac seems to have hoped to use Red's quest as the novel's central line and then to relate other symbolic elements and patterns to it. Perhaps he felt that these other elements would compensate for the seeming lack of external event, that they would establish the richness of Red's internal life. In the 25 March 1949 entry, Kerouac reminds himself that the book is to be structured not only by the events of the quest but by places as well. He writes that the book is to explore not only the opposition of town and city, of Galloway and New York, but great rivers like the Mississippi and Susquehanna and valleys like the San Joaquin. In the early April continuation of the March notes, Kerouac asserts that three factors will unify *On the Road:* the American seasons, American places, and Red's attempt to recover his inheritance. Red's travels will be simply the vehicle for presenting these other elements.

In these April notes, Kerouac also makes it clear that he means for Red's quest to have historical significance. Red's lost inheritance is figuratively to be America's lost inheritance, its lost innocence. One segment of the April notes compares the contemporary stampede for success with the perversion of pioneering spirit by the 1849 rush to California for gold. In the entry, Kerouac describes at length pioneers en route west to homestead abandoning their wagons and families to ride off for Sutter's Mill at the word of gold. Kerouac then compares these gold-seekers to intellectual liberals who have also lost their souls because of their fascination for solutions that are nothing but false glitter.

Kerouac's journal notes of March and April 1949 show that traveling with Cassady in early 1949 had clearly complicated Kerouac's sense of his road material and moved him from a strictly factualist approach toward the world of the child and the romantic. However, it was not until the summer of 1949 that Kerouac actually seems to have begun drafting a version of *On the Road* based on these notes. In April 1949, Harcourt Brace accepted *The Town and the City*, and Kerouac worked throughout the month trimming the 1,100-page manuscript for publication. Only after he had moved to Denver in May was Kerouac ready to begin again with *On the Road*. Most likely he completed less of this second draft than the thirty thousand words of the November 1948 factualist version, but in letters to Ginsberg and Elbert Lenrow,[16] his instructor in the American novel course at the New School, Kerouac describes the work in progress and sends on an excerpt of some seven hundred words that describes Red the night before his release from jail. As the passage opens, the inmates are going to sleep, that point in time when they are closest in spirit to the world of the child. Red in his bunk listens to the conversations around him, his attention drifting from those closest to him and then listening to those farther and farther away, until the voices become so indistinct that they are like waves. This sense of the sea like ebb and flow of sound leads Kerouac to equate the jail with a ship under sail.

Once Kerouac introduces the metaphor of the jail as a ship, everything else all but disappears. The passage from that point on largely ignores the initial setting of the jail and proceeds to survey the New York neighborhoods visible, presumably, from Red's cell window. This voyage of New York moves on a swell of long vowel sounds and by means of an associative logic controlled by the sound and by the emotional resonances of words more than by their explicit meanings. Kerouac uses unusual words such as *rumorous* and then echoes them with words such as *murmurous*. He uses a variation of Whitman's title phrase "Out of the Cradle Endlessly Rocking" to affect the phrase later in the passage that characterizes the neighborhood of Rockaway, and similarly subsumes the Jamaica neighborhood with images of lights and blinking mystery to evoke the image of a Caribbean night. Throughout, Kerouac attempts to create a lyric, imaginative world that overcomes the actual scene of the external world.

The example of Melville probably helped shape the style and strategy of the passage describing Red's night in jail. The previous fall, Kerouac and Holmes had audited Alfred Kazin's Melville course and were "tremendously impressed" by Melville and by Kazin's enthusiasm for him.[17] In his work journal and letters from 1948 and 1949, Kerouac talks about "Bartleby the Scrivener," *Pierre, The Confidence Man*, and "The Encantadas"; and in the letter to Lenrow, Kerouac introduces the piece about Red's night in jail by saying that he found himself turning *On the Road* into a project with a Melville-like character even though he had not set out to do so. A week later in the letter to Ginsberg, Kerouac again cites Melville and claims that the jail scene is evidence of the seriousness of their stylistic attempts to move beyond ordinary usage to create a prose that, like Melville's, not only dealt with the world but was poetic as well in its pure attention to the nature of language. Holmes recalls that Kerouac at this point was particularly taken with "The Pacific" chapter of *Moby-Dick,* and Kerouac's description of Red's last night in jail resembles this Melville chapter in its sound and rhythm and also in the way the lyric flight of associations begins in the novel's plot, transcends it, and then returns to it. However, in Kerouac's passage, the opening is an awkward attempt to reach the point where the jail transforms into a ship, and the ending a jolting reentry into the world of the plot. Moreover, the passage is most compelling when Red is least integral, even though he is ostensibly the one looking out the window and transforming the city; and Red's passivity and the passage's awkward opening and closing have the effect of suggesting to the reader that the writer feels his hero does not understand the significance of his own thoughts.

In the journal notes of March and April, Kerouac is unsure about how to manage the fictional representation of inner and outer worlds, and in the July letter to Ginsberg, Kerouac's attempt to recount the series of visions Red will have later on in his last night in jail underscores Kerouac's uncertainty over the relationship of fact to fantasy, as does his final summary of the book's action in the same letter. In this summary, Kerouac cites a series of symbolic figures that Red will encounter, and seems more aware of the difficulties of the quest and the ambiguities of inheritance than in March and April. Red will no longer find his father immediately, and the act of searching itself has assumed a more central role. Kerouac is also no longer so sure that the end will be bliss and insight. But his sense of how to present his material has nearly disappeared into a tenuous dream world. The only narrative action is contained in one short phrase about dusty trials and wild rides. This vague sense of

Red's physical world is quite unlike the detailed world of *Moby-Dick* with its seamless continuum from the supernatural to the factual. In his zeal to break out of the limits of ordinary prose, Kerouac seems, in these 1949 notes for and fragments of an *On the Road* emphasizing the inner world of the child, to forget what the Melville of *Moby-Dick* never forgets, the necessity of grounding the fictional world.

Kerouac may have drafted no more of this second *On the Road* than appears in the July letters to Ginsberg and Lenrow. Shortly after these letters, he left Denver to find Cassady in San Francisco, and the two of them began their second cross country trip together, described in part three of the published *On the Road*. But by February 1950 when Kerouac next comments on the book, there is renewed interest in the naturalistic side of writing and very likely some recognition of what had gone wrong with the book the previous summer. In a letter to Ginsberg, Kerouac writes that *On the Road* is coming along wildly and with a wonderful intricacy (Kerouac to Ginsberg, February 1950, GA). Kerouac then explains that the situations used in the book are now entirely fictional, totally imaginary, though certainly expressing his concepts and his sense of life. He advises Ginsberg that the key to fiction is first to be clear about the ideal and eternal relationships of the characters so that one may manipulate the necessay naturalistic elements to evoke the ideal relationships for the reader. In the letter, Kerouac gives an example of this precedure when he explains to Ginsberg his ideas about businessmen. Kerouac claims that they are driven by their sense of guilt, and he plans to dramatize this by having an appropriate figure wake with a scream in his motel room and reveal his sense of crime, and the visions that go with it, to a listener there with him.

The impulse for *On the Road* in this letter is still what Kerouac refers to as metaphysical, but naturalistic material is now seen as a pragmatic necessity even though, in the notes of March and April and the work of July, Kerouac still has little sense of how he will use naturalistic material to reveal the metaphysical. His sense of the book still seems to require a narrator who exists solely to record the businessman's spieled vision. Whatever became of the scene with the businessman confessing in the night is unclear. It seems likely, though, that this work of February 1950 stalled out just as the work of the previous summer, and there is little to indicate Kerouac's progress on *On the Road* from this point through November 1950. In May 1950, he was off again for Denver to work on the book, but aparently managed little before Cassady arrived and the two began the trip to Mexico City described in part four of the published *On the Road*. According to Charters, Kerouac's stay in Mexico was a period of heavy drug usage that stretched him nearly to the breaking point, and it is unlikely that Kerouac worked much on his Road book until he returned to New York and a more ordered existence in October 1950.

From his return to New York in 1950 until the completion of *Visions of Cody* in 1952, Kerouac's work on *On the Road* centered around his attempt to master first-person narrative. In *Pic, On the Road,* and *Visions of Cody*, the final three versions of his Road book, Kerouac develops an increasingly flexible and intense sense of voice. In retrospect, it seems inevitable that Kerouac's desire to comment on the outer world of the adult and reveal the inner world of the child would lead him to adopt the first person, but the shift from the third-person voices of the factualist and metaphysical versions to the first-person voice of *Pic* seems to have been almost an accident. On his return from Mexico, Kerouac was less attracted by the directness and flexibility of the first person than he was by the possibility of looking at the road through the eyes of a child in order to pull back from the emotional extremes of Mexico and recover a certain degree of innocence.

Pic's narrator and hero is a Negro boy of ten who tells his story in dialect. Kerouac talks about the project in a 4 November 1950 letter. A woman named Ellen Lucey had written to congratulate Kerouac on *The Town and the City* and to ask about his relationship to the characters in that book. Kerouac claims that like Francis Martin he was a despairing intellectual and that like Will Dennison he had experienced the affliction of morphine. But Kerouac goes on to point out that his present work is in marked contrast to the world of Martin and Dennison. He writes that his second book is presently one-third completed and that it traces the story of a Negro boy as he and his brother hitchhike from North Carolina to the West Coast and then back. Kerouac identifies this Negro boy with Peter Martin, the character in *The Town and the City* most closely modeled on himself. Kerouac claims that he feels as if he were black and more particularly as if he were a child.[18] The way the letter unfolds suggests that the last line of the letter might just as easily have read, "And especially I'd *like* to feel like a child."

Kerouac does not explicitly identify *Pic* as a version of *On the Road*. But he does call the work his "second novel," and Holmes recalls that Kerouac, "dissatisfied with the time it was taking him to get to the 'road' material, concluded that the 'self-conscious novelization' type of treatment that he was using was wrong [and] veered off into what would become *Pic*," which was never finished and led into the "version we now have"[19] as *On the Road*. Also, the material of *Pic* overlaps with the other versions. It is a story of hitchhiking, and the "Ghost of the Susquehanna" incident, already conceived as part of the book by 1949 and repeated as the climax of part one of *On the Road*, is an important episode in *Pic*. Although *Pic* belongs in the succession of *On the Roads*, textual questions make its precise relation to the other versions a bit unclear. Grove Press labeled it "Jack Kerouac's Last Novel" when they published the book in 1971. This seems to imply that the book was the last book that Kerouac wrote, but Grove apparently meant that *Pic* was Kerouac's last unpublished novel since Kerouac's letter to Lucey and the text itself suggest that the *Pic* of 1950 and that of 1971 are largely the same.

Pic opens in rural North Carolina. Pic, an orphan, lives with his elderly grandfather. On the grandfather's death, Pic is taken in by other relatives who resent the economic burden and have some undefined grudge against Pic's dead parents. The situation is altered when Pic's older brother Slim, a jazz musician living in New York, arrives, and offers to take Pic to live with him and his wife. When the family refuses, Slim resolves matters to everyone's satisfaction by kidnapping Pic and heading back to New York. In New York, Slim in unable to find work, and when the rent comes due, he decides to move to California. His wife will go on ahead by bus. Slim and Pic will hitchhike.

This actions takes up some ninety pages. The actual "road" sequence takes only twelve, mostly given to the encounter with the "Ghost" outside of Harrisburg, Pennsylvania. After the "Ghost," there is a brief conclusion in which Slim and Pic go into a church to rest and are approached by a priest who puts Pic in the choir as a soloist and gives Slim temporary employment as a janitor. At the end of their labors, Slim and Pic are given a hundred dollars, take a Greyhound, and within a page are on the coast. The ending is, at best, abrupt, and makes what is now *Pic*, with the exception of the conclusion, seem like the setup for the longer piece that the letter to Lucey suggests will describe the brothers' trip to the West Coast and back.

The manuscript published by Grove may be the unfinished work from 1950, or it may be a work from the last year or so of Kerouac's life based on the earlier work. Probably it is some of each. *Pic* as printed would make about a third of a novel, and it breaks off (disregarding for the moment the final chapter) at the point where, if continued, the story would move into the world of the road. According to the letter to Lucey, this nonexistent part should be the major section, but according to Holmes, each of the early *On the Roads* stalled before reaching the description of life on the road. The text itself suggests that the book's final chapter was added at a later date. At the end of chapter thirteen, after Slim and Pic have first been misdirected by the "Ghost" and then redirected by a passing motorist, Pic tells the reader, "we was talking about that Ghost of the Susquehanna for the next three months I tell you when we got to Sheila in San Francisco.[20] Pic's precise meaning is obscured by the dialect. He may mean that they (he, Slim, and Sheila) talked about the Ghost for three months after reaching San Francisco, or he may mean that they (he and Slim) talked about the Ghost for the three months it took them to reach the coast. Kerouac's original conception—where travelling, rather that arriving, is central—points to the latter even though it conflicts with the printed ending.

When working on a manuscript, Kerouac tended to push straight ahead. Letters mentioning current work usually mark points of indecision, and the letter to Lucey probably comes at about the end of the work on *Pic*. In *Jack's Book: An Oral Biography of Jack Kerouac*, Barry Gifford and Lawrence Lee, reporting apparently from an interview with Kerouac's third wife, Stella, write that, "At the very end of his life, when the words were gone," Kerouac "resurrected *Pic*," "padded it to novella-length and sold it to Grove Press." According to Gifford and Lee, the original ending in which Pic and his brother are picked up by "two older travelers named Sal Paradise and Dean Moriarity" was dropped at this time at the request of Kerouac's mother, who then "helped [Kerouac] write the final scene, in which a priest saves the boy from a wasted life on the Road."[21] The book does not seem padded, but, even if Kerouac revised the 1950 work, its general import for *On the Road*'s development would be the same.

Pic is in many ways Kerouac's least autobiographical book. The persona of Pic, though it may have its genesis in wish fulfillment, is distinct and separate from Kerouac. Pic speaks in his own voice and tells his story for his own reasons. Pic is probably modeled on Huckleberry Finn. In Twain's book, Huck is ostensibly the perceiving agent, and his naiveté, a function both of his youth and his position outside the social hierarchies of the Mississippi Valley, leads him to notice and comment on the absurdities, immoralities, and discontinuities of the world which he observes but to which he does not belong. Also, Huck's closeness to the natural world of the river (at least partly the product of his relationship with Jim) enables Twain to counterpoint natural and social orders. Pic, like Huck, is outside the normal social hierarchy and is free to move, with his brother, from one situation to another, reacting spontaneously to whatever comes before him whether it is a truck driver or his first cup of coffee. Pic's dialect is also reminiscent of *Huckleberry Finn*, and Kerouac, like Twain, at times exploits his persona's language by allowing Pic to make puns, of which Pic himself is unaware.

Pic is a distinct step forward from the fragments of 1949. The first-person narrator allows Kerouac to emphasize the minute and complex reactions of his hero to the world around him—that is, to focus more on the hero's process of perception than on his physical actions. Pic, the child, tells the story of what passes before him, mingling fact, fantasy, and sensation. Pic's fantasies and observations come seemingly firsthand and unmediated. He has no self-consciousness about his way of perceiving and combining the elements around him, and his directness largely does away with the need in the earlier version to break in and clarify what is "really" happening in the character's mind.

Pic, like Huck, is able to shift easily and continuously from recording events in the outside world to sharing the vitality of the inner world, and back again.

Although the shift to the first person increased Kerouac's narrative fluidity and allowed for the delight in detail that was so important to him, the choice of a child for a persona also created problems. Huck Finn is again useful. Unlike Pic, Huck is old enough to act on his own. He can run away and, when things break right, scheme along with any character in the book. Pic, though, is too young to act on his own. He is passed from grandfather to aunt to brother and cannot initiate action. He is limited to the world that passes before him, and his youthfully limited understanding makes the actual social world in *Pic* much more constricted than in either *Huckleberry Finn* or *On the Road*. *Pic* allowed Kerouac for the first time in his work on *On the Road* to bridge between inner and outer, imaginary and physical, but *Pic* also cut Kerouac off from the social, as distinct from the simply physical, reality of the outer world. He had cut himself off, that is, from the outer world, the world of the adult, just as in the factualist conception of *On the Road* he had cut himself off from the redeeming world of the child.

The Ghost of the Susquehanna incident reveals Pic's specific limitations as a narrator. In *On the Road*, the encounter is eerie and frightening, and it fits into major thematic patterns having to do with the search for lost fathers, the confrontations with false guides, and the recognition of aging and death. In *Pic*, the encounter is quaint. Pic says of the Ghost, "That man was so funny, that was why Slim was followin him and talkin to him so" (*Pic*, 107). Supposedly, adult readers making allowances for the child's perspective are to understand that Slim follows out of more than just amusement, but the indirection necessary to maintain the integrity of the persona makes it difficult for Kerouac to admit to his reader what it is that captivates Slim. Pic's own response at the end of the encounter shows

Kerouac straining against the limitations of his narrator.

> "Well," Slim said, "it *was* a ghost." And he worried
> himself to death standin there with me in those fearful
> woods, at midnight, trying to figure where we was and
> how we got lost. All I could hear now was the pat of
> the rain on a million leaves, and the chug-chug across
> the river, and my own heart beatin in all that open air.
> Lord it's somethin. (*Pic*, 109)

We might accept this from a Huck Finn but not from a
character as young as Pic, and the vague response leaves the
encounter's significance still very much in doubt.

Whether Kerouac recognized these problems and abandoned *Pic* because of them, or simply dropped the book
because of general dissatisfaction with it is a matter for con-
jecture. Either way, he stopped working on the manuscript
and, within a few days, drifted into an affair that led to his
marriage in the middle of November. Kerouac and his wife
settled in a Greenwich Village loft, and Kerouac took a job
as a script synopsizer for a movie company. According to
Charters, Kerouac actually worked primarily on *On the
Road*. Circumstantially, this work seems to have been closer
to the pre-*Pic* conception than to *Pic* itself. If Kerouac had
come to feel that *Pic* was a dead end, he would be as apt to
return to the earlier third-person work as to push forward to
something else, particularly if he assumed that his problems
with the manuscript came from the adoption of a first-
person voice rather than from the adoption of a child as his
persona.

Possibly Kerouac returned to the work he had done from
1948–49. A statement from the dust jacket of the British edition of *The Town and the City* is perhaps relevant.
Presumably adopted from a letter of Kerouac's to the
publisher, the statement reads:

> [Kerouac] is now working on a novel whose background is the recurrence of the pioneering instinct in American life and its expression in the migration of the present generation; a book provisionally entitled *On the Road*.[22]

This appeared in June 1951 and very possibly dates from early 1951. Another scrap from early 1951, a Guggenheim application, also suggests that Kerouac's next move was back to his earlier senses of the project and third-person narration. Kerouac writes that he is working on the third version of *On the Road* and that the book will be the first of a series of interrelated texts organized according to an overall plan that he intends to be his life's work. *On the Road* and the books to follow will, according to Kerouac, be a classification of people and types of experiences that characterize his generation.[23]. Holmes's recollections of Kerouac's work at this time suggest that the work of early 1951 after *Pic* had much in common with the earlier work of the 1948–49 journal. In *Nothing More to Declare*, Holmes writes:

> When he came by in the late afternoon, he usually had new scenes with him, but his characters never seemed to get very far beyond the many layered New York milieu a well-made novel seemed to demand as a contrast to all the footloose uprootedness to come. He wrote long intricate Melvillian sentences that. . .(to him) always got stalled in the traffic jam of their own rhetoric.[24]

In a recent letter, Holmes characterizes this "Ray Smith" material as "very good in a traditional, family-novel fashion." "New York milieu" and "family-novel" style recall the November 1948 "Road," and "intricate Melvillian sentences" brings to mind the work on "Red" from summer 1949.[25]

The opening page of the 1948 "Road journal" may also be significant. For all the disorder of his personal life, Kerouac took particular care of his papers. Charters, when she visited Kerouac to prepare a bibliography of his work, was struck with this and remarked in her introduction on the orderly arrangement of his notebooks. She describes the cover to the *Doctor Sax* notebook and the changes of title from "The Myth of the Rainy Night" to a "Novella of Children and Evil" to the final title, and how the earlier titles had been crossed out to leave only the final one.[26] The opening page of the 1948–49 "Road journal" shows similar changes. In the upper right-hand corner in large letters, Kerouac has written "John Kerouac," and below that in ink extending the width of the page, "Journal during first stages of 'On the Road.'" The journal's text begins immediately below this heading.[27] This seems to have been the page's original state. The signature "John Kerouac" could not have come much later than November 1948. Kerouac began using "Jack Kerouac" on his work no later than February 1949, the beginning of his spring term at the New School. Two other entries on the first page seem to have come later as indexing notes. The first simply notes in the space between the signature and first line, "1948–49," but squeezed between the date and first line in smaller printing is the designation "(Ray Smith)." The position and writing suggest that Kerouac added this after he had finished the journal to identify the material as a general group of work, which indicates that he returned to his earlier conceptions of the book hoping to rework and salvage at least some of the work from 1948 and 1949.

There is also evidence that Kerouac eventually viewed all of the work, except for *Pic*, that preceded *On the Road* and *Visions of Cody* as one group of manuscript. In June 1952, Holmes had sent Kerouac a chapter of what later became his second book, the jazz novel *The Horn*. In response, Kerouac writes that Holmes seems to have found his mature voice. Kerouac states that the writing of *The Horn* is quite different from the Spontaneous Prose of his present work, but that it is quite similar to what he was attempting to do earlier with *On the Road*. Kerouac characterizes this earlier work for Holmes by stringing together in one unpunctuated phrase the names of Ray Smith and Red Moultrie, the heroes of the 1948 and 1949 versions respectively.[28]

Again, in June 1955 in a letter to Ginsberg, Kerouac refers to *Beat Generation* and then identifies it as the Ray Smith *On the Road*. *Beat Generation* may, in fact, have served as the basis for the play Kerouac later worked on under the same title. The third act of that play in turn was the basis of the film *Pull My Daisy* by Robert Frank and Alfred Leslie.

Whatever the precise nature of the Ray Smith work of early 1951, it amounted to a move back toward the more "traditional 'novelistic' form of *The Town and the City*," which, as Holmes notes, simply "was not fluid enough to contain the formlessness of the experience [that Kerouac] was attempting to set down."[29] Kerouac's successive "Roads" had brought him full circle from the naturalistic conception of November 1948 through the romantic work of 1949 and *Pic* and finally back to the naturalistic project of classifying the experiences of a generation. As Holmes hints, Kerouac's problem was to avoid the imitative fallacy. A tightly structured, objective book seemed necessary to establish the thematic significance of such matters as the corruption of the pioneering instinct by the fascination for success and money, and the subsequent loss of personal and national inheritance. And yet such distance and control kept proving incompatible with the fluidity of the road experience.

Through early 1951, Kerouac "grew moody and perplexed"[30] as he tried to push ahead with his book. Then in

March he entered a VA hospital for treatment of his recurring phlebitis. Charters characterizes the stay as again a time of stocktaking. When Kerouac was released, he was ready to begin with yet a new sense of *On the Road*. He had decided to abandon the Ray Smith material, center the book on Neal Cassady, make it more autobiographical, and shift from the third person back to the first. This time, though, his persona would not be a black child but a version of Kerouac himself. As a result of these decisions, Kerouac in three weeks of April 1951 drafted what would finally be published in 1957 as *On the Road*.

The increased importance of Cassady may have been due in part to Kerouac's wife. Fifteen years after the fact, Kerouac claimed to have written *On the Road* "for my new wife, to tell her what I'd been through."[31] On another occasion, he recalled:

> She'd come home from her four-hour waitress job and she'd always want to know all about Neal and what we'd done. "What did you and Neal really do?" she'd ask, and I'd write it for her, and she'd come home and laugh at what I'd written. I'd sit behind a big screen and yell, "Coffee," and her hand would come around the corner holding a cup.[32]

Prior to the April 1951 work, what Cassady and Kerouac had "really" done was still something different than what was happening in the "Melvillean" work that Kerouac was showing Holmes, but the scraps that Kerouac was writing to entertain his wife were apparently more successful than those which were to be a part of the novel.

Charters suggests as well that Cassady may have helped incline Kerouac to make his Road book more autobiographical. In the biography, Charters discusses the impact on Kerouac of a long letter from Cassady. This letter, sometimes referred to as the "Joan Anderson letter," has since been lost, but apparently detailed much of Cassady's own history. Charters writes:

> What excited Jack in reading the letter wasn't only the way Cassady was writing. Jack had been getting the letters for years and already had a sense of Neal's style. What was new for him was reading an extended narrative about Cassady's adventures. Neal's autobiographical style was exactly what Kerouac had been fumbling toward himself in his grandiose plans to be a writer.[33]

This perhaps overstates the matter, but Cassady's writing in the surviving letters and his one book, *The First Third*, is certainly autobiographical. A letter from Cassady to Kerouac in December 1950 clarifies matters:

> I know it's the style to create a fiction of a bunch of characters thrown together in a composite—like Wolfe or Proust did. But, how for one as just straight case-history? I know, none of the characters would stand up—no one person has all the necessary attributes to hold water in a novel.[34]

Kerouac could agree with both of Cassady's propositions, and in part his problem was to find a way to write a "case-history" that would have the "necessary attributes" to make successful fiction. Perhaps Kerouac realized that this might be done by telling the story in his own voice but, instead of telling strictly his own story, combining it with someone else's story and taking the role of narrator—taking, that is, the role of Smitty, the hero's Boswell. As a result, the *On the Road* of April 1951 was neither strictly case study nor autobiography. Or rather, it was both: a case study of Cassady told in Kerouac's own voice as part of his own autobiography. It was in some way Kerouac's response to Cassady's example and request, combined with elements and concerns that dated back to the earlier "Roads" including factualism and vision.

✗ The April 1951 work on "On the Road" has become something of a legend. In later years Kerouac and some of his friends characterized the April work as a conscious act of literary revolution, a decision to write spontaneously and solely from inspiration rather than from preconceived notions about one's material. At the time, though, Kerouac's decision to attempt to write his book at high speed was more ⸗n act of desperation than a demonstration of aesthetic pri..ciples. Holmes recalls that in early April Kerouac "sat down in disgust and frustration and batted out the first draft of the version we have now."[35] Kerouac announced,

> "I'm going to get me a roll of shelf-paper, feed it into the typewriter, and just write it down as fast as I can, exactly like it happened, all in a rush, the hell with these phony architectures and worry about it later."[36]

And apparently this is precisely what Kerouac did, typing steadily onto a roll of "shelf-paper" or "teletype paper," and drawing heavily on a supply of benzedrine and his ability to type one hundred words a minute. But Kerouac's comments to Holmes suggest that initially Kerouac thought of this April 1951 experiment, what he later called the twenty-day *On the Road*, as a ploy to clarify his thoughts that would in turn allow him to write his book, rather than as an attempt at writing the book itself.

Holmes actually may have planted the idea for what might be termed the "Scroll experiment" in a letter to Kerouac dated 27 December 1950. Holmes had written in hopes of being of some help to Kerouac in his troubles with *On the Road*. Holmes starts by citing the recording of Benny Goodman's Carnegie Hall concert and claims that Goodman's playing on the record is better than anything else in his career. He talks about the "living and strident" tone of one solo that comes from the same "triumph of material over form" that shapes "the rhetoric of Melville and Whitman."[37] Holmes sees Goodman's solo as a useful example for Kerouac in his uncertainty about how to shape the pieces of the various *On the Roads:*

> In [*The Town and the City*] the form was implicit in the material. Perhaps you did not worry over much about it. Perhaps you let the great flood of material simply take you and find and form itself. You told me, one of the first times I met you, "You know, John, I haven't *got* form really. But I think my book has *deep* form." That stuck in my craw, and I think it is true of you, and true of many American writers. Those that have plagued their minds with form have produced but stunted garden flowers that have no magnificence, none of that exultant always-blooming burst and power of really great American writing. But, now, in *"On the Road"*, you are struggling with the difficulties of form and mould. Where to put all this vast heap of material? How shape the mountain to a hill the eye can contain . . . I have seen you attack your great lump of clay . . . . But always, though it may have satisfied me or someone else, it did not settle your mind. Something had been stripped away, you had not gotten the perspective right. You began again. No one could say you have not been tireless, patient, persevering. But it has resisted your head.

Holmes goes on to urge Kerouac:

> Go back to the moment (if this can be done) when "On the Road" came to you out of nowhere. Go back to that instant, and remember it in all the naked excitement it possessed then . . . Think only of your feelings and

believe in them. Turn neither right not left! Start writing some night, in this reverant [sic] mood, and go on. Fill your head (and page) with everything you can think of, in its natural order, in the beauty of its happening, and then worry about the rest.

This is apparently what Kerouac did, and the result initially surprised and excited him. He had set out on a compositional exercise and found unexpectedly that he had the book itself. But he soon began to have his doubts. In her biography, Charters reports an interview with Robert Giroux, the Harcourt, Brace editor who had earlier accepted *The Town and the City:*

> Robert Giroux remembers that Kerouac phoned him from the loft in great excitement to say that he'd just finished *On the Road.* The next day he appeared at Giroux's office with the huge roll of paper under his arm and threw it across the floor shouting, "Here's your novel!" Jack had pasted the sheets of teletype paper together—Giroux said they felt rubbery, like Thermo-fax paper—to make one big roll. Giroux was so startled that he said the wrong thing: "But Jack, how can you make corrections on a manuscript like that?" Later he realized that Jack was in a state of ecstacy [sic] and wanted a ceremonial reaction, dancing around the paper carpet of manuscript. Kerouac drew back, obviously hurt at his editor's response. Belligerently insisting he wouldn't change a word for anyone, he rolled up his manuscript and disappeared. Giroux heard nothing more from him for several years.[38]

Kerouac, though, remembered Giroux glancing through the scroll and exclaiming, "My God Jack this is like Dostoevski." He also remembered Giroux's judgment that the Harcourt,

Brace sales department would find the book unsalable.

The differences in recollection between Giroux and Kerouac may be explained in part by Holmes' memory of the matter. He recalls Kerouac typing "the huge roll" onto standard 8½-by-11-inch sheets, revising the manuscript as he typed. According to Holmes, Kerouac then formally submitted the manuscript which was in turn formally rejected by Giroux. Probably Kerouac took the manuscript to Giroux twice, once in scroll form and then again after it had been typed and revised. Possibly the initial trip to Giroux's had been simply to show the manuscript for encouragement before proceeding to the final stages of work. Certainly, Harcourt, Brace was less positive in its response than Kerouac had hoped.

It is worth noting that Kerouac in recalling the encounter with Giroux says nothing about being unwilling to revise. The scroll experiment had been a ploy to work through a conceptual bind, and Kerouac emphasizes Giroux's positive response that the book was Dostoevskian and the sales department's negative judgment that the book was unsalable. Kerouac had moved closer to his artistic voice with the scroll than he had hoped. Yet Harcourt, Brace led him to feel that, if anything, he was actually farther away from being a salable writer than two years earlier with *The Town and the City*.

Sales were important to Kerouac for several reasons. Nearly thirty, he had yet to establish to himself that he could make a living as a writer or as anything else. He had been depending alternately on his mother, wife, and friends for support. Moreover, Kerouac was ambitious. He wanted to be not simply a successful writer or a good writer, but a socially significant writer. As early as the summer of 1949, he had projected *On the Road* as an opus. In his letter to Ginsberg that summer, Kerouac writes that he hopes with *On the Road* to define the post–World War II generation and establish its prominence in order to trigger the change that seems to come every two decades (Kerouac to Ginsberg, 5 July 1949, GA).

But to have the social impact of a book like *The Sun Also Rises* or to become a public personality like Ernest Hemingway, it was necessary for *On the Road* to sell. According to Holmes, he and Kerouac had often talked about the "isolation of the American artist," the isolation of a Poe or Melville, and the encounter with Giroux confronted Kerouac personally with the possibility that he might succeed artistically and yet fail in every other way. For Holmes, this problem became the seed of his novel *The Horn*, which dramatizes the effects of neglect and misunderstanding on that most American of artists, the jazz musician.[39] For Kerouac, it raised the question of how he should revise his scroll experiment. He could emphasize the book's "poetic" concerns and in all likelihood make it even less salable, or he could emphasize the "prose" level of plot and character, increase the book's commercial viability and risk lessening its depth.

Within a few days of finishing the scroll, Kerouac was contemplating changes. In a letter to Cassady dated 7 May 1951, Ginsberg wrote:

> the writing is dewlike, everything happens as it really did, with the same juvenescent feel of spring: the hero is you, you are the hero, beginning with appearance on scene 1946. Jack needs however an ending. Write him a serious self prophetic letter foretelling your future in fate, so he can have courage to finish his paean in a proper apotheosis or grinding of brakes. He is afraid to foretell tragedy, or humorable comedy, or gray dawn or rosy sunrise, needs help to understand last true longings of your soul, yet, though he surely knows.[40]

And then after the encounter or encounters at Harcourt, Brace, "Kerouac decided his marriage was over" and moved back to Long Island and " 'the woman that wanted him most,' " his mother.[41] By July, he and his mother had left the city for Rocky Mount, North Carolina, where they spent the rest of the summer with Kerouac's sister and her husband. By mid-July, Kerouac had decided to rework the April scroll extensively. One factor was perhaps the advice of Rae Everitt, Holmes's literary agent. After Giroux rejected *On the Road,* Holmes took it to Everitt and, sometime in June, Ginsberg relayed Everitt's comments to Kerouac.

> She thinks: this will be hard to sell, but will try. Difficult because needs lots of revision, needs editor interested and competent and willing to spend time. First part unnecessarily long, whole book (450 pages) should be cut to 300 . . . . Not necessarily interested in those type characters but recognize your interest and possible possibility of making a whole novel about same . . . I mentioned crucial scene in Frisco with women denouncing Neal, she thought it was the thing, recognized it also, wished whole novel were like that, full of illumination (my phrase) and at grips with subject (her phrase). Thought many long parts of latter end were at grips with subject, you found your meat, etc. I also suggested fuller character study needed, she agreed. Believed jazz scenes were worth publishing whole book as is for their sake (maybe a slite exaggeration my phrasing); I agreed they were best on great jazz in American literature. (Ginsberg to Kerouac, 1951, H.R.C.)

Kerouac's response was less precipitous than his apparent response to Giroux. In July, Kerouac wrote to Ginsberg that he had decided to cut *On the Road* extensively and to insert new sections that he had begun composing (Kerouac to Ginsberg, July 1951, GA).

115

In spite of his reply to Ginsberg, Kerouac did not fully agree with Everitt. In a letter to Holmes dated 14 July 1951, Kerouac talks extensively about his work, and some of his plans seem intended to make *On the Road* even less appealing to a publisher. Kerouac writes that he partly approves of Ginsberg's and Everitt's critique, but he also complains that Everitt wants him to simplify the book.[42] Kerouac says that he has written an honest book, and he links its difficulties to his adherence to what he identifies as William Blake's "crooked road of prophecy." To Kerouac, Everitt seems to want a road with all the curves straightened out of it, an option Kerouac finally cannot accept.

In the letter, Kerouac talks briefly about the possibility mentioned to Ginsberg of revising the manuscript by cutting and pasting in new sections. As he explains, this would involve removing the material from the early sections of the book that do not directly involve Cassady, and using them as the basis of a separate novel about Kerouac's experiences in California on his first trip west. Kerouac refers specifically to the material involving the Mexican girl Terry and Remi Boncoeur. Kerouac would then replace this material in *On the Road* with scenes of Cassady's youth. These, he writes, he has already completed as part of his effort to understand Cassady's full character and complete significance. Yet Kerouac's sense of the effect these changes might have on the book is mixed at best. He seems to feel that they may patch up his manuscript but that they will not result in the full rendering of Cassady that he explains he wants. That can only be done by placing his representation of Cassady amid a series of intensely realized, imaginary figures. This ideal Cassady would have to come later, Kerouac admits, and that leaves him for the present with a book, *On the Road*, that is untrue according to the imaginative and artistic richness of the experiences, and at the same time a true representation of what actually occurred.

Throughout this letter to Holmes, Kerouac struggles to understand and express what is true and untrue in his sense of his experiences. In a sense, he is close to a kind of artistic despair. He feels that his understanding of Cassady and the America that Cassady represents is fundamentally a lyric truth. To write it in manageable form would trivialize it. To write it with regard only for its inner truth would distort its reality. It is this tension between the symbolic truth of the inner world of the child and the realistic truth of the outer world of the adult that leads Kerouac to assert that he must purify himself until he can

> tell the truth (all of it in every conceivable mask) and yet digress from that to my lyric-alto knowing of this land . . . a deep-form bringing together of two ultimate and at-present conflicting streaks in me.[43]

This recognition leads Kerouac to assert that, after meditating on his soul as a writer for a week and a half, he is once more full of joy and ready to begin a new book, a jazz novel to be called *Horn* which will be constructed imaginatively and will not be spontaneous and unmediated like *On the Road* . But this resolve to begin again shows Kerouac quite unsure about the implications of writing spontaneously. *On the Road*'s lyrical quality is a result of its lack of artifice, yet the book is to be made more lyrical by introducing imaginary figures. In the next sentence, the book is said to be false as art yet true to what happened. Kerouac vacillates between the notion that the artistic manipulation of his material is necessary to reach Cassady's depths, and the sense that this sort of conscious manipulation is what characterizes the commercial fiction that he thinks Rae Everitt wants *On the Road* to become. To the extent that he identifies spontaneity with having composed the scroll version of *On the Road* at high speed, it is actually a factor that reinforces the naturalistic dimension of the book. It guarantees that the scroll *On the Road* will be what happened even though it will also be untrue to the depth and meaning of the material. However, to the extent that Kerouac sees spontaneity as a matter of being free from society's perceptions and of looking freshly at his material, the implications are positive and actually lead away from the simplified roads of conventional fiction to the "crooked road of prophecy." Again, it was not until *Visions of Cody* that Kerouac realized that speed was not an absolute requirement for spontaneity. Until then, he was left to struggle with the revisions of the book, trying to find a way to give it the depth that would satisfy himself and the tightness and polish that would satisfy a publisher.

In spite of these confusions, the letter to Holmes establishes two important points about *On the Road's* development. First, here in 1951 and well after drafting the basis of what is now *On the Road,* Kerouac is still troubled about the relationship of his writing to the dichotomy—first defined in 1948 to Ginsberg—between the truth of the outside world and the truth of the inner world of the child, expressed here as "lyric-alto knowing." Kerouac here shows a new sense that the two must be brought together and reconciled even though he is uncertain about how it is to be managed. Second, Cassady has an increasingly central role in Kerouac's sense of his Road book. There is no mention of road material as such in the letter, only the notion of *On the Road* plumbing Cassady's depths and the eventual hope of doing this perfectly. Homes writes,

> The experience [Kerouac] flings into ON THE ROAD was always associated in his mind with Neal; the vision of America and the West and the footloose life of ROAD all came initially from Neal—that is, it was Jack's fascination with Neal's persona that opened all that up to him. So that after he had gotten down the surface of the life, the "road experience," he found that

he hadn't really caught the kernel towards which that experience had been driving him all along—that is, the (to him) mystery of Neal's character, the sources of his freedom, what drove him, etc. I think it was out of this feeling that he hadn't accomplished what he'd wanted to in ROAD that he gravitated naturally back to Neal (in life) and thus went on writing about him.[44]

Also, the letter to Holmes shows that Kerouac is beginning to see his search for purity of perception and expression as more important than his attempt to establish himself as a commercially viable writer. He is beginning to sense the doubly dualistic tension of his writing up to that point. Writing was, on one hand, an act of perceiving the internal and exernal worlds. On the other, it was an act of self-affirmation and a gesture toward the social world, a gesture potentially though not necessarily self-aggrandizing. In questioning his motives for writing, Kerouac is also beginning, in this letter, to feel the need to discover new ways to address his audience. Near the end of the letter, he writes that he hopes, when he goes to California, to use Cassady's new tape recorder for experimenting with narrative technique.

With the return to Long Island in the fall, Kerouac's uncertainties about *On the Road* were intensified by the possibility of publishing the April scroll more or less as it was. Ginsberg, who at times served his friends as an informal agent, had secured a deal for Kerouac with Ace Books. Ace, which specialized in drugstore paperbacks, had already agreed to bring out Burrough's first novel, *Junkie*, and the offer to Kerouac was for a three-book option to begin, tentatively, with *On the Road*. Kerouac, though, seems no longer to have been sure that he wanted to publish the April manuscript. He apparently had not progressed very far with his plans for inserts, but he was sure enough that the book needed a major reworking to hold off Ace

Books, even though his mother had decided to give up her job and their flat to accept her daughter's invitation to live in Rocky Mount. Kerouac was not included in the invitation, and the pinch was both psychological and practical. His ties to his mother were exceptionally strong, and her decision left him feeling betrayed and with no place to live. Without finding a job or selling the book, Kerouac had no way to pay the rent.

Kerouac apparently vacillated over Ace Book's offer until at least October 1951, when he discovered what he first called sketching and later termed Spontaneous Prose. As Kerouac recalled it, when the breakthrough came on 25 October, it was so sudden and exhilarating that Ace Book's interest in *On the Road* did not matter, and as Kerouac sketched whatever he encountered, *On the Road* ceased to be a traditional survey of travelling and became instead a project that consciously and unconsciously evoked Cassady in his many dimensions (Kerouac to Ginsberg, 18 May 1952, GA). That is, with the discovery of Spontaneous Prose, Kerouac's Road book turned away from what is now *On the Road* and developed into what is now *Visions of Cody*. In the letter to Ginsberg, Kerouac refers to his book interchangeably as *On the Road* and as the book about Cassady. That the transition he talks about refers to what are now *On the Road* and *Visions of Cody* is underscored by Kerouac's preface to the 1960 edition of *Excerpts from Visions of Cody*, where the terms he uses to describe *On the Road* are virtually identical to those that describe *On the Road* before the discovery of sketching in the May 1952 letter to Ginsberg, and the terms Kerouac uses for *Visions of Cody* are virtually identical to those he uses for the *On the Road* after sketching. In the 1960 preface, Kerouac writes,

Visions of Cody is a 600 page character study of the

hero of *On the Road* . . . . I wanted to put my hand to
an enormous paean which would unite my vision of
America with words spilled out in the modern spontaneous method. Instead of just a horizontal account of
travels on the road, I wanted a vertical, metaphysical
study of Cody's character in its relationship to the
general America.[45]

On the Road, no matter how speedy its composition, was
not "spontaneous," and it is clear that sketching or Spontaneous Prose means much more to Kerouac than a recipe
for a style. The decision to sketch was Kerouac's declaration
for the truth of "lyric-alto knowing," even if it obscured the
truth of what happened and resulted in Ace Books
withdrawing its interest in his work.

Sketching meant a new relationship for Kerouac to his
writing. Writing was no longer "horizontal"; it was "vertical" and involved "wild form," a form "beyond the
novel." In a letter to Holmes written 3 June 1952 shortly
after finishing *Visions of Cody,* Kerouac writes:

> What I'm beginning to discover now is something
> beyond the novel and beyond the arbitrary confines of
> the story . . . into realms of revealed Picture . . . *wild
> form,* man, wild form. Wild form's the only form holds
> what I have to say—my mind is exploding to say
> something about every image and every memory . . . I
> have an irrational lust to set down everything I know
> . . . at this time in my life I'm making myself sick to
> find the wild form that can grow with my wild heart
> . . . because now I KNOW MY HEART DOES
> GROW . . . .[46]

Kerouac's decision was, in effect, an act of faith. To push
"beyond the arbitrary confines of the story" would undercut
his ability to function as a commercial writer (note the

twenty-year lapse between *Visions of Cody*'s composition and publication), but it would lead to "revealed Picture" and the assurance that his "HEART DOES GROW." Kerouac's decision to sketch meant trusting his own artistic impulse over any preconceived or learned sense of what writing novels involved.

Contrasting the notion of "wild form" and "revealed Picture" to earlier Road book attempts suggests the specific meaning of sketching for Kerouac's work. In earlier versions of *On the Road*, Kerouac's desire to write a book that would make him a literary and public personality in the manner of Hemingway is a constant presence. In each conception of the book, Kerouac stands outside the world of the novel, albeit at less and less distance, attempting to translate his experiences into fiction. In each case, his incomplete understanding of the material, the process of translating it, and his own conflicting motives resulted in what Kerouac saw as a falsification of his experience. Sketching involved a different relationship between the writer and his material. It meant choosing to stand inside the fictional world and, in Holmes's words, "dismantle all his hard-learned 'artistries' . . . to free the whole range of his consciousness to the page."[47] With sketching, Kerouac was recognizing that the move from the distant persona of Pic to the closer one of Sal had still left him in an ambiguous relationship with his fictional world.

In *The Town and the City* and the earliest "Roads," Kerouac only dimly perceived the interaction of theme, experience, and point of view, and he adopted strained and overly indirect fictional voices in his desire to write significant fiction and avoid simple autobiography. In *Pic* and *On the Road*, Kerouac moved progressively closer to autobiography until in *On the Road* he managed to explore both his romantic and naturalistic impulses for the first time. But the persona of Sal did not allow Kerouac to explore fully the interaction of these two. *On the Road* summarizes Sal's education and looks back from a point where it is supposedly completed. The naive Sal is unable to anticipate the mature Sal, and the mature Sal cannot return to his earlier perspective without seeming to regress. The counterpoint between persona and earlier self creates certain ironic possibilities but does now allow Kerouac to explore the relationship directly. He can only imply the relationship of naturalistic and romantic perspectives by juxtaposing and repeating key images and events. This invests the book with a certain intricacy, but it is still essentially fictional in a traditional sense and is not the world of Spontaneous Prose that emerges in *Visions of Cody*, where the material is autobiographical but the energy that shapes the book is not. Oddly, *Visions of Cody* is more self-centered and yet less ego-centered than the earlier versions of the Rood book. It is concerned with the interaction of perception and imagination that takes place in language and with the nature of consciousness, and not with the history of the self.

The distinction between "horizontal" and "vertical," the notion of standing inside, of "dismantling," is clarified further by returning to the May 1952 letter to Ginsberg. Kerouac explains that sketching came about when his friend Ed White suggested casually that Kerouac should simply sketch, in the manner of a painter except using words, things on the street. Taking his cue from this chance comment, Kerouac explains that when he tried it the world seemed to come to life before him and that, facing reality with total honesty, it was as if angels of vision were coming to him. By writing without concern for shame and without preconception but with intense concentration on what was present, Kerouac explains that he was at times inspired to the point of losing all awareness that he was writing. And in closing, Kerouac points out that he realizes that the automatic writing of the later Yeats is in some sense a source for what he is doing (Kerouac to Ginsberg, 18 May 1952, GA). The same almost religious emphasis on honesty, purity, and truth found in the July 1951 letter to Holmes is apparent in this description of sketching. In addition, this letter shows that sketching is centered on the moment of perception in a way quite unlike the earlier fictionalizing. Rather than viewing writing as the translation of already perceived experience into language and structure, sketching views writing as the process of recording the artist's act of perception or interpretation of that experience. It is in this sense that Kerouac puts himself inside his fictional world in sketching. He defines writing as the process of recording the associations that grow from an initial perception. Writing might even be said to be synonomous with or a means to perception. In this sense, value or analysis is no longer that which the writer holds and then sets out to embody, but rather that for which the writer is searching in the mediation which is the act of writing.

Kerouac's decision to sketch meant accepting the various dualities of his impulse to write and, instead of trying to avoid them, making them the focus of his writing. It meant viewing writing as a way to explore the tensions of his own responses to the world. This meditational aspect of Kerouac's sense of "Yeats' trance writing" is clearer in the 1958 "Essentials of Spontaneous Prose." Its first tenet, "*Set-up*," stipulates:

> The object is set before the mind, either in reality, as in sketching (before a landscape or teacup or old face) or is set in the memory wherein it becomes the sketching from memory of a definite image-object.[48]

From this "image-object," the sketching writer, with his mind properly purified and obeying the "laws of *time*" follows the "free deviation (association) of mind," "beginning not from preconceived idea of what to say about image but from jewel center of interest in subject at *moment* of writing."

The sketching impulse, the associational spiral, the swim out from the "jewel center" of the "image-object" had been a tendency in Kerouac's work as early as *The Town and the City*. What is missing, for instance, in the description that opens that book, is the specificity and initial focus demanded in sketching. The description of New York as seen by Red in his cell is another example that prefigures sketching. The actual description, the play of images and the puns on geographical names, creates a charged, metaphorical realm. Kerouac is "swimming in a sea of English with no discipline other than rhythms of rhetorical exhalation and expostulated statement."[40] Although the result is engaging literary play, the transition from the ostensible setting of Red's cell to the passage is awkward, and the narrative perspective is unclear. The "spontaneous" passage conflicts with the "fictional" world around it.

A comparison of passages from *On the Road* and *Visions of Cody* illustrates what Kerouac means by Spontaneous Prose and also clarifies what he means by "horizontal" and "vertical." In both books, Kerouac describes his first meeting with Cassady in passages that begin with essentially the same phrase: "I first met Dean" (OR, 3), and "I first met Cody."[50] Both passages present the same situation and many of the same details. Yet the effect is quite different. In *On the Road* there are two views of Dean: Dean as Sal saw him at the time of the incident, a "young jailkid shrouded in mystery," a "young Gene Autry . . . a sideburned hero of a snowy West (OR, 4–5), and Dean at the time Sal narrates the story who is largely undefined. Sal says simply that the "sideburned hero" existed "when Dean was not the way he is today."

In *Visions of Cody*, the contrast between the young, pure Dean and the later, less positive Dean disappears. Cody to Jack Duluoz is a multifaceted presence. Like the young Dean, Cody is "a Nietzschean hero of the snowy wild West," but he is also threatening:

In the door he stood with a perfect build, large blue eyes full of questions but already thinning in edges, at edges, into sly or shy, or coy disbelief, not that he's coy, or even demure; like Gene Autry (exact appearance) with a hardjawed bigboned—but he also at that time bobbed his head, prided himself on always looking down, bobbing, nodding, like a young boxer, instructions, to make you think he's really listening to every word . . . . Cody I had expected to be, from reading a letter he wrote from Colorado Reformatory, a kind of small, thin, shy guy with dark hair and a poetic sadness in his jailness, like a sick criminal genius, or a saint, an American young saint, one who might even be boring and eventually turn to some strange Seventh Day Adventist type religion, like you meet in bus stations in Minneapolis, with wide eyes of fire and a phony phenomenality, turning his body to religion or just sadkid goop; but Cody was dishonest looking, a thief, a car thief, and that's exactly what he was, he had already stolen over five hundred cars (and served time for some of it); not only a thief, maybe a real angry murderer in the night. The "kid" I had imagined from his letter, I never imputed any kind of crime for—other than some kindly Robin Hood-type theft, giving a widow, exit, giving a widow a window, sadly in the late afternoon. Cody was serpentine he was not sad—Cody had long sideburns like certain French Canadians I used to know in my boyhood in Lowell, Mass. who were real tough, sometimes were boxers, or hung around rings, gyms, garages, porches in the afternoon (with guitars), sometimes got shiny boots and motorcycles and rode voyages as far as Fall River and New York just to be on Times Square in their buttons a half hour, and had the best looking girls, and you saw them the couple coming up from the dump and the river at night along the baseball fence as nonchalant as nothing had happened, he just threw away the rubber and his dark eyes flashed across the night. Cody was vigorous, his actions were tamed to his will—the "kid" never had a chance; I thought of Cody immediately as a lion tamer, he looked a little like Clyde Beatty had looked to me in the great circus in Boston, from a distance, stiff and strong, the visiting Ringling of thunderous May night. I didn't think of Cody as a friend. (VC, 338–39)

This passage catalogues Duluoz's initial responses to Cody according to the logic of "Essentials of Spontaneous Prose." It begins with the concrete and specific scene (albeit as it exists in Duluoz's memory) and then moves farther and farther afield, more and more totally into the imagination, before finally attaining a moment of insight or recognition, "I didn't think of Cody as a friend." That is, the passage begins with the *"Set-up"* of a specific "image-object" and then proceeds "swimming in sea of English," to work outwards "from jewel center of interest in subject of image at moment of writing" by a logic of "free deviation (association) of mind" until reaching "peripheral release and exhaustion."[51]

As the passage moves out from the initial description, it goes through five phases. Duluoz begins with what he "had expected [Cody] to be." This is followed by a return to the reality of the situation, "but Cody was dishonest looking," which differs from the initial "image-object" in being more concerned with the stereotype Cody projects than Cody himself as an actual presence. The third phase is also concerned with stereotype, but this time the stereotype that emerges from Duluoz's discarded expectations. The fourth segment returns to the actual impression Cody makes: "Cody was serpentine he was not sad." This time, though, Duluoz approaches his impression of Cody by paralleling it with his childhood memories of "real tough" French Canadians. And in the passage's final phase, reality, stereotype, and memory fuse in the image of Clyde Beatty which yields the discovery, a surprise for Duluoz as well as the reader, that Duluoz did not always think of Cody as a friend. Each segment of the passage has a distinct logic, and yet each builds from what precedes and leads into what follows. Each turn establishes a different relationship between Cody, the "image-object," and the speaker, and each relationship implies a different time perspective until these merge in the final segment.

Several factors keep the passage from seeming random or becoming confusing. Most importantly, everything relates to the "image-object" of Cody standing in the doorway. This remains a stable point of reference. Secondary but still important is the way each segment is characterized by a distinct style and syntax. The first segment, Duluoz's expectations, is one long run-on sentence tied together by parallelisms and coordinates. The end of this headlong rush is marked not only by a semicolon but by three sharp syllables, "sadkid goop," that brake the passage, as Kerouac puts it in "Essentials of Spontaneous Prose," "like a fist coming down on a table with each complete utterance, bang!" By contrast, the second is composed of short, staccato phrases that open out and conclude in a long flowing phrase. The third is somewhat fragmented, almost as if Duluoz is losing his train of thought. The fourth segment returns to the run-on syntax of the first, but this time units of stressed monosyllable like "real tough," "Times Square," and "baseball fence" break up and balance the long phrases to create a slow, dreamy pace that underscores the sense of memory. The tone is reinforced by the alliteration in the middle lines where Kerouac mixes hard and soft g sounds with r's. The fifth and final segment is again up-tempo, but without the breathlessness of the first or the staccato of the second. Rather, the movement is quick and purposeful. The segment opens with four short declarative sentences. The fifth sentence begins like the first four, presenting the image of Clyde Beatty, but then spills out into "the Ringling of thunderous May nights," before the pattern reasserts itself with a final declarative sentence. As Kerouac puts it in "Essentials of Spontaneous Prose,"

> follow roughly outlines in outfanning movement over subject, as river rock, so mindflow over jewel-center need (run your mind over it, *once*) arriving at pivot, where what was dim-formed "beginning" becomes sharp-necessitating "ending" and language shortens in race to wire of time-race of work, following laws of Deep Form, to conclusion, last words, last trickle—Night is The End.[52]

In the description of Cody, Duluoz responds excitedly to the "image-object," falters and slows as he reaches for the meaning of the image, and slows further as he drops into childhood memories. These memories then pivot the passage and begin the "race to the wire" and the conclusion which reveals something new about the initial "image-object."

The description of Cody is a unified meditation on a problematic image. The passage has no narrative action and little or no "horizontal" or linear motion from one point to another. Rather, it relies on the associational logic of the speaker to build up the implications of the initial image. The passage's motion is "vertical," a demonstration of Burroughs' "factualist" argument that a single "fact" exists simultaneously on more than one "level." The description of Cody is not unusual in *Visions of Cody* for either its control or intricacy, but its parallel in *On the Road* suggests the danger of equating spontaneous prose too simply with speed writing. *On the Road* was drafted quickly but not "spontaneously." As the name *sketching* suggests, spontaneous prose is spontaneous in that it records the writer's response to an image and subject at the moment of writing. As Kerouac writes in "Essentials of Spontaneous Prose," "begin not from preconceived idea of what to say about image but from jewel center of interest in subject of image at *moment of writing.*"

The sketching aesthetic to come is prefigured as early as 1948 with Ginsberg's interest in Cezanne. In his *Paris Review* interview, Ginsberg dates his interest in Cezanne as "around 1949 in my last year at Columbia, studying with Meyer Schapiro,"[53] but 1948 is apparently the correct date because Kerouac had read Ginsberg's paper for Schapiro's course in September 1948. Ginsberg was intrigued by Cezanne's cultivation of visual perception. In the *Paris Review* Ginsberg states:

> I was reading his [Cezanne's] letters and I discovered this phrase again, *mes petites sensations*—". . .I have worked for years trying to," I guess it was the phrase, "*reconstitute* the *petites sensations* that I get from nature . . . ." And what does he say finally—in a very weird statement which we would not expect of this austere old workman, he said, "And this *petite sensation* is nothing other than *pater omnipotens aeterna deus*".[54]

The phrase *petite sensation* became a kind of code word for Ginsberg and Kerouac. In 1948, Ginsberg writes Kerouac, "I am at home under the watchful paternal eye, developing my petite sensation and imitating Cezanne."(Ginsberg to Kerouac, 1948, H.R.C.). And the first entry in Kerouac's 1948–49 "Road journal" closes, "We need our *petit* absorptions like campstools in the wilderness."[55]

The landscape painter's communing with his subject anticipates the act of meditation in the *Set-up* of the Spontaneous Prose writer, and in a 1955 letter to Cassady's wife Carolyn, Kerouac writes that the afternoon scene where he is is like a landscape from the Netherlands and that he feels like a Cezanne when he goes to write in the woods and meditate (Kerouac to Carolyn Cassady, April 1955, H.R.C.) For Kerouac, Cezanne's example validated the perceptual moment as a subject of thematic significance in and of itself. In a letter of September 1948 responding to Ginsberg's lengthy Cezanne paper, Kerouac writes that the paper's way of approaching the act of seeing has led him to see light and contour in a more intense and true way (Kerouac to Ginsberg, 18 September 1948, GA). Elsewhere in the letter, Kerouac calls this type of seeing a spiritual aesthetic. This does not necessarily mean that Kerouac agreed with Cezanne that the *"petite sensation* is nothing other than *pater omnipotens aeterna deus,"* but this interest in the question of perception locates the sketching aesthetic in its proper framework.

Details of Ginsberg's paper itself suggest several connec- tions with spontaneous composition. The paper's title, "Cezanne's Comedy," anticipates Kerouac's later descrip- tion of his work as "one enormous comedy, seen through the eyes of poor Ti Jean (me). . .seen through the keyhole of his eye."[56] And Ginsberg's quotations from Cezanne's letters and notes point toward sketching. The headnote to the paper, from a 1904 letter of Cezanne's to Bernard, reads:

> "The artist must scorn all judgment that is not based on intelligent observation of character. He must beware of the literary spirit which so often causes painting to deviate from its true path—the concrete study of nature—to lose itself all too long in intangible speculation."[57]

At another point, Ginsberg quotes Cezanne's "drawing is merely an outline of what you see," which almost implies an identity between the perceptual and artistic (or recording) act. For Ginsberg's Cezanne, the primacy of perception over "speculation" is the key to art. Speaking of a Cezanne canvas, Ginsberg writes, "All the marks on the paper are specific *signs* of a sensation of direction of form." To Ginsberg "this use of sight as another language to express understanding" leads to "an example of a *pure* image, or a true image, rather than a synthesized, untrue, impure image." In this state, Ginsberg feels that "the form equals the art equals the image and all are resolved and one." This foreshadows Kerouac's interest in the "image-object," and for Ginsberg, "there is a concentric flow" that parallels the writing outwards involved in spontaneous composition.

Ginsberg's interpretation of Cezanne surprisingly has much in common with Burroughs's factualism. Burroughs writes:

> All arguments, all non-sensical considerations as to what people "should do" are irrelevant. Ultimately there is only fact on all levels, and the more one argues, verbalizes, moralizes the less he will see and feel of fact. (Burroughs to Ginsberg, 9 November 1948, GA)

And again in 1950, Burroughs writes Kerouac:

> [Ginsberg's] dichotomy between "regular life" and visions is not only unnecessary it is inaccurate. I mean it does not *in fact* exist. "Either . . . or" is not an accurate formula. Facts exist on infinite levels and one level does not preclude another. Insanity is the *confusion of levels*. . . . The insane are *too much* concerned with "regular life": that is with money, sex, digestion, illness, and the impression they make on others. These "facts of life" frighten the insane, and no man can detach himself from what he fears. In consequence the visions of the insane are unspeakably dreary.[58]

As in Ginsberg's sense of Cezanne, the emphasis is on the

perception of "fact" in and of itself with as little preconception or intellectualization as possible. In each case, a tyranny of fact is avoided by the insistence that fact and the perception of fact can exist on more than one "level," more than one plane.

In Ginsberg, the "concentric flow" ties all together, but Burroughs does not define the relationship between levels, which is perhaps one reason for Kerouac's trouble in adapting Burroughs's factualist perspective for *On the Road* in November 1948. With sketching, though, Kerouac had finally found a way to utilize factualism by combining it with Ginsberg's sense of a concentric flow to the artist's creative impulse.

Sketching is important not only for an understanding of Kerouac's work but for what it indicates about Kerouac's relationship with other Beat writers. All too often Kerouac is approached simply as an impressionistic and less thoughtful version of Ginsberg and Burroughs. Through their emphasis on such European intellectual figures as Freud and Spengler, Ginsberg and Burroughs were certainly instrumental in giving Kerouac terms for his own dislocation, but it was Kerouac who developed a sense of language, a style in the richest meaning of the term, that in turn enabled Ginsberg and Burroughs each to discover their own voice. Ginsberg has pointed out a number of times how Kerouac and the example of Kerouac's work encouraged him to abandon the derivatively traditional style of *The Gates of Wrath* in favor of the style of *Howl and Other Poems*:

> Jack always accused me of stealing from him, & rereading 20 years later I see now how much it was true, my Greyhound poem taken from his description of dock-loading ship *President Adams* [in *Visions of Cody*] for instance, 'cept his is half a decade earlier . . . . His phrasing was archetypal for this moment of

133

consciousness enlarging in wonderment to notice Americanist minute particulars aside from the centers of Attention-Power. . . .[59]

And Burroughs's factualist novel *Junkie* apparently follows the factualist *On the Road* just as that first *On the Road* derived from Burroughs's pronouncement. Just as sketching is partly an outgrowth of factualism, *Naked Lunch* comes in part from the example of the sketched *Visions of Cody*. While composing *Naked Lunch* in Tangiers, Burroughs wrote Kerouac:

> I have been attempting something similar to your sketch method. That is, I write what I see and feel right now trying to arrive at some absolute, direct transmission of fact on all levels.[60]

There is certainly no reason to minimize Kerouac's debt to Burroughs and Ginsberg, but neither is there any reason to ignore the equally important impact of Kerouac and his work on his more critically respected colleagues.

Although the breakthrough of October 1951 marks a turning point in Kerouac's development, sketching was not initially the complete model for writing that influenced Burroughs and *Naked Lunch*. The articulation of the sketching insight into a way of writing books of "wild form" took some six months. Kerouac's earliest sketches, written between late October and early December, were largely drawings in words of immediately present objects or scenes such as subway stops, Poughkeepsie backyards, and diners. Like an actual sketch or painting, these "sketches" have little or no ostensible narrative "voice."

This period of sketching seems to have ended when Kerouac's mother was ready to move to Rocky Mount. Kerouac still had not realized that the new work would necessarily become the basis of a new version of the Road book, and to support himself, he decided to ship out with Henri Cru, a prep school buddy who appears in *On the Road* as Remi Boncoeur. When he failed to get a berth in New York, Kerouac proceeded overland to California to meet Cru's ship. On the way, he visited Cassady, then living in San Francisco with his second wife and working as a Southern Pacific brakeman. Kerouac spent several weeks with the Cassadys, working as a baggage handler for the Southern Pacific, and then tried again at Christmas to ship out with Cru before settling back in with the Cassadys. Cassady got Kerouac work as an apprentice brakeman, and the visit became a five-month stay during which Kerouac drafted *Visions of Cody*.

At least as late as December 1951, Kerouac was still searching for the direction his Road book should take. In a response, apparently, to an attempt by Carl Solomon to find out what Kerouac had done with *On the Road*, Kerouac writes that he has not left Ace Books but that his book is as yet unfinished and that he is trying to make some money on his own (Kerouac to Solomon, 27 December 1951, GA). The book Kerouac refers to may be the scroll and his plan for cuts and insertions, the Cody version, or some intermediate stage. It is also possible that Kerouac is simply covering up for his own uncertainty. In his letter to Ginsberg, Kerouac dates the beginning of the Cody version of *On the Road* as 25 October 1951, the beginning of the sketching experiments, and he calls the Cody *On the Road* the Neal book. But that letter, written in May 1952, probably reflects hindsight since Kerouac initially had no sense that sketching would lead to a book. Later in the above letter to Solomon, Kerouac writes that he intends to put off his Dean Pomeray book and instead begin right away on his own book about the red brick of Lowell because he has realized that his work about Cassady has turned out, oddly, to be about himself. Dean Pomeray is an amalgam of Dean Moriarity and Cody Pomeray, Cassady's names respectively in *On the Road* and

Visions of Cody, but the key is the reference to red brick. Kerouac used red brick imagery briefly in *The Town and the City* but uses it extensively in the second section of *Visions of Cody*. This suggests that Kerouac was caught between his sense of his road material as something related to Cassady, and something related to himself at the time of the Solomon letter. It also shows him caught between revising the April scroll and pushing ahead with the new material, of retreating in the direction of a salable manuscript and following the sketching breakthrough of October into new dimensions of the material.

One thing may clarify Kerouac's comments to Solomon. Charters reports that Kerouac told Solomon sometime in the fall of 1951 of plans to write another book about Cassady as a follow-up to the April scroll version of On the Road. It may be that this book was to focus on Cassady's Denver youth and to use some of the inserts about which Kerouac had written Holmes. It may be, as well, that this project was to be the second of Ace Book's three-book package. If this is the case, Kerouac's letter to Solomon in December 1951 is actually explaining his tardiness with two manuscripts, the version of *On the Road* derived from the scroll that Solomon had already seen and that Kerouac was supposedly revising, and the Neal book Kerouac had also proposed. What Kerouac actually seems to have discovered is that his plans for the Neal book were a way of temporarily ignoring his dissatisfaction with the scroll *On the Road*.

Several factors apparently combined to motivate Kerouac to begin *On the Road* again and draft what is now *Visions of Cody*. One was his determination not to be motivated by commercial considerations, evident in the July 1951 letter to Holmes; another was the excitement over sketching. Living with Cassady, also, gave Kerouac a chance to study Cassady in a new context, which may have encouraged him to see Cassady himself as increasingly central to the book and the act of being "on the road" proportionally less so. Kerouac's access at this time to drafts and fragments of Cassady's *The First Third*, which details Cassady's Denver childhood, may also have played a part in the shift. Finally, it should be remembered that the tape recorder was a very recent development in 1952, and Cassady's tape recorder perhaps encouraged Kerouac in his interest in experimenting with narrative technique. Certainly the tape recorder influenced the shape of *Visions of Cody*. The book's third section is comprised entirely of transcribed and edited tape recordings of Kerouac, Cassady, and their friends, and the experiment with the tape recorder may have been the final push for Kerouac to break with the work of the scroll. The sections of *Visions of Cody* prior to the tapes read as if they were written initially without a design in mind for a specific book. They read as if they were selected, edited, and arranged from material already at hand when Kerouac realized the shape the book should take. The sections that follow the tape all seem as if they were written with the book's final design in mind. They build from the earlier sections to the book's closing section, a narrative of Kerouac's trips with Cassady which comprise parts two, three, and four of the version published as *On the Road*.

Precisely when Kerouac realized he was working on yet another version of his book is unclear, but it was certainly before March 1952, when he wrote to tell Holmes that the new *On the Road*—that is, *Visions of Cody*—was finished. Kerouac writes that the new *On the Road* is dramatically better than any of the earlier versions. He asks Holmes to tell Ginsberg that he has absolutely attained the quintessence of his voice, and so much so that at some future point he will inevitably look back with consternation and chagrin that he can no longer write at such a pitch.[60] Several things make it clear that Kerouac is talking about what is now *Visions of Cody* and not the *On the Road* published by Viking. Kerouac copies out two lengthy examples of his new *Road* book for Holmes, and both, with minor differences in

137

phrasing and punctuation, are in *Visions of Cody*. The second of these, labeled by Kerouac as the conclusion to *On the Road*, corresponds to the last two pages of *Visions of Cody*. Similarly, in his 18 May letter to Ginsberg, Kerouac quotes passages now found in *Visions of Cody* that he identifies as part of *On the Road*. Kerouac may be quoting passages that were once in *On the Road*, deleted at a later date, and then used in *Visions of Cody*, but this seems unlikely. The passages Kerouac sends Ginsberg and Holmes are intended to show them what is best in the book, and they could easily have been incorporated in the published *On the Road* had Kerouac chosen to do so. The ending of *Visions of Cody*, for instance, is stronger than the ending of *On the Road* and could simply have been substituted for the one in *On the Road*.

A 7 April letter to Solomon about *On the Road* also seems to be about what is now *Visions of Cody* rather than *On the Road*. In the letter, Kerouac worries that Ace Books may refuse to publish the manuscript intact. He therefore proposes that Ace issue two different editions of *On the Road*. The entire manuscript would appear in hardcover form and make the literary reputation of Kerouac and the firm. The narrative segment that begins with Kerouac encountering Cassady in 1947 and includes their trips together would be a much shorter book, an inexpensive paperback to make money. Kerouac asserts that he will not stand for Ace bringing out only a partial, paperback edition. Kerouac's comments to Solomon make no sense if they are applied to what is now published as *On the Road*. *On the Road* is one continuous narrative, but *Visions of Cody* is almost entirely plotless except for the concluding sections, which condense about two hundred pages of *On the Road*'s action into sixty pages. Since the pages of *Visions of Cody* are large and the print relatively small, this concluding section would make a twenty-five-cent drugstore paperback of typical length for the early 1950s. It would be about the same size as

Kerouac's *Tristessa*, which Avon Books published in 1960 with a cover and price designed to have precisely the appeal that Kerouac proposes for this Ace Books paperback of *On the Road*.

A letter of 13 June 1952 to Homes also indicates that the *On the Road* of 1952 is what is now *Visions of Cody*. Kerouac writes to ask if Ginsberg has gotten the manuscript of *On the Road* which had been mailed from Mexico. Kerouac writes that he is afraid that the manuscript is lost. Later in the Letter, Kerouac refers, to illustrate a point, to the earlier *On the Road* written in three weeks during the spring of 1951.[62] This certainly suggests that the *On the Road* of June 1952 which Kerouac had sent to Ginsberg is not the April scroll, the basis of what was finally published as *On the Road*, but a new version.

Some commentators have claimed that *Visions of Cody* is simply scraps left over from *On the Road*, others that *Visions of Cody* is a sequel to *On the Road*.[63] But Kerouac's correspondence and the way *Visions of Cody* reworks entire passages from *On the Road* show that *Visions of Cody* was a finished and independent text, and was to replace the work now published as *On the Road*. When Kerouac writes to Ginsberg in May 1952 that the whole of *On the Road* is inspired and compares its rush of language to *Ulysses*, Kerouac means *Visions of Cody* (Kerouac to Ginsberg, 18 May 1952, GA).

Kerouac felt that he had broken through to a major achievement with *Visions of Cody*, but he also recognized that the book's experimental quality would make its reception uncertain. In the May letter to Ginsberg, Kerouac nearly begs him to read the book through, lamenting that neither Cassady nor Burroughs had found time to do so. In another letter, Kerouac claims that *On the Road* is a book of greatness, but worries that no one will publish it.

As Kerouac feared, even Ginsberg, his most enthusiastic reader, thought the book "a holy mess." After first receiving the manuscript, Ginsberg writes to Cassady,

> it's great allright but he did everything he could to fuck
> it up with a log of meaningless bullshit I think, page
> after page of surrealist free association that don't make
> sense to anybody except someone who has blown Jack.
> I don't think it can be published anywhere, in its pres-
> ent state. I know this is an awful hangup for everyone
> concerned—he must be tired too—but that's how it
> stands I think. Your tape conversations were good
> reading, so I could hear what was happening out
> there—but he put it in entire and seemingly ununified
> so it just skips back and forth and touches on things
> momentarily and refers to events nowhere else in the
> book; and finally it appears to objective eye so diffuse
> and disorganized—which it is, on purpose—that it just
> *don't make.* . . . He was not experimenting and explor-
> ing in new deep form, he was purposely just screwing
> around . . . . Not purposely, I guess, just drug out and
> driven to it and in a hole in his own head—but he was
> in a hole.[64]

Ginsberg's opinion of the book did eventually change. His
introduction to *Visions of Cody* in 1973 is as positive as the
earlier letter is negative. Still, Ginsberg's letter suggests how
the April scroll came to be published as *the On the Road*.
The response of Kerouac's friends to the Cody *On the Road*
was so negative that Kerouac apparently never bothered to
submit it to a publisher. Instead, he seems to have followed
the advice of his friends and begun circulating, with
Ginsberg's and Holmes's help, the text derived from the
April scroll. What is now *On the Road* was placed first with
a literary agency and then eventually at Viking Press.

Kerouac's return to the April scroll version in no way
indicates that he agreed with his friend's assessment of the
Cody *On the Road*. He perhaps accepted their judgment

that it was unpublishable because of its seeming formlessness, occasionally opaque language games, and its sexual explicitness, but he continued to believe in the book. His sense of the relationship of the two versions to each other is indicated by the correspondence. Through the summer of 1952, Kerouac talks only about *On the Road*, using both the Road book and the Neal book as synonyms. After the summer of 1952, Kerouac distinguishes between the two versions, referring to the scroll version as *The Beat Generation* and the Cody version as *Visions of Neal* and *Visions of Cody*. Kerouac may have continued to think of the Cody version as *On the Road* well after he gave up hope of publishing it. In his essay "The Origins of the Beat Generation," he writes:

> in 1955 I published an excerpt from *Road* (melling it with parts of *Visions of Neal*) under the pseudonym "Jean-Louis," it was entitled *Jazz of the Beat Generation* and was copyrighted as being an excerpt from a novel-in-progress entitled *Beat Generation* (which I later changed to *On the Road* at the insistence of my new editor).[65]

Visions of Cody, or *Visions of Neal*, may still have carried the title *On the Road* as late as when Kerouac assembled this jazz piece.

Whatever *Visions of Cody*'s title in 1955, Kerouac still had high regard for the book and continued to feel the same way about it even after *On the Road* was published. In a letter to Lenrow early in 1958, Kerouac asserts that *Visions of Cody* is his greatest work,[66] and an anecdote of Holmes demonstrates the extent of Kerouac's commitment to the *Visions of Cody* version of the Road book. Several years after *Visions of Cody* was finally published, Holmes, Ginsberg and others gathered in Lowell, Massachusetts, for a Kerouac festival. Along with the standard eulogies and reminiscences, the festival featured a kinescope of Kerouac reading on the "Steve Allen Show" shortly after *On the Road*'s publication. The camera shows Kerouac holding a copy of *On the Road*. But as Holmes and Ginsberg watched the show at the festival, they realized that Kerouac was actually reading from a typescript of *Visions of Cody* pasted into the copy of *On the Road*.[67] Apparently neither Allen nor his audience knew the book well enough to realize they were being treated to a version of the work other than the one currently the center of controversy. Kerouac's performance was a protest, though so quiet that even friends failed to notice until much later, at being made a media image instead of recognized as a writer, and a signal as to what he himself believed to be the nature of his achievement.

Chapter Three

The Redeeming Eye

The discovery of sketching freed Kerouac from the need to translate his experience into fictional figures which then had to be manipulated like the markers in a board game. It freed him to concentrate on the interplay of perception and imagination, and the way this interplay assumed substance in language. It may seem that this should make *Visions of Cody* simpler than *On the Road,* but *Visions of Cody* is a difficult text, an elaborately literary text whatever its status as "fiction." Part of *Visions of Cody*'s difficulty comes from the way the sketching perspective encouraged Kerouac to treat language as a subject in and of itself. Part of the difficulty comes from the way sketching insists on the writer's continually discovering the terms of his interest in his material. And part of the difficulty comes from the fact that sketching is an approach to style. "Essentials of Spontaneous Prose" says a great deal about how to write a passage but nothing about how to construct a book. And because of this, *Visions of Cody* is not only about the discovery that happens from sketch to sketch, but also about the discovery of how to

143

organize sketches and sketching into texts of "wild form." In this sense, *Visions of Cody* turns out to be a book structured by the actual search for the book.

Initially, the problems and possibilities of Spontaneous Prose as the basis for books of imaginative prose can be clarified by considering briefly two contemporary parallels to Spontaneous Prose, jazz and Action Painting. In the Action Painting of Jackson Pollock, there is no pretense of the artist's objectivity or distance, and the impression of the artist's involvement in his canvas is one aspect of the power of the finished painting. In a sense, the artist becomes a performer even though the viewer never sees the performance as it takes place, but sees instead the record of the performance, the record of a dance that took place in color and the texture of paint. Pollock does not represent objects or interpret them. His performance, the interplay of emotion, imagination, and an intense focus on the medium of the art itself, results in an object that has something of the same density, complexity, and even arbitrariness of natural objects, and the objectlike quality of the canvases can be seen in the importance of scale and texture to their effect. Ultimately, it seems that Pollock's genius has something to do with his sense of how to approach time through space, and motion through inanimate object.

If a Pollock canvas is the record of a dance in color, *Visions of Cody* is the record of a dance in language. There is the same intense focus on the medium of the art and the imagination, the same sense that texture and motion or the implication of motion is more important than overall architecture. There is the same presence of the personal, the performer. And both Pollock and Kerouac are more concerned with discovering new combinations in their material and selves through the risk of improvisation than with representing or interpreting the world. In Action Painting and Spontaneous Prose, the artist does not start out in possession of a reality to communicate. He must discover the world and record the process of his discovery.

The improvisational nature of Action Painting and Spontaneous Prose is, of course, suggestive of jazz, and both *On the Road* and *Visions of Cody* contain scenes where an improviser takes a phrase, explores it, and expands it into something new and vital. But jazz is also relevant to Spontaneous Prose and *Visions of Cody* in other ways. In his *Paris Review* interview, Kerouac cites jazz as an influence on his sense of measure:

> *Interviewer:* What about jazz and bop as influences . . .? *Kerouac:* Yes, jazz and bop in the sense of a, say, tenor man drawing a breath and blowing a phrase on his saxophone, till he runs out of breath, and when he does, his sentence, his statement's been made . . . that's how I therefore separate my sentences, as breath separations of the mind . . . .[1]

Moreover, the sound of jazz is important. A jazz musician establishes his identity not only through his melodic inventiveness, but also by developing his own sound and tone. And Kerouac's descriptions of jazz performances call attention to this, at times characterizing the musician in terms of his sound even more than his formal inventiveness. A jazz man's "sound" is his signature, the distillation of personality.[2]

For a prose writer, Kerouac places unusual emphasis on sound. It not only exists to reinforce or intensify the subject of a passage, it may become the subject itself. Sound may itself carry thematic weight the way texture does in painting in general and Action Painting in particular. It is no accident that many passages in *Visions of Cody* and the work immediately following turn out to be metrically regular and use sound patterns to delineate structure.[3] Nor is it an accident that the first perceptive critical response to Kerouac as an artist, Warren Tallman's "Kerouac's Sound,"[4] should have this focus.

The example of jazz also illuminates Spontaneous Prose in

another way. Any highly improvisational art risks becoming so diffuse that it seems arbitrary and loses its power to give the impression of performance. In the jazz that Kerouac knew best, the swing music of the late thirties and the bop of the forties, two factors unify improvisational performance. The most obvious is the use of widely known melodies or conventional chord patterns as a starting point, to be elaborated and modified but to remain an implicit reference or center. The role of melody or theme in jazz of the thirties and forties is roughly equivalent to the role of the "image-object" in Spontaneous Prose. The second factor that unifies a jazz performance is the vocabulary of the musician. Any jazz improviser, even the most inventive, a Lester Young or a Charlie Parker, comes to have not only his sound but phrases, rhythmic ideas, and ways of attack that are peculiarly and recognizably his own. It might even be said that the greater the performer, the more noticeable, the more indelible are these tendencies. Rather than marking the musician's limitations, these devices become the means of his expression as he discovers new combinations among them and new ways to fit them to the disparate materials that serve as his improvisation's starting point. They become his means for annexing larger and larger bodies of the public music into his own private, yet accessible world. They become the means of both the artist's renewal and the renewal of the music. In Kerouac's Spontaneous Prose, quirks of syntax, favored sounds, meters, and individual words like *gray* and *sad* that are used and reused in different contexts parallel the jazz musician's vocabulary and make Kerouac's performances as instantly recognizable (and as impossible to copy) as those of Coleman Hawkins, Young, or Parker.

The paintings of a Pollock or the recordings of a Parker form an impressive body of work, but each body of work is essentially a collection. Even though Pollock's painting shows development, there is no inevitable structure that determines that one canvas must be dealt with before or after another. Each canvas is an independent performance, and this is also the case with Parker. "Ko Ko" and "Au Privare" do not have to be approached in terms of each other, and the primary sense of architecture is that of sequence within an individual piece, of chorus following chorus. But this raises the question of whether it is possible to organize an extended work of imaginative prose, a novel (if that term is treated flexibly), along such principles. Certainly "sketching" is an adequate model for a scene or passage, but it is no more clear that one could sketch a novel than sketch a large mural. A mural might be elaborated from a series of sketches, but only with some method of structuring that in its synthetic quality would differ considerably from the spirit of sketching.

Several factors suggest Kerouac's awareness of the formal problems implied by sketching. Kerouac subtitled *Mexico City Blues,* a 1955 collection of poetry, *241 Choruses,* and Holmes recalls that Kerouac "never thought of the opening sketches of *Visions of Cody* as being publishable."[5] The gap between the "discovery" of sketching in 25 October 1951, which Kerouac later cited as the beginning of *Visions of Cody,* and Kerouac's actual awareness that the sketches were the start of a new book sometime in early 1952 also indicates his uncertainty over how his new sense of writing should be managed. Unfortunately, there is little to indicate Kerouac's sense of the solution to these problems. In a letter to Holmes written on 3 June 1952, while working on *Doctor Sax,* Kerouac talks about *"wild form"* but does little to define it. There is the same emphasis on the spiritual as in the initial definition of sketching, and the claim that *"wild form"* involves "something beyond the novel and beyond the arbitrary confines of the story,"[6] but Kerouac is too excited to go into detail. That *"wild form"* relates to sketching and Spontaneous Prose is clear from a second letter to Holmes later that month, in which Kerouac complains that editors reject his work because they are concerned only with the action of the plot. Kerouac senses that these editors make no effort to get beyond the surface of his style and therefore do not see how the structure of the books exists implicitly, as both Burroughs and Kerouac say, "on all levels" and not just the level of story action.[7]

Even though Kerouac nowhere articulates his ideas about how sketches should be structured into books of wild form, his strategies can be derived from the texts. Most simply, Kerouac seems to cluster sketches together that share a common theme. This creates, in effect, a mosaic where the sketches shape a larger picture, and individual sketch relates to individual sketch in much the same way that the segments of a single sketch relate to each other and the "image-object." This strategy is apparent in the sketches on pages 70–78 of *Visions of Cody.* The three sketches deal with Kerouac's horror of the inevitability of physical decay, his ambivalence over sexuality, and his conviction of the impossibility of a man and woman bridging the distance between them.

The first sketch opens with a description of a vacant lot in Denver where Cody and his poolroom buddies are standing. As Kerouac catalogues the debris, he creates an ominous anticipation, almost in the way a camera might in a Hitchcock film, by transforming ordinary objects through an intense and inexplicably prolonged look at them.

> Crap in weeds was an old map, Cashmere Soap paper, bottom glass of a broken bottle, old used-out flashlight battery, leaf, torn small pieces of newspaper (someone had saved a clipping and then torn it), nameless cardboards, nameless mats of hay, light bulb cardboards, old Spearmint Gum wrapper, ice cream box cover, old paper bag, weeds with little bunched lavender shoots and Rousseau-like but October rusted leaves—old cellophane—old bus transfer ticket, the strange cor-

rugated cardboard from egg crates, a rock, pieces of brown beerbottle glass, old Phillip Morris flattened pack—the roots of weeds were purple borscht color and left the matted filthy earth like tormented dog cocks leave the sac—sticks—coffee container—and an empty pint bottle of Five Star brand California Sherry drunk by an old wino of the road when things were less grim. (VC, 70)

The portent of the catalogue leads to the admission that someone has discovered a miscarried fetus in the field and that the crowd has "come snooping to see it." The catalogue, it turns out, has detailed the "embarrassed" but intense scanning of the ordinary "to pick out the spot," a situation that makes the details of things discarded by people and nature particularly right.

This is the "image-object" that governs the first sketch, and Duluoz responds:

what a forlorn thing it is and frightening that the nameless soul (the thing created by the terribleness of a womb which when it does halfway the work or even complete work takes the melted marble of man's sperm which is a kind of acceptable substance, say in a bottle, and transforms it by means of the work of some heinous secret egg into a large bulky piece of decayable meat—) that this nameless little would-have-been lay, spilling out of that grocer's bag, grocer's wrapping, under a tree that by dry Autumn had been turned almost the same shade of red, turned thus instead of by wet and secret wombs—Girls are frightening when you see them under these circumstances because there seems to be a kind of insistence on their part to look you in the eye to find out that personal thing about you which is probably the thing that you expect and burn and kill to find *in them* when you think of penetrating

149

> their thighs—that secret wetness of the woman is as
> unknown to you as your eyes are to her when they're
> confronted by a miscarried whatnot in a field under
> dark and mortal skies—(VC, 71)

When the sketch next jumps to a description of "those
tremendously frightening two-lane bumpy roads" (VC, 71)
of the West, there at first seems no connection between this
new scene and the scene in the field. But the repetition of
the word *frightening* suggests the unity which Duluoz then
establishes more firmly by recalling driving these roads with
Cody as he simultaneously imagines Cody driving them to
get away from the "miscarried whatnot." These "Western
roads are lonelier to ride than any," but isolation and open
space eases the emotional pressure and allows a sense of
escape from what has just been "confronted." This
withdrawal leads at least temporarily to a kind of renewal
which is suggested by Duluoz's changing sense of landscape
and space as Cody drives. At first, the landscape itself seems
not only frightening but anthropomorphic. It reflects the
scene in the vacant lot: "a sad cut of earth, a hair head of
grass on a lump of sand, then endless range" (VC, 71). This
in turn is replaced by a sense of space, of vista, as night and
the "great flat spaces" absorb the distant headlights, and
Cody drives "calm and relaxed and perfect." And finally the
revitalized landscape loses its frightening aspect and
becomes simply "tufts of bunchgrass on nobs of dry dead
earth flashing by in the night in swift blurrily fanning succession . . . while the fellows gabbled and drank beer and
sent cans banging into the abyss" (VC, 71–72).

This excitement leads directly to the arrival of Cody and
his buddies at a whistle-stop north of Denver to visit a pair
of girls who "were not exactly the usual American girl team
of the pretty one and the ugly one because in this case the
older one was extremely attractive herself" (VC, 72).
Kerouac first describes the whistle-stop, giving it a kind of

half-cheerful, half-sad seediness typified by the house, "somewhat sooty from railroad and therefore deliberately painted bright red window frames" (VC,72). He then expounds on "the older one" and turns finally to her younger friend:

> the epitome of the cute little sexy fleshpot of honey, gold and shiny hairs that you see in illustrations of Coca-Cola girls at fountains with equally pretty rosy boys and so much so, so startingly what the guys wanted that immediately they were terrified to see it staring them in the face, the bird in the hand—with her pudgy arms that gave promise to the genuineness of two beautiful tits protruding from deliciously soft cashmere sweater and her arched eyebrows and plum little foolish assy mouth. (VC, 73)

The initial image of the vacant lot and miscarriage leads from fear through isolation, calm, excitement, and back to fear, from human death through ongoing nature to the glossy ideal of an advertising image which combines isolation and excitement and a hint of decay, of excrement. In fact, the final phrase, "plump little assy mouth" is so unexpected one tends to read it as "sassy mouth." Yet, "assy" is so startlingly right that there can be no question what Kerouac intended. But with this, the image of poster girl and "terrified guys," the scene freezes to a tableau, and Kerouac in effect writes himself to a standstill without reaching the ostensible action of the scene, the encounter of Cody and his buddies with the two girls.

Kerouac's response is simply to break off the sketch. He announces, "I'll start again." The emphasis on images in Spontaneous Prose does not lend itself directly to narrative per se, and the sketch that builds from the Denver vacant lot illustrates Holmes's observation that the real events in Kerouac are events of consciousness. Narrative is simply one element among several that the speaker weaves together in responding to the initial stimulus. Kerouac does not use the images of the sketch to illuminate the story but the elements of the story to illuminate the images, and when the line of imagery leads no farther, he simply shifts to something else whether the action of the plot has been fulfilled or not. In the sketch under consideration, the line of imagery ends before the energy of the initial image has been fully resolved, and so Kerouac circles back to start over from a second image-object that condenses and recasts the details of the first sketch.

> The house where the girls were . . . was located prac-tically under a watertank of the U.P. railroad that passed right by and left that dark dirt which is like the concoction of an artist's palette after a short rain, the black color artists use to depict night, gloom, maybe evil. . . . A fitful moon was all that was left of that entire day's wild light (poolhall chinks of light, miscar-riage field purples and iron file skies) and now nobody could see anything except the shape of the house, a few brown lights in it, and the hanging pendant globe of a street lamp. . . . (VC, 73)

This leads to a fuller description of the girls and poolroom buddies. Details from the previous sketch are repeated and glossed, but again, before the action starts, Kerouac breaks off, announcing that, "These imaginings lead me back-wards to my one and original poipose" (VC, 75). He re-minds the reader that the narrative is subordinate to the speaker by referring to the narrative, slight as it is, as "imaginings." It is as if the speaker's attempt to imagine fic-tional equivalents for his concerns threatens to take on a life of its own, a life that is finally stereotypical and threatens to trivialize the initial image.

At first, the third sketch, the "original poipose," seems to have nothing to do with what precedes it. It discusses "dirty old voyeurs on Times Square" and the use of cheesecake photos: "Cody used to say 'Have this picture, I've used it' " (VC, 75). But as Kerouac illustrates the use of a soft-core pornographic shot, his fantasies explore the root of sexual ambivalence, the link between sadism and masochism, fact and fantasy, and the gulf between a media-packaged, commercial sexuality and "decayable meat":

—little black and white books nudged among many in a Times Square or Curtis Street bookstore window draw us to see the thing in lurid white, somehow interests us more than color, in black and white the thigh is all the whiter, the background all the darker and evil— . . . I even know this is infinitely more delicious than touching Ruth's [Ruth Maytime, the famous Hollywood actress] breast itself (though I'd do anything for the chance) . . . —the dirty magazines of boyhood become the religious publications of manhood—to stop joking—one pull on that cloth and a great breast plops out . . . holding us captive and especially because we know it'll never happen, it's only a picture, but IF IT DID!—if so, a magnificent bouncing jelly-like white-as-snow warm strange Ruth-personal breast with a nameless but revealing nipple which would tell us everything we need to know . . . and if she complains it's her fault, I didn't ask her to have three-fifths of her living breast that I want to nudge between my lips photographed, she offered it herself and I'm sure God will reward her for doing it—Ah that breast! It is such a casual breast, it just went swimming with her, her hair's wet, she's cutting a cake on Orrin Wynn's yacht, Edgar Bones the idiot is husbanding cutely at her side—her mouth is done up into what is supposed to be a smile but is really a great bit of desire and shuddering sensual bitterness (she's

> really *cutting* the cake) . . . —This pix is black and
> white, this breast is gray—there is more reality in gray
> for me (and for Cody too) because I was brought up in
> the balconies of B-movie theaters. Ah the holy contours
> all we men know— (VC, 76–77)

The gray pictures perpetually promise a revelation, a fulfillment, they can not deliver and that may not exist. Yet this
flight into illusion or fantasy may be the only way to clothe
the ultimate nakedness of the raw fetus. The speaker both
believes in the escape of a gray photographic world and
knows it for a pathetic sham. The part playful, part
desparate, part insightful fantasy of Ruth and the ultimate
breast does not answer the initial image, but it does provide
a temporary release from it and a point of rest, without
falsifying the initial image as the endings of the two
previous sketches threatened to do.

A reader expecting a novel organized around plot might
miss the relationship among these three sketches. Yet they
function as a unit, and Kerouac uses even what initially
seem like discontinuities as part of the exposition, an indirect exposition managed in terms of image and emotion
rather than action and concept, but coherent exposition
nonetheless. Still, grouping sketches around a theme or
image is not finally sufficient to structure a *Visions of Cody*
or account for "wild form." If it were, "wild form" would
be essentially an extension of the serial logic of a jazz
performance where solo follows solo, returning always to
the same theme and unable to extend beyond it. Robert
Creeley remembers an early fifties rumor that someone
named Kerouac had written an entire book about a blinking
light,[8] and such a book could be structured on a jazz model.
But it is probably more intriguing in prospect than in ac-
tuality, and the rumor probably derived from the several
sketches in *Visions of Cody*'s first section that deal with
lights and reflections.

The most useful analogue for understanding Kerouac's sense of structure and "wild form" is film. In Holmes's *Nothing More to Declare*, one provocative piece, "A Decade of Coming Attractions," deals with the effect of film on the generation which grew up during the thirties and came of age during the Second World War. Holmes writes that the movies were

> the sharing of an initiation rite with your contemporaries (like suffering the same trauma and being supplied with the same clues to its cure), for the movies of the thirties constitute, for my generation, nothing less than a kind of Jungian collective unconscious, a decade of coming attractions out of which some of the truths of our maturity have been formed.[9]

Kerouac nowhere talks explicitly about structure in terms of film, but the references in the books are extensive and suggestive. Many are primarily thematic. In *On the Road*, Hollywood is a source of romantic and falsifying fantasies about America that Sal must outgrow as part of his education, and in *Visions of Cody* Kerouac uses for illustration types of films, grade B westerns for instance, or specific scenes, "railroad tracks . . . (like the can jungle place *My Man Godfrey* wanted to go back to after he got his fill of Park Avenue in a tremendously Hollywoodian naive Depression movie that was nevertheless naively true . . .)"(VC, 79). But some references go beyond this and suggest Kerouac's interest in film as a medium. In *Doctor Sax*, the child Jackie understands the disastrous extent of the flood in his town only when he begins to visualize it as a scene he might see on the Saturday newsreel, and in *Visions of Cody*, Kerouac imagines Cody as looking

> like the Hollywood stunt man who is fist-fighting in place of the hero and has such a remote, furious,

anonymous viciousness (one of the loneliest things in the world to see and we've all seen it a thousand times in a thousand B-movies) that everybody begins to be suspicious because they know the hero wouldn't act like that in real unreality. (VC, 48)

These references involve film as a metaphor for seeing and suggest that film affects not only what we see but how we see it, and it is a short step from this to the idea that film might also affect the way we organize what we see.

In her study *The Age of the American Novel: The Film Aesthetic of Fiction Between the Two Wars*, the French critic Claude-Edmonde Magny speaks of

the cinema's profound modification of our collective sensibility, a modification that has taken place without our even being aware of it. We no longer perceive in the same way as we did fifty years ago; specifically, we have gotten into the habit of *having stories shown to us* instead of hearing them narrated. This must naturally turn storytelling technique upside down.[10]

Magny also observes that just as film in the twenties

is trying to escape from the pure narrative and break out of its old grooves, the novel also seems with Dos Passos and Joyce, to have a parallel ambition: to escape from the linearity with which it was apparently cursed by its material conditions of perception and to strive for the simultaneity of polyphonic music or painting. . . . The novelistic prose of Joyce tries to give us a synoptic view, a simultaneous perception of the consciousness of various characters; the film, of course, in conformity with its point of view, presents us with the simultaneity of their different behaviors. At the same time, Joyce tries to give us the interpenetration of present and past, which his belief in "unconscious" authorizes him to seek technical expression for.[11]

And Magny talks of the tendency to eliminate "the anonymous narrator . . . from the modern novel" and substitute "the use of the camera lens, a retina on which everything must register."[12] Magny writes:

> We have finally become aware that each scene in a novel—like each image in a film—bears the imprint of its point of view, has an origin that will make itself sufficiently evident by itself. Every scene in a novel is now understood to be as basically *relative* as a photograph.[13]

Magny's discussion parallels comments of Kerouac. Her sense of the impulse to "escape" . . . linearity" in favor of "simultaneity" suggests the contrast between the "horizontal" nature of *On the Road* and the "vertical" nature of *Visions of Cody*. Her sense of scenes in novels as photographs has the same emphasis on the visual image as sketching. And her sense of the substitution of the "camera lens, a retina" for the narrator anticipates Kerouac's description of his work as "one enormous comedy, seen through the eyes of poor Ti Jean (me) . . . seen through the keyhole of his eye."[14]

In *Visions of Cody*, the most extended look at film, "Joan Rawshanks in the Fog," occurs when Duluoz, walking in the Russian Hill area to see the sun set on the Golden Gate, happens on a Hollywood crew making elaborate preparations to film a very brief segment for a Joan Crawford film. In the scene Crawford, "Joan Rawshanks," runs up a driveway, struggles a frightened moment with the door to an apartment house, and disappears inside. Duluoz joins the "interested neighbors in an unofficial spectacle (impulsive, organic spectacle)" (VC, 280), and watches the crew film the scene three times. For Duluoz, the encounter reveals the artistry and elaborate manipulation behind what ultimately appears on the screen. Not only are there the cameras, director, and actress, but also an army of technicians and hangers-on, truckloads of equipment, and an entire neighborhood nearly immobilized so that the unreality of the movie can project the proper reality.

> in back where the angry technicians muster and make gestures in the blowing fog that rushes past kleig lights and ordinary lights in infinitesimal cold showers, to make everything seem miserable and storm-hounded, as though we were all on a mountain top saving the brave skiers in the howl of the elements, but also just like the lights and the way the night mist blows by them at the scene of great airplane disasters or train wrecks or even just construction jobs that have reached such a crucial point that there's overtime in muddy midnight Alaska conditions . . . . (VC, 275-76)

> and everybody watching (crowds in the cold fog, hand in pockets, like little kids at the back end of semi-pro football games . . . (with a cat . . . wielding those strange riddled cardboards they use for estimating the inch-ounce of light they want, though how can anybody detect that when the picture finally flashes on the screen;) (VC, 277)

> I had never imagined them going through these great Alexandrian strategies just for the sake of photographing Joan Rawshanks fumbling with her keys at a goggyfoddy door while all traffic halts in real world life only half a block away and everything waits on a whistle blown by a hysterical fool in a uniform who suddenly decided the importance of what's going on by some convulsive phenomena in the lower regions of his twitching hips, all manifesting itself in a sudden freezing grimace of idiotic wonder just exactly like the look of the favorite ninny in every B-movie you and I and Cody ever saw . . . . (VC, 286)

Duluoz is particularly struck by the disparity between the actual filming, "the take," and the product to be made from it. Duluoz sees the take as a performance. It has an audience, and the performer must manipulate the materials at hand for the purposes of the imagination. As Rawshanks prepares for a take, Duluoz even calls out to her as he might to a horn player, "Blow, baby, blow" (VC, 281), and he compares the take itself to a bullfight in its use of the "allotted moment":

> it surprises you that the actual kill is a distant, vague, almost dull flat happening like when Lou Gherig [sic] actually did connect for a home run and the sharp flap of the bat on ball seems disappointing even though Gherig [sic] hits another home run next time up, this one loud and clout in its sound, the actual moment, the central kill, the riddled middle idea, the thing, the Take, the actual juice suction of the camera catching a vastly planned action, the moment when we all know what the camera is germinating, a thing is being born whether we planned it right or not; there were three takes of every area of the action. . . . (VC, 281)

But cinematic performance is distorted by repetition. By the third take, Rawshanks has the scene "almost as perfect as a vaudeville act," and this strips the performance of legitimacy even as it heightens the persuasiveness of the illusion Rawshanks is to project in the final film:

> she goes to the door, fumbles, gets the keyhole, plunges into the keyhole, with rapture, like she was coming, she has that awful ugh desperation we all saw at this moment, the door won't yield to her first tug, gad, the door is closed, obstreperous, you can feel it in the crowd, their hostility for that door is already aroused and the picture isn't even cut yet or the film dry;

> they're going to hate that door en masse opening night; it's just a door, though; I see Joan tugging at it, she tosses her frightened face to the sky, the overhead, actual, creamy concrete garage ramp light on the ramp steps; two tugs, three, the door finally opens, the crowd cheers scattered and forlorn in the rainy dismalities; and Joan has made her third Take—The camera men suddenly begin mutilating and dissecting parts of their equipment and camera . . . . (VC, 289)

Film values illusion and perfection over the immediacy valued in jazz performance. Rawshanks is not playing to Duluoz and the crowd but to some unseen future audience. Duluoz feels "the embarrassment" of Rawshanks "plain as day fabricating tears on her arm" (VC, 281), but realizes that her artistry is simply the raw material for the larger process that results in the product of the finished film, a product elaborately synthetic and constructed but seeming absolutely real and unmediated to its audience. In the final cut, Rawshanks will cease to be an actress making an audience believe she is a frightened woman. She will be simply and totally a frightened woman, and the audience will even tend to lose its awareness of itself as an audience as the members of it slip into their dreamlike identification with the personality on the screen.

It is significant that Duluoz refuses to resolve the conflict between performance and product, take and finished film, simply by substituting the director or producer as artist in place of the actress. The process Duluoz encounters is too indirect, too vast and intricate, to be controlled by a single vision. He notes at one point that

> at first Joan apparently wanted to weep in this scene, the young director dissuaded her; this explains the early head on hands business, she was fixing up to cry, in fact the scene was run off and shot and Joan, weep-

ing, ran up the ramp to the door; nope the director
made her do this over again, substituting for the tears a
frightened run . . . (doesn't it seem as though the script
would have been materially altered on the point of this
decision about whether to cry or be frightened? . . .
(VC, 279)

Duluoz sees filmmaking as corporate in its reality even if it
attempts to project an aura of individualism to its final audience. To Duluoz, there is finally not a director in the
singular but "directors," "the great generals of the vast activity" who sit "under the tent" (VC, 279) like a military
headquarters staff. And this staff has both bureaucratic and
militaristic overtones. He senses them manipulating the
spectators, "not for kicks but in serious fascistic interest in
crowds" (VC, 280). And even this staff is finally not in control. Rather it is the technicians:

> they're the backbone of Hollywood for the movies have
> nothing now but great technique to show, a great
> technique is ready for a great incoming age, and these
> workmen of the progress of machine to aid and relieve
> the world, these ambiguous wonderers at the limits of
> set and imposed but useful and will-get-you-there (ho
> ho) task huddled in the night doing their work behind
> the fuffoonery and charaderees of Hollywood so mad,
> Hollywood, the Death of Hollywood is upon us . . . .
> (VC, 284)

And these technicians seem ultimately disinterested in the
particular project on which they are working as they amuse
themselves at the expense of the local police and wait for the
job to be over. They have little in common with Duluoz's
fantasies of what filmmaking would be like:

> when I thought of Hollywood camera crews I always

pictured them in the California night, by moonlight, on some sand road back of Pasadena or something, or maybe in some tree-y canyon at the foot of the Mojave Desert, or some dreaming copse like the one in Nathanael West where the cowboy who kills the chicken is pausing suddenly at eventide . . . best of all I thought of them in the San Joaquin Valley of California . . . where maybe actually an old Italian fruiterer lives with fatwife and dogs but in the moonlight it looks like the corral of a cursed homesteader; and on the soft dust of the star-white dirtroad in the moonlight softly roll the big pneumatic tires of the camera truck, about forty miles an hour, scooping up a low cloud for the stars . . . and on the road itself Hopalong Cassidy, in his white hat and his famed pony, loping along intently with beck and bent. . . . (VC, 285)

In spite of his distaste for its corporate dimension, Duluoz's response to his encounter with filmmaking is by no means entirely negative. For one thing, corporate Hollywood must still look to its audience for its material. The western, for instance, can not completely subvert its folkloristic and democratic dimension: "it isn't that Hollywood has won us with its dreams; it has only enhanced our own wild dreams, we the populace so strange and unknown, so incalculable, mad, ee . . ." (VC, 285). But also the encounter underscores for Duluoz the contrast between the often anticlimactic reality of the event itself and the intensely realistic illusion of the event in the constructed work. Duluoz realizes that the mediation of the camera makes certain events available emotionally that would otherwise be too real to be grasped.

I looked anxiously everywhere not only for a better place to see from, but up at the apartment house where the old ladies wrung their hands in hysteria. Apparently (for they could have drawn their blinds or rigged something up) they wanted actually to see what was going on in the street, what the actual hysteria of the scene being filmed, in which subconsciously I sensed their belief; so that in the midst of some awful sprawl Kleig-light grayscreen gangster extras getting all wet and bloody in the street with ketchup as the camera actions, the old ladies would come plummeting down from their five-story window in a double wild believing religious hysterical screaming suicide which would be accidentally filmed by the expensive grinding huge cameras and make a picture so stark that for another century Hollywood tycoons would feature this film as the capper to an evening of dominoes and deals, for relaxation of the nerves; two wild women flying in the night suddenly into the area of the lamps, but so suddenly as to look to the eye like rags, then instrumentations of the eyeball, then tricks of the camera, then flickers of electricity, then finally humanizations in twisted hideous form under the bright glares of the wild fear of old women in America, plunk on the ground, and Joan Rawshanks in the fog, not smiling, or fabricating tears, standing, legs aspraddle in a moment of dubious remembrance . . . . (VC, 282)

As Duluoz imagines the scene, the film is more unsettling and bleak than the event itself. The camera's ability to record the details of the jump creates a contrast between the abstract progression of the fall and the stark, suddenly humanized vignette that results from it. What for Rawshanks would be a moment of bewildered hesitation would be for the film viewer a moment of horror.

Kerouac's sense of the film is shown not only in Duluoz's explicit comments but in the way the entire episode is rendered. Kerouac sees the encounter cinematically and organizes it through narrative techniques such as crosscuts and dolly shots that Magny argues have been borrowed by

novelists from film. Like a camera, Duluoz alternately
sweeps different areas of the scene and moves in for close-
ups. And like a film editor, Duluoz intersperses the main
drama with bits of subsidiary dramas among the onlookers
and crew. And he flashes back and projects ahead, sup-
plementing what can be observed with hypothetical
histories and imagined outcomes. Magny suggests that such
an approach reveals the paradoxical effect of the camera.

> On the one hand, cinema is dominated by its desire for
> hyperreality, because its mechanical means of
> reproduction encourage it to become more objective
> than nature itself; but on the other hand, its creator
> must regain his liberty so that he may leave his mark on
> the work and raise it to the level of art, and this will be
> made possible by the camera's mobility which provides
> a counterbalance to the hyperobjective method. The
> contemporary novel tends more and more to the same
> basic duplicity.[15]

Magny clarifies the nature of this duplicity when she comments on "ellipses," her term for the personalizing techniques of cinema. She writes that "ellipses,"

> understood in the broadest sense as a choice of
> elements . . . allows the presentation of raw material
> ordered in terms of a desired specific artistic effect,
> that is, of meaning. It consequently permits the rein-
> troduction of the author's subjectivity and will,
> whether that *auteur* be director or writer. By means of
> this will, art accentuates and invigorates the paradox
> that is the very principle of perception: vision is the ar-
> bitrary act of will par excellence, that by which we
> choose to see right-side up the objects which in reality
> are painted upside down on our retinas. The right to
> an arbitrary vision of the world is the most sacred, the

most inalienable right of man. Art only proclaims out loud this too-often-forgotten right.[16]

In effect, Magny argues for a dialectical relationship between the objectifying presence of the camera and the subjectifying presence of the author through his selection and arrangement of the material recorded. The precise terms of the exchange between camera and creator may be open to debate, but Magny's analysis underscores the fact that making a film involves two distinct classes of activity: First gathering raw material, footage, and then selecting and arranging this material into a final product, the film itself. And it is this dual nature of filmmaking that suggests the nature of "wild form." Like a film, *Visions of Cody* is constructed through the calculated arrangement of discrete, spontaneous performances; and it is this arrangement, what might be called construction, that creates an ordering intelligence and purpose behind the fragmentary surface of the sketches.

Nothing establishes that Kerouac viewed "wild form" in terms of the cinematic metaphors of "Joan Rawshanks in the Fog," but several factors suggest that it is appropriate to do so whatever terms Kerouac himself may have used. "Joan Rawshanks in the Fog" is pivotal structurally and thematically in *Visions of Cody* even though it does not deal with Cody. It marks the first emergence of what becomes Kerouac's full mature style, and it must have been written at about the time that Kerouac finally decided that the pieces he had been drafting since the previous summer would become a new version of *On the Road*. The episode also suggests Kerouac's awareness of the thematic significance of formal problems. His awareness of filmmaking as a process underscores his concern with the distortions introduced by artistic techniques, and yet his belief in their necessity. And the dialectic between performance and construction, or something quite like it, seems to have been the

key to a possible mediation between the truth of real life
and the truth of art, that would retain the immediacy and
directness of actual experience while giving it the intensity
and sense of value and order that comes from the imagination.

Visions of Cody and *On the Road* have the same source,
but the two books develop very differently. *On the Road*
takes the form of an initiation. Sal's failure to appropriate
the world of Dean Moriarity educates him in the symbols
and patterns of his culture. Sal's counterpart, Jack Duluoz,
traces his isolation and confusion to his travels with Dean's
counterpart, Cody Pomeray, and seeks to overcome these by
understanding the process of his own perception and imagination. *Visions of Cody* is still concerned with America,
but with America experienced directly rather than through
the mediation of cultural archetype. The shift in emphasis
from *On the Road* to *Visions of Cody* is evident in the way
the two books utilize other texts and art forms. In *On the
Road*, Sal's reference to the film *Sullivan's Travels*
characterizes his actions. In *Visions of Cody*, "Joan
Rawshanks in the Fog" explores the relationship of perception to imagination. References in *On the Road* tend to be
confined to characters, actions, and structures of classic
American fiction, and these highlight Sal's encounter with
the tradition. References in *Visions of Cody* are broader in
scope, moving across genre, medium, and tradition. Instead
of to Twain and Melville, they are to Joyce, Whitman, and
Celine, and these figures are typically evoked for their sense
of language or for their sense of the process of the imagination. It might be said, a bit simplistically, that *On the Road*
is interested in literature while *Visions of Cody* is interested
in the literary, and that *On the Road* is more interested in
interpreting an experience and *Visions of Cody* more interested in how to express it.

In a sense, *Visions of Cody* centers on what *On the Road* points to and then ignores. Both books have a young writer for their narrator. In *On the Road*, this detail is almost gratuitous. It is announced as one of Sal's central motivations and then dropped. In *Visions of Cody*, though, this aspect of Duluoz is a major factor. Duluoz is as much concerned with exploring the nature of language as in understanding Cody. This gives *Visions of Cody* a double focus. It is a book about Cody and simultaneously a book about the problem of expressing Cody. Kerouac suggests this dual sense of the project in his preface to the 1960 edition of *Excerpts from Visions of Cody*: "I wanted to put my hand to an enormous paean which would unite my vision of America with words spilled out in the modern spontaneous method."[47] Kerouac here makes clear that *Visions of Cody* emerged not only out of his interest in Cody but out of his interest in mastering Spontaneous Prose, and *Visions of Cody* can be approached as a series of technical experiments that are visible in the book's series of narrative voices.

Kerouac's concern for voice is not surprising. From the omniscient third person of the earliest version in 1948 to the first-person narrator of what is now *On the Road* in 1951, Kerouac seems to have searched for increasingly greater flexibility and immediacy, and in *Visions of Cody*, he uses a series of voices apparently to overcome the limitations of any single voice. Each voice defines a different aspect of Duluoz's relationship to Cody, and the voices as a group define a debate over the strengths and weaknesses of various approaches to fiction, a debate that parallels the conflict in "Joan Rawshanks in the Fog" between the intensity of the consciously constructed aesthetic object and the somehow not real enough truth of naive documentary. In a sense, Kerouac is concerned with the relationship of style to vision, and the centrality of this issue in *Visions of Cody* makes clear that a piece like "Essentials of Spontaneous Prose" is an attack on outmoded or petrified conventions, not a denial of the intricacy of the aesthetic process itself.

Each of *Visions of Cody*'s five major sections is marked by its own voice, and this defines the logic of the "visions" just as Sal's education defines the logic of the trips in *On the Road*. This is not to say that *On the Road* and *Visions of Cody* are similar structurally, only that the narrator's concerns, not the hero's, order the books. *On the Road* follows chronologically the stages of Sal's education. *Visions of Cody* moves contrapuntally in the manner Ezra Pound ascribes to *Ulysses*: "What is James Joyce's *Ulysses*? This novel belongs to the great class of novels in sonata form, that is, in the form: Theme, countertheme, confrontation, development, finale."[18]

Visions of Cody begins with Kerouac's initial sense of sketching. Isolated and lonely, Duluoz wanders New York City translating whatever he encounters into images that seem at first to be independent of rhetorical purpose or narrative design. The second section, though, assumes precisely what the first avoids, the narrator's right to authority over his reader. The second section counters the idiosyncratic and self-reflexive "voice" of sketching with the omniscient third-person voice of traditional fiction, just as it counters the inactive, purposeless Duluoz with the dynamic Cody. As Kerouac recounts Cody's Denver adolescence, he freely directs the reader's attention, locating the action in time and space:

> Around the poolhalls of Denver during World War II a strange looking boy began to be noticeable to the characters who frequented the places afternoon and night and even to the casual visitors who dropped in for a game of snookers after supper when all the tables were busy in an atmosphere of smoke and great excitement and a continual parade passed in the alley from the backdoor of one poolroom on Glenarm Street to the backdoor of another—a boy called Cody Pomeray, the

son of a Larimer Street wino. Where he came from
nobody knew or at first cared. Older heroes of other
generations had darkened the walls of the poolhalls
long before Cody got there; memorable eccentrics,
great poolsharks, even killers, jazz musicians, traveling
salesmen, anonymous frozen bums who came in on
winter nights to sit an hour by the heat never to be seen
again . . . (VC, 47)

The sketching of the first section allows Kerouac to deal
with the significance of images for the speaker. The strategy
of the second allows him to deal with the significance of the
material for the reader. In the first case, the voice is freed
from its obligation to an audience, and in the second it is
bound to it.

The first two sections establish what Pound would call
theme and countertheme, and these two elements, one
Duluoz and the imagination and the other Cody and the
real world, come together in the third and longest section of
Visions of Cody when Duluoz, driven by the dislocation
revealed in the first section and drawn by the Cody he
describes in the second, joins Cody in San Francisco.
Kerouac constructs this encounter out of transcriptions of
taped conversations between Duluoz and Cody. Stylistically
it is the simplest section of the three, but rhetorically
perhaps the most complex. First, there are two voices,
Duluoz and Cody, each an audience for the other and each
unaware of the audience provided by the reader. Second,
there is the mechanical voice of the tape recorder that exists
only for the audience and author. This voice is unaware of
itself, and the impersonal accuracy of the machine replaces
the distortions of both the introverted imagination of the
first section and the extroverted imagination of the second,
thus creating a minimalist counterpoint to the imaginative
density of both sketching and traditional fictional voices.
And third, Duluoz's and Cody's debate over the difficulty of

relating their experiences to each other in a way that would adhere to the truth while conveying the intensity of the experience underscores the thematic implications of the tape experiment by suggesting that the bond between friends may itself rely on a narrative act subject to the same conflict between accuracy and intensity as the novel. The confrontation in the third section is in fact several confrontations. The reader must confront the disparity between the Duluoz and Cody of Duluoz's imagination and the Duluoz and Cody of the ordinary social world documented by the tapes, while Duluoz must face the conflict between himself and Cody which is both the conflict between himself and another and the conflict between the Cody he finds in San Francisco and the one he previously imagined.

The movement of the first three sections shows Kerouac's search for a way to establish the rhetorical directness and authority necessary to the horizontal activity of narrative while maintaining the vertical intricacy and freedom of his initial sense of sketching. Part of Kerouac's difficulty in this comes from his unwillingness to have the narrative itself predetermined by conventions of plot or by the reader's assumptions about the "authority" of the writer's voice, or to have the narrative world reduced merely to a naturalistic account of what happened. This struggle is apparent in the relationship of the first three sections and in the movement within each of the sections. In the first, the individual sketches are essentially imagistic and vertical, but as a group they define a fictional situation that Kerouac finally makes explicit by inserting a letter from Duluoz to Cody. The letter explains what has been going on without actually introducing the controlling voice of a narrator. In the second section, Duluoz's narrative of Cody's youth tends to digress into extended imagistic passages that build from the details of the fictional world and finally squeeze the narrative out altogether, only to be replaced in turn by narrator-less journal entries. The tape transcripts themselves are entirely without artifice. Yet as Duluoz probes to possess Cody's experience, Cody continually reminds him of both the limits of documentary and the falseness of art.

Kerouac develops the confrontations of the tapes in the fourth section, the "Imitation of the Tape." Here, the voices of the first three sections are brought together and internalized within Duluoz, who is now alternately and in combination sketcher, storyteller, and recorder of what can be heard and what can be imagined as heard. The two segments that conclude the section show the result of this synthesis. "Joan Rawshanks in the Fog" and the group of "Visions of Cody" imply a new style, both "modern" and "spontaneous," that bridges between naive documentary and solipsistic artifice by seeing them as interdependent and self-correcting. This development enables Kerouac for the first time to establish a hierarchy among the various Codys of Duluoz's imagination and of the world, and this is the development, to use Pound's terminology again, that enables Kerouac, as a finale, to assume the voice of the fourth section and in *Visions of Cody*'s closing to narrate the trips previously detailed in parts two, three, and four of *On the Road*.

Sketching, as Kerouac first describes it and as it exists in *Visions of Cody*'s first section, is made possible by an almost complete disregard for the reader. The writer's attention must be on the material at hand if he is to free himself from conventional expectations and discover (rediscover) the world and his relation to it. Grammatically, these first sketches are first person, but as narrative they are voiceless or, perhaps more accurately, prior to voice. The "I" in the sketches does not admit the existence of a reader. To acknowledge a reader would be, in effect, a backward glance breaking the attention to the image-object and the process initiated by it. The sketch of "an old diner" that opens the book shows the rhetoric, or lack of it, that is typical of sketching.

This is an old diner like the ones Cody and his father ate in, long ago, with that oldfashioned railroad car ceiling and sliding doors—the board where bread is cut is worn down fine as if with bread dust and a plane; the icebox ("Say I got some nice homefries tonight Cody!") is a huge brownwood thing with oldfashioned pull-out handles, windows, tile walls, full of lovely pans of eggs, butter pats, piles of bacon—old lunchcarts always have a dish of sliced raw onions ready to go on hamburgs. Grill is ancient and dark and emits an odor which is really succulent, like you would expect from the black hide of an old ham or an old pastrami beef—The lunchcart has stools with smooth slickwood tops—there are wooden drawers for where you find the long loaves of sandwich bread—The countermen: either Greeks or have big red drink noses. Coffee is served in white porcelain mugs—sometimes brown and cracked. An old pot with a half inch of black fat sits on the grill, with a wire fryer (also caked) sitting in it, ready for french fries—Melted fat is kept warm in an old small white coffee pot. A zinc siding behind the grill gleams from the brush of rags over fat stains—The cash register has a wooden drawer as old as the wood of a rolltop desk. The newest things are the steam cabinet, the aluminum coffee urns, the floor fans—But the marble counter is ancient, cracked, marked, carved, and under it is the old wood counter of late twenties, early thirties, which had come to look like the bottoms of old courtroom benches only with knifemarks and scars and something suggesting decades of delicious greasy food. Ah!

The smell is always of boiling water mixed with beef, boiling beef, like the smell of great kitchens of parochial boarding schools or old hospitals, the brown basement kitchen's smell—the smell is curiously the hungriest in America—it is FOODY instead of just spicy, or—it's like dishwater soap just washed a pan of hamburg—nameless—memoried—sincere—makes the guts of men curl in October. (VC, 3-4)

This is not stream of consciousness, something written to suggest the mental processes of a character, but what might be termed stream of attention since the passage records a process which is conscious, directed, and focused on the physical world. Details pile up in the order they strike the sketcher's senses, and the passage is emphatically present tense, moving from the immediate scene, through association, to a recognition of and release from the initial interest in the diner. Syntax is condensed as it might be in note taking, and the "I" is mostly omitted, again, as it might be in a note to one's self. Even the few instances of "you" underscore the way the sketches ignore the reader's existence. When Duluoz notes, "where you find the long loaves," he is not acknowledging an auditor but simply substituting the colloquial "you find" for the more formal "one finds."

The relationship of writer, text, and reader in a sketch such as this is somewhat paradoxical. It is as if the sketcher compensates for his austerity toward his reader with an almost overripe sense of language. The sketches, though they do not actually use a speaking voice, have a strong sense of words as voiced objects. In a phrase like, "stools with smooth slickwood tops," the alliterative *s*'s mix with the long and short vowels to create a strong cadence and an aural texture that imitates the texture of the object. Perhaps most importantly, the refusal to acknowledge the reader seems to allow the sketcher to evoke emotions so textural in nature that they typically can not be narrated to another. In *On the Road* when Sal resorts to words such as *gray* or *sad*, it is usually his admission that the experience has outstripped his ability to express it. But details like "FOODY instead of just spicy" actually give some precise emotional

173

life to a phrase like, "—nameless—memoried—sincere— makes the guts of men curl in October." Part of the success of the diner sketch and others like it in expressing these emotions and textures may come from the way the reader looks through the eye of the sketcher rather than looking at the I. The perceptions come to the reader through a human presence which allows emotional involvement, but for the span of the sketch ego and identity are temporarily suspended. This allows the reader to experience the sketch as if he were unfolding the details and emotions himself. In a sense, neither the sketcher nor his viewer the reader exists for the other, and yet they are intertwined.

Sketches like the diner sketch are self-contained and self-fulfilled, and one reviewer has suggested they be read as individual prose poems. This approach, though, ignores the way the sketches function in the book as a whole. Individually, they do function almost entirely vertically, but, considered as a group, narrative elements are apparent. The narrative is subordinate to the imagistic movement of the individual sketch, but it is strong enough to stamp the first section as more than simply a collection and to enable it to define the whole book thematically in the same way that Sal's initial solo trip defines *On the Road*. In part, the sketches' narrative element comes from Kerouac's apparent manipulation of them after the actual sketching. Each sketch is a discrete performance, but these performances are arranged to suggest actions for the sketcher. Duluoz wanders back and forth from his home on Long Island to Manhattan, going in and out of the subway and places open to someone with an excess of time and a shortage of money. In some cases, events are implied but omitted. At one point, the sketcher progresses from "an old El station on Third Avenue and 47th" to "Third Avenue and 9th Street" where he sketches "a beat employment agency" from the exterior and then from the interior. Finally, the scene shifts to "the men's room in Third Avenue El." The sketch in the men's room associates the "wainscot effect" of the walls with Denver "flophouses" leading to the image of a cheap restaurant where bums sit, "heads bent in pitiful congregation, the needs and necessities, no 'dining' here" (VC, 6–7). The grouping and tone, what is seen and how it is seen, suggest that Duluoz has come into the city looking for work, failed, and fears becoming a derelict.

Kerouac also suggests a narrative dimension through the occasional references to Cody. The sequence detailing Duluoz's trip to the employment agency begins:

> In the autumn of 1951 I began thinking of Cody Pomeray, thinking of Cody Pomeray. We had been great buddies on the road. I was in New York and I wanted to go to California and see him, but I had no money. (VC, 5)

There are only a few of these comments. Kerouac distinguishes them from the sketches by using that most common tense for narrative, the simple past, rather than the present tense of sketching, and they were probably inserted at the time Kerouac selected and arranged the sketches as a section. "Manhattan Sketches," published in 1963 in the anthology *The Moderns*,[19] points to this conclusion. The piece takes eight of *Visions of Cody*'s opening sketches, changes the order, modifies the opening phrase in some, and deletes, with the exception of one brief phrase, all references to Cody. As a result, sketches that seem to come from several different forays into town in *Visions of Cody* are arranged to imply a single trip on a single evening from a cafeteria in Manhattan out to Long Island. Which arrangement reflects the "actual" experience is not important. Probably neither corresponds to the original situation, but the alternative versions show Kerouac's willingness and ability to manipulate the sketches for different effects.

Finally, even though the sketching perspective does not

emphasize the sketcher as a narrator or character, the personality, the I behind the eye, is implied by what is sketched and by the motifs, textures, and patterns that repeat over the course of the sketches just as habits of phrasing repeat in a jazz musician's solos and identify who is playing. In *Visions of Cody*'s first section, many sketches are of places where people tend to gather without interacting—a diner, subway station, different cafeterias—and this suggests Duluoz's isolation and his desire for contact with those that pass through his field of vision. His baroque feel for the physical detail of ordinary scenes attempts to make the inanimate world yield the emotional sustenance one would normally seek from other people. When Duluoz does sketch people, he chooses subjects he cannot approach and who are unaware of him: a black worker asleep in a subway car, an old woman on the street, a famous jazz musician. In contrast, the physical world for him at moments seems "an all-out promise of joy" and even gains the voice the people lack:

> happens to be a fog—distant low of a klaxon moaning horn—sudden swash of locomotive steam, either that or crash of steel rods—a car washing by with the sound we all know from city dawns—reminds me of Cambridge, Mass. at dawn and I didn't go to Harvard—Far far away a nameless purling or yowling of some kind done either by (raised, vibroned) a train on a steel curve or skidding car—grumble of a truck coming—small truck, but has whistle tires in the mist—a double "bop bop" or "beep beep" from railyards, maybe soft application of big Diesel whistle by engineer to acknowledge hiball-on-the-air from brakeman or car knocker—the sound of the whole thing in general when there are no specific near-sounds is of course sea-like but also almost like the sound of the living structure, so as you look at a house you imagine it as adding its breathing to the general loud

hush—(ever so far, in the hush, you can hear a tiny SQUEE of something, the nameless asthmas of the throat of Time)—now a man, probably a truckdriver, is yelling far away. . . . A cluster of yellow November leaves in an otherwise bare and sheepish and castrated tree send up a little meek PLICK as they rub together preparing to die. When I see a leaf fall, I always say goodbye—And that has a sound which is lost unless there is country stillness at which time I'm sure it really rattles the earth, like ants in orchestras. . . . A car door slamming, the click, the velvet modern hinge-click before the soft slam—the soft cushioned new-car slam, flump—some man in hat and coat up to something pompous, secret, sheepish—The area breathes; it seems to want to tell something intelligible to me— (VC, 9-10)

Duluoz's acute sense of detail gives the night and fog a life. "The area breathes" and even gives back to Duluoz a sense of recognition by wanting to "tell" him "something intelligible."

Not only do the sketches as a group reveal Duluoz's predilection toward certain settings, they also reveal his fascination with certain textures and tones. The sketches, for instance, stress the colors gray and brown and use them in so consistent a manner that they take on specific values. Gray is associated with the oppressive and urban present. It is the color of worn-out things which somehow continue on after death. When Duluoz looks at a hotdog stand next to the "Capricio B movie," he stresses its

counter topped by a marble so old it has turned gray and chipped . . . and beneath, an ancient woodflap once used to close place at night, now nailed under Coca-Cola [sign], is so weatherbeaten and old, and was once painted brown, that it now has a shapeless

177

color like shit against the gray, almost shit-gray
sidewalk. . . . (VC, 4)

Sooty white lettering "makes a dirty sad effect" (VC, 5),
and in "the men's room in the Third Avenue El . . . a big
coathook decked with soot (like snow that's fallen on a twig)
and fully a foot long, [is] like seeing an enormous
cockroach" (VC, 6). For Duluoz, much of the city's
brightness is an attempt to cover over the gray. He notices
"tinfoil (attempt to brighten window sensationally,
drastically like they do in wildest modern stores" (VC, 5).

Brown implies a positive sense of aging and is associated
with dreams, memories, and things that gain value with
age. In St. Patrick's Cathedral at dusk, Duluoz watches the
"windows grow rich, brown, dark, secret, get better with
age of light like wine with age of Time" (VC, 28), and the
altar of St. Joseph, "a humble self-admitting truthful
Saint," is "a symphony in brown." In the "old El station on
Third Avenue . . . the fantastic ceiling of carved wood" and
the "carved raw buttresses like Victorian porches" give
Duluoz the sense that "the place is so brown that any light
looks brown it it—It's fit for the sorrows of a winter night
. . ." (VC, 5). Brown may be sorrowful, but gray is despair.
Brown suggest loss, but loss redeemed by human contact
and usage. Brown is the actual loss of gray transformed by
the imagination.

The tension betwen gray and brown is apparent in
Duluoz's account of the "mahogany darkness" of his first
study:

> Whether her cherry trees were in bloom or not it was
> brown in this room—when my father had rheumatism
> in it the sheets of his sickbed made it gray—now this is
> an "inexpressibly delicious" old memory like old
> port—nothing in California matches it. I rolled my
> glassies for the first time on the jagged wood of the

desk—it was when I got idea for racing, they meandered a race under my eyes—it was a gray day—the whole idea of the *Turf* must have come to me like (as just now and not since 1948) that so-seldom experience of seeing my whole life's richness swimming in a palpable mothlike cloud, a cloud I can really see and which I think is elfin and due really to my Celtic blood—coming only in moments of *complete inspiration.* . . . In my life I number them probably below five—at least on this level— (VC, 27)

And although brightness intensifies gray's negativity, its effect on brown is positive:

A glittering counter—decorative walls—but nobody notices noble old ceiling of ancient decorated in fact almost baroque (Louis XV?) plaster now browned a smoky rich tan color—where chandeliers hung (obviously was old restaurant) now electric bulbs within metal casings or shades—But general effect is of *shiny food* on counter . . . as brilliant as B-way outside! . . . Huge salads, cottage cheese . . . flaky rich Napoleons . . . enormously dark chocolate cake (gleaming scatological brown)—of deepdish strudel, of time and this river. . . Then the serious business, the wild steaming fragrant hot-plate counter—Roast lamb, roast loin of pork, roast sirloin of beef. . . . But most of all it's that shining glazed sweet counter—showering like heaven—an all-out promise of joy in the great city of kicks.
. . . (Poor Cody, in front of this in his scuffled-up beat Denver shoes, his literary "imitation" suit he had wanted to wear to be acceptable in New York cafeterias which he had thought would be brown and plain like Denver cafeterias, with ordinary food)— (VC, 10–11)

Here, a texture like "browned a smoky rich color" suggests a sense of time as depth that reinforces Duluoz's delight and establishes continuity with the past. It enables him to savor his pleasure in "the glorious cafeteria of Cody's first New York vision . . . in late 1946 all excited" (VC, 10), in spite of his recognition of its "sad" transitoriness.

Duluoz's use of gray and brown defines a basic dichotomy: the real world and present afflict him with isolation and loss, while memory and imagination give him vitality and connect him to his surroundings. Memory and imagination affect the movement of time for Duluoz. Time as he experiences it with others is fragmented and moves too fast; but memory and imagination, though solitary activities, slow time and allow possession of the moment and by implication of human community as well:

> people in cafeterias smile when they're arriving and sitting down at the table but when they're leaving . . . they pick up their coats and things with glum faces (. . . which is a special glumness that is disappointed that the promise of the first-arriving smiling moment didn't come out or if it did it died after a short life)—and during that short life which has the same blind unconscious quality as the orgasm, everything is happening to all their souls—this is the GO—the summation pinnacle possible in human relationships—lasts a second—the vibratory message is on—yet it's not so mystic either, it's love and sympathy in a flash . . . more so reminds us that the moment is ungraspable, is already gone and if we sleep we can call it up again mixing it with unlimited other beautiful combinations—shuffle the old file cards of the soul in demented hallucinated sleep— (VC, 15)

Slowing time to "call up" the "ungraspable" is reminiscent of the tenor man's paradoxical performance and "IT" in *On the Road*. But in *On the Road*, Sal describes the performance in order to study and interpret this paradox. In *Visions of Cody*, Duluoz himself attempts to perform. The sketches embody the conflict of "IT." They are performances, not comments on performance.

Sketching's identity as performance helps account for the variety in the first section. As an activity, a way of responding to time and identity, sketching is fundamentally the same whether one sketches something physically present, a memory, or a fantasy—or, for that matter, something physically present as memory or fantasy. Close attention to the activity of perception, memory, or imagination in each case requires connecting discrete elements that would otherwise remain fragmentary and beneath the threshold of awareness. The relationship of perception, memory, and imagination is particularly clear in the ending of the sketch in St. Patrick's Cathedral:

> And now finally the window is so *out* that the bottom glass reflects *brownly* the lights that just came on for an imminent service.
>   These glass windows refract NIGHT too for now I see nothing but the rich dim recollections of what at dusk was a Rembrandt barrel of ale in a Dublin saloon when Joyce was young, the hint so vague it's like people in a dark room wearing phosphorescent rims and all involved in some drama so tragic that the light of day can't shine on it—only the inward light of night—
> (VC, 31)

Details of the window give way to "dim reflections" which in turn lead to "the inward light" before the priest destroys the sense of connection by reintroducing society's time, "mixing theological verities" with "Old Soldier crap."

The window not only shows the interaction of perception, memory, and imagination in sketching, it suggests a

181

metaphor for the eye of the sketcher. The window simultaneously reflects and refracts. It is both mirror and lens. Making light inside and outside the church available at the same time, it transforms the actual lights into the brown light of memory and "the inward light of night." Similarly, the sketcher himself is simultaneously mirror and lens, a window at the meeting place of the actual world and the imaginative inside world. Kerouac develops this interplay more fully in Duluoz's sketch of "the immense plate glass window" of a Sixth Avenue cafeteria:

> inside neon tubular lights reflected in the window and they in turn illuminating the Japanese garden walls which are therefore also reflected and hang in the street with the tubular neons (and with other things illuminated and reflected such as that enormous twenty-foot green door with its red and white exit sign reflected near the drapes to the left, a mirror pillar from deep inside, vaguely the white plumbing and at the top of things upper right hand and the signs that are low in the window looking out . . . are also reflected and hanging but only low on the sidewalk because also they're practically against it)—so that a great scene of New York at night with cars and cabs and people rushing by and *Amusement Center, Bookstore, Leo's Clothing, Printing,* and *Ward's Hamburger* and all of it November clear and dark is riddled by these diaphanous hanging neons, Japanese walls, door, exit signs— (VC, 16)

Duluoz is particularly interested in the way the glass allows the outside in, yet projects the inside out. He notes with amazement a "reflected mirror pillar" that the cafeteria lights seem to make hang in the streets where it, though not actually there, reflects back an image of "the tubular neon, the real one inside" (VC, 17).

The glass gives Duluoz the feeling that the letters of the signs "are shifting their depths as my eyes rounden—they dance—through them I know the city, and the universe" (VC, 18). Ostensibly, "them" refers to the letters, but it also refers to the sketcher's eyes. They too "dance," and it is finally "through them" that Duluoz "know[s]." In sketching, the novel is a mirror of inside and outside worlds. It is a window that not only allows one to see in and out, but that also projects the image of the inside onto the outside and vice versa. This creative dimension of the glass, of the eye that is the novel and the sketcher both, is suggested by the way, when Duluoz shifts his gaze six inches, he finds a "miraculous mirror" which reflects through the window and allows him to see "to places I can't even see" (VC, 18). This grace of the window and the eye gives Duluoz his "great immortal metropolitan in-the-city feeling that I first dug (and all of us) as an infant . . . smack in the heart of shiny glitters" (VC, 18).

Duluoz's fascination with "these confusions of reflected light" recalls Kerouac's and Ginsberg's interest in Cezanne and "les petites sensations." Like Cezanne, Duluoz here seems able to shift his attention slightly and discover yet another world existing alongside or within the one he has been regarding. The physical world to the eye is not separate from the imagination. The two interpenetrate. When a light in a window across the street is turned off, for Duluoz

> the mirror pillar is suddenly revealed all the way to its entire length because my attention had been on the actual window and the reflected pillar was just barely touching the edge of the window and I didn't know it. (VC, 17)

The interaction of inner and outer worlds on the window of the eye demonstrates Kerouac's solution to the problem of responding to the actual world and the imaginative world. Sketching transforms both into image and, as image, they are free to coexist. They become "the old file cards of the soul" to be shuffled into "beautiful combinations."

For Duluoz, sketching allows escape from the recognition "that the moment is ungraspable." Sketching, by balancing between the actual and the imaginative, functions like memory and makes the world, "the flash," "memoried and human." But there is a cost. To be "as an infant" in "the heart of shiny glitters" is available only to "*incurable* sitters" who renounce action and identity and become passive enough, transparent enough, that light can pass out and in. In Emersonian terms, it means becoming a "transparent eyeball." Kerouac shares with Emerson a sense of the exhilarations of the moment when vision is so comprehensive it implies a union with the world beyond self, but Kerouac, or at least Duluoz, is also troubled about the price in a way that the Emerson of *Nature* is not. To be a "transparent eyeball" is to "see all" and be "nothing."[20] Or as Duluoz claims, "I accept lostness forever. Everything comes to me because I am poor" (VC, 33). In both cases, vision comes only after social identity and social relationships disappear. As Emerson says,

> standing on the bare ground,—my head bathed by the blithe air and uplifted into infinite space,—all mean egotism vanishes. I become a transparent eyeball; I am nothing; I see all; the currents of the Universal Being circulate through me; I am part or particle of God. The name of the nearest friend sounds then foreign and accidental: to be brothers, to be acquaintances, master or servant is then a trifle and a disturbance.[21]

Identity is at least partly a social construct, and to be aware of it and of social relationships is to be aware of time and therefore of limitation. To renounce identity may not actually allow an escape from time and limitation, but it does mean an escape from the awareness of them.

This implies that to be the heroic individual of the American romantic tradition, one must give up the possibility of identity. Whatever Emerson's sense of this may be, for Duluoz it is finally a problematic exchange. He is exhilarated by the momentary freedom of ecstatic vision and troubled by the loss of identity and the isolation that are corollary. To be a "transparent eyeball" is finally to be invisible, or visible only from light that one traps from elsewhere. In his "lostness," Duluoz goes about "dressed like a bum with a seedy envelope" (VC, 24) unable to approach those he encounters, and his ambivalence about this is apparent in the way he interprets a jazz solo by George Handy, who in "sadomasochistic modernity" rejects "the joy of bop . . . which existed naturally in his heart for the glooms and despairs and great disappointed deaths, the deadly loss of ego, the last acknowledgment of self" (VC, 24–25). To renounce ego is perhaps heroic. It leads to the ultimate and visionary self beyond identity, but the cost of this rebirth is isolation, invisibility, and the death of joy. The freedom of being outside society is also the burden of being without identity. To be free of physical constraint is to risk being trapped alone in the imagination.

Kerouac's awareness of this cost is visible in his arrangement of the sketches to imply a narrative to Duluoz's encounter with romantic vision. Initially, the sketches show Duluoz overcoming his isolation from a world that offers him no role to play or place to be by losing himself in the visual richness of the physical world. This immersion enables him to discard identity altogether and with it his anxiety about his place in society. Duluoz's immersion in the visual allows him to recover his vitality, but it also leads him to value the imagination more than the world, which results, finally, in an even greater isolation. The farther Duluoz pushes into pure vision and his own imagination, the less the objects he encounters have human meaning and the less they can redeem him with a sense of engagement. The process that enables Duluoz to recover the physical, pushed too far, leads to losing it. The "flash" ceases to be "memoried and human." Without engagement and a sense of the new, the exhilaration over the "beautiful combinations" that come from "shuffl[ing] the old file cards of the soul" (VC, 15) becomes instead "my own personal tragedy," and, when Duluoz then "catches" himself "in the act of shuffling the file cards of the memory or the mind under the deck" (VC, 41), he feels it is a "desperate" activity, that he has "done wrong" to himself. In the first case, Duluoz merges "soul" and world through discovering new combinations. In the second, he is trapped in his own "memory" which reduces "shuffling" to an obsessive and regressive defense against the world, a kind of imaginative masturbation that substitutes for the earlier love and must lead, Duluoz suspects, to emotional impotence and the loss of the ability to sketch.

By the end of the first section, Duluoz can only dream passively until he is reawakened by "a great American intersection . . . the openspace whiteness which is always situated *exactly halfway* between the country and downtown" (VC, 37–38). This reminds Duluoz of Cody and Denver so strongly that he resolves to "go to the Coast without money anyway" (VC, 38). He announces in his letter to Cody,

> I'm completely your friend, your "lover," he who loves you and digs your greatness completely—haunted in the mind by you (think what that means, try to reverse, say, supposing you referred all your sensations to somebody and wondered what they thought about it) . . . supposing each time you heard a delightfully original idea or were given such an image that makes the mind sing you immediately slapped it over like one

of these new office roller files to check with the CODY THING, that is, the Cody constellation, and then on another level checked it emotionally like to measure its amounts of awe that you would bring to it. (VC, 39)

Duluoz here makes explicit what the brief, inserted references have implied, that is, that Cody has been a key in Duluoz's rejection of ordinary society for vision and that Duluoz looks to Cody as a way of understanding and correcting his own situation. Duluoz seems to suspect that Cody has renounced society, yet retained identity. Cody is active and visionary, not passive and visionary or prone to Duluoz's paranoia. And Cody is of the West with its mythic past, open space, and social fluidity. Duluoz sees that if anyone can overcome the conflict between being an individual and having identity it is someone like Cody. And even were this not so, Duluoz looks to Cody as his one chance to overcome isolation, to establish community and still remain true to his own individualism.

In the first section, Kerouac subordinates the sketches' narrative element to the imagistic movement of the individual sketches. Yet the "I" made possible by narrative is finally a necessary condition to the eye of the sketcher. The impact of immersing in the immediate interplay of perception and imagination comes in part from the sketcher's recognition that suspending, being released from, ego and identity is necessarily temporary. When the demands of real time and the need for a place in society are dismissed entirely, the escape into the eye leads not to vitality and discovery but to compulsive repetition, a sense, as Duluoz says, of being "haunted." The narrative element of the sketches, in effect, demonstrates what the individual sketches would not; that is, that the dialectic activity of sketching, the interaction of inner and outer, is grounded in an awareness of this dialectic in a more comprehensive form as the unresolvable opposition between the imagination as authority and the world as authority, between the enacting of self as an individual free of society and the possession of identity within and from society.

Even though it is the implied narrative of Duluoz's sketching that points to the dialectic of individual and identity, imagination and world, it is important to recognize that Duluoz is not the "I" of the opening section. Duluoz experiences the conflicts and enacts the process, but he is not necessarily aware of their implications, at least not for the book. If he were, he would be, rather than a character, the book's narrator, its Sal Paradise, and Duluoz's social existence, his identity, would then subsume the inner world into the outer and explain away the dialectic by denying one of its terms. This would trivialize the interchange fundamental to sketching and collapse the first section in on top of itself. If construction were primary and narrative established more directly, the reader's recognition of the world and of identity would reduce the creation of image to a symptom of a particular character. If performance were primary and the sketcher more simply visible in his activity, the individual and imagination would overwhelm the narrative and establish the sketcher in a privileged position with the reader that would obscure the full implications of the search for vision.

In effect, there can be no narrator in a traditional sense in a wild form work of Spontaneous Prose without creating what Jacques Derrida would call a "center" for the "structure" that is the text, at which point *Visions of Cody* would become either traditional fiction in the sense of *On the Road*, or simply autobiography. Derrida writes:

> At the center, the permutation or the transformation of elements . . . is forbidden. At least this permutation has always remained *interdicted*. . . . Thus it has always been thought that the center, which is by definition unique, constituted that very thing within a

structure which governs the structure, while escaping structurality. This is why classical thought concerning structure could say that the center is, paradoxically, *within* the structure and *outside* it. The center is at the center of the totality and yet, since the center does not belong to the totality (is not part of the totality), the totality *has its center elsewhere*. The center is not the center. The concept of centered structure—although it represents coherence itself, the condition of the *episteme* as philosophy or science—is contradictorily coherent. . . . The concept of centered structure is in fact the concept of a freeplay based on a fundamental ground, a freeplay which is constituted upon a fundamental immobility and a reassuring certitude, which is itself beyond the reach of the freeplay.[22]

In this sense, the "I" of the first section that organizes and establishes the significance of the activity of sketching must emerge out of a dialectical play, itself the structural equivalent of the thematic tension between inner and outer, between the acts of performance and construction, if it is to respond fully to the inner and outer worlds, the worlds of child and adult.

In the first section, the performed sketches evoke an imaginative presence, and the constructed narrative revalues it in terms of the world. The combination defines the "I" that organizes the book. The separate, spontaneous sketches, performance, embody the energy of the individual. Like an improvised jazz solo, they suspend the laws of society's time so that the imagination may shape time to its laws. The selection, modification, and arrangement of sketches—in short, the perspective of construction—-recognizes society and identity, adheres to the actual, and accepts the logic of sequence and duration. Duluoz is the side that emerges from construction, an identity that suggests Kerouac's sense of how the activity of the transcending imagination appears to society. The other side of the "I" is in some sense Kerouac himself, the individual existing totally in the action of the imagination. This aspect of the "I" is entirely self-absorbed but inherently without egotism or name since it is prior to identity. If Duluoz controlled the book, it would be a study of the socially ineffectual artist. If the nameless, childlike individual controlled the book, it would be impressionistically vague and solipsistic. But each aspect of the "I" grounds the other. The logic of performance vitalizes the social, and the logic of construction focuses the imagination.

In a sense, the "I" of *Visions of Cody* is in fact Kerouac, but Kerouac as the product of the unnamed self and the self named by society. Kerouac does not project a version of himself into the book to act out his concerns as he does with Sal in *On the Road*. Rather, he creates himself through the book and the tension of performance and construction, inner and outer, individual and identity. There is, in other words, no implied Kerouac whose understanding transcends the text. This does not mean, though, that *Visions of Cody* is simply autobiographical. It is not the self narrating its history, nor the self reporting the equivalent of its undigested dreaming. It is the self evoked and explored through the interplay of different perspectives, and this process leads to a clarity and depth beyond the capability of the normally fragmentary self. As a result, the "I," the Kerouac in the book, is actually more real than the Kerouac behind it, and the understanding of the Kerouac of the text transcends that of the Kerouac outside it. In a sense, the text becomes the author. Kerouac in the fullest sense is the book. And the actual Kerouac exists primarily as the energy and materials that merge in performance and construction.

This sense of the text as in some way its own author, its own authority, suggests one reason for Kerouac's uneasiness with any single narrative point of view, since a single perspective would point to a single and limiting understanding outside the text. Also, because Kerouac had already begun to submerge the limited self into the text in *On the Road*, the tendency of readers to reverse the process, to view the text as limited and submerge it into a presumed all-encompassing self in order to fix their attention on Kerouac as a personality is unfortunate though somewhat understandable. It misses the thrust of Kerouac's writing and reduces him to the partial existence he was trying to overcome. This view overvalues identity and mistakenly sees it as opposed to, rather than derived from, society. Kerouac's readers have too often romanticized the resulting destructive conflict between self and society as proof of a transcendent identity (itself a contradiction in terms). Kerouac may have made this same mistake at times in his own life, and it may have contributed to his self-destructiveness. But this does not justify reducing his best texts to the partial understanding of an actual Kerouac, rather than respecting the more comprehensive nature of what he was able to perform and construct.

The interplay of performance and construction established in the first section is present throughout *Visions of Cody*. It underlies each section and functions as an organizational presence in place of an author or narrator. This means that the reader must remain suspended between two antithetical principles, and the elaborate indirection of the narrative in the first section, the sketcher's firm refusal to acknowledge his audience, suggests Kerouac's sense of how easy it would be for the reader to simplify the text if the dialectic itself, in either its structural or thematic form, were established any other way than as a function, a set of vitalizing relationships. Moreover, the reader's task is made even more difficult by the way the terms that express this basic structural and thematic function evolve as the book progresses, and as new material is annexed. This progressive element is illustrated by the different implications of image and narrative in the first and second sections. The function of performance and construction, inner and outer, remains constant, but the relationship of image and narrative to these dialects shifts. In the first, image is performance. Narrative is construction and implies the perspective of the outer world. In the second section, though, not only is the narrative of Cody's youth the dominant line and image the counterpoint, but narrative is actually treated as performance. The "I" still exists as the middle term of unnamed self and social identity, of performance and construction, but the "I" has enlarged its sense of image, narrative, and voice in a way that reflects and assumes the developments of the first section, making it possible for Kerouac to approach the action of the text more directly while still maintaining the critical balance between inner and outer.

Without the "I" of the first section, the narrative of the second could not function as it does. The third-person voice that presents Cody's story would be perceived as an omniscient narrator beyond the text. Instead, the seemingly omniscient voice points within the text to the "I." The world of the narrative is implicitly an imaginative act, a performance motivated by the longing for Cody elaborated in the letter that closes the first section. Duluoz's letter signals a shift to an overtly narrative concern and leads the reader to expect either an account of a trip west to, or an encounter with, Cody. Instead, though the novel does shift from sketching to narrative, Duluoz disappears, and the encounter takes place in the imagination. It is as if Duluoz, unable to join Cody quickly enough in the actual world, projects a Cody that can be possessed immediately. In this sense, the narrative is a "vision of Cody," a creation of the imagination within the text, even though its traditional, realistic form implies the history of a real Cody available in terms of vision as actual, physical sight.

Besides defining the possible terms of Duluoz's interest in

Cody, the letter anticipates the shift to narrative by demonstrating Duluoz's ability to treat narrative as an imaginative projection:

> I think of Frisco, I think of the evening I'm going to ar-
> rive, shh, I creep up the street taking in not only every
> aspect possible all the sensations round me but refer-
> ring them to earlier personal tiptoeings around my
> beloved and spectral and soon to be holy Frisco . . .
> digging the street, digging available indications of
> what's going on in your house from a block away (ac-
> tually understanding in myriad rapid thought
> everything I sense as it stands in front of me and ac-
> tivates all around, in portable breast shirtpocket
> notebooks slapping), advancing little by little to the
> point of knocking on the door which will be exactly like
> those hot summer afternoons when I used to pretend
> that I was dying of thirst in the desert but an Arab
> chieftain found me . . . and laid a glass of water in
> front of me, but said "You can only have it if you sur-
> render your fort and your men, and do it on your knees
> abjectly" and I agree . . . seeing the glass, the dews of
> the foggy rim, the ice clinking, and plunging for it . . .
> that moment of actually taking the first sip and ap-
> preciating water itself *playinly*, whee, wow, you know
> what I mean, that's how I'm gonna knock on your *door*
> *which ain't any door*. (VC, 42–43 [italics added])

In addition to presenting what amounts to a sketched narrative, the letter also reveals that in at least one case,
Duluoz takes a sketch from the period of the first section
and his own experience and shifts it in time and place to use
as a seed for the narrative of Cody in the second section. In
the letter, Duluoz claims to Cody, "I dig like you did, I dig
jazz, a 1000 things in America, even the rubbish in the
weeds of an empty lot, I make notes about it, I know the

secrets" (VC, 40). Duluoz here locates the origin of the sketch of the empty lot where Cody and his buddies are imagined to witness the discovery of the miscarried fetus.

This comment might be seen as carelessness on Kerouac's part, an indication that the text is, in fact, a random assemblage. But there are indications that Kerouac deliberately lets the contradiction stand as an indication of the process of the book's composition. The catalogue of the empty lot begins the unit of three sketches discussed earlier that end with Duluoz's fantasy about cheesecake photos, his "one and original poipose." In effect, the unit moves from a sketch to narrative and back to a sketch. The sketched image initiates the possibility of action which is then followed out descriptively and leads to a final sketch, itself possibly from New York and the sketchings of October or November 1951. Cody and friends are nearly extraneous to the sketch of the empty lot, but the empty lot provides impetus for the narrator's fantasy of their trip to the whistle-stop and the two women which in turn establishes significance of the description of "dirty old voyeurs."

Two things suggest that the "I" is purposefully calling attention to itself as the source of what is represented as Cody's experience. First, these sketches mark the point where the "I" explicitly reenters the text in the second section and briefly mixes narrative and sketched image. And second, Kerouac underscores the importance of this mixture by the way he disrupts the third sketch—the Times Square sketch, itself a digression from the narrative—to insert a parenthetical narrative fragment as a further digression. From describing the "nameless but revealing nipple" of the "strange Ruth-personal breast," the passage jumps to:

> (the exact nipple will tell us more than Ruth's entire life story, "Around the beauty parlors of Brooklyn during World War II a strange energetic young lady began to be noticeable to the characters who frequented the

places afternoon and night and even to the casual
visitors . . ."—the first glimpse of it and we've finally
seen her soul, its perfection and its imperfection, its
confession, its secret girlish shame, which is best of all
what we want). . . . (VC, 76)

This beginning of a history of Ruth can only owe its existence to the "I." The quotation marks within the paren-
theses indicate the dependence of the third-person voice on
the speaker of the sketch, the "I." Ruth has no history other
than as a manifestation of the "I." She reveals the imagining
author, not the world, and the reader is asked to remain
aware of this, not ignore it or forget it. Even were the story
completed, it would remain a performance catalyzed by the
sketched image, in effect an image sketched on a broader
scale than a single object. It would be action treated as object or, perhaps more precisely, action existing in order to
evoke objects transformable into sketched images. Ruth's
story may be a joke, a digression within a digression, but it
indicates the way Kerouac in the second section treats narrative as an imaginative, not a mimetic, act.

It is no accident that the fragment of Ruth's history
parodies the beginning of Cody's history that opens the second section:

Around the poolhalls of Denver during World War II a
strange looking boy began to be noticeable to the
characters who frequented the places and even to the
casual visitors who dropped in for a game of snookers
after supper. . . . (VC, 47)

The telling of Cody's youth reflects the "I" even more than
it does Cody. And this is the case whether the "I" is explicit
about his presence, as in the sketch of "dirty old voyeurs," or
retires behind the temporary screen of a seemingly impersonal third-person voice. In the tape transcripts of the third

section, Kerouac includes an exchange between Cody and Jack Duluoz in which Duluoz describes writing several of the narrative pieces from the second section. Duluoz talks about how he has "picked up on images" of Cody's youth and "projected" them from his own imagination into pieces of narrative:

> JACK. You should have seen what in imagination, man, I wrote a thing about you and him [Cody's father] and Old Bull Lewis, Old Bull Balloon, and I changed his name to Old Bull Lewis because he was supposed to be a farmer, had a farm, outside of town, Alameda there, and I said, "The three of them got in the car for some unknown—well they got a lot of ah, wire together and, and screen, they got together, and they got a—they went out to Nebraska to sell these flyswatters, made these little flyswatters . . . †the car like a potato bug crawled eastward for no reason under the huge skies"—all that kind of shit?
>
> CODY. And it's just what happened, see, I remember that trip.
>
> JACK. Carl Rappaport was all hungup on the way that I had picked up on the images, of what you told me about yourself, and projected them on the wall, all ballooned up—
>
> CODY. Enlarged, yeah
>
> JACK. . . . and cracked, crazy, (Cody laughing) Old Bull Balloon, see? Who was actually the guy?. . . that went with you. . .
>
> CODY. Well, he was a guy either named Blackie or, ah, something like that, but he was a tough, muscular—
>
> JACK. Listen. . . I had a guy called Rex. . .a bum, he

---

†In Kerouac's tape transcripts, ellipses indicate pauses. Asterisks (*) indicate that a portion of the transcript has been omitted.

was a buddy of your father's, but I know there was no
guy called Rex but do you know why I called him Rex?
CODY. No
JACK. I said "Because he was no king, he was a guy
who never wanted to grow up and so an American
who, ah, never, ah, outlived the desire to grow up and
so lay on the sidewalk"—you know, like we all want to
lie down on the grass on the sidewalk, and there's
a—at one point your father, Cody, see, Old
Cody's—he's lying under a pool of piss under old Rex,
something, under the *ramps.* . .
CODY. (*laughing bemused*) I've seen him lying in
many a place like that, but this guy going to Nebraska
was like I say tanned and muscular and. . .very emi-
nent, he wasn't in the depths of alcohol like my father
although he was a complete wino and drank all day
and everything, but he was young, he was only about
thirty or so, see—
JACK. Oh yeah? (VC, 178)

What has been presented in the second section as continuous
and impersonal narrative is here shown to be Duluoz's
romanticized fantasies originally conceived independently
of the text and then arranged, revised, and assembled. The
"I" is the performer, the editor, and in effect the subject as
well, even though the narrative presents the actions of Cody
and his world.

The letter that closes the first section, the digressions
within the second, and the material in the tape transcriptions
all point to Kerouac's expectation that the narrative of Cody's
youth be approached not simply for what it says about Cody
but what it implies about the "I" who invents it. In Cody,
Duluoz creates a kind of alter ego. Cody is dynamic, visible,
and decisive. He is precisely what the "haunted" Duluoz is
not. With "no mother" and an absent wino father, Cody has
developed by his own genius and not that of society. He is

197

heroically himself, shaped by his own law even if that places him in conflict with the law of society.

> It [Cody's face] is a face that's so suspicious, so energetically upward-looking like people in passport or police lineup photos, so rigidly itself, looking like it's about to do anything unspeakably enthusiastic, in fact so much the opposite of the rosy Coke-drinking boy in the Scandinavian ski sweater ad, that in front of a brick wall where it says *Post No Bills* and it's too dirty for a rosy boy ad you can imagine Cody standing there in the raw gray flesh manacled between sheriffs and Assistant D.A.'s and you wouldn't have to ask yourself who is the culprit and who is the law. (VC, 48)

And Cody is competent to make his way in the real world. He may be in opposition to society's self-protecting laws, but he is able to work around them and function in a "practical way." "At fifteen this child had the regimen of his life worked out . . ." (VC, 56), and Cody's 7:00 A.M. to 11:00 P.M. routine is a complete round of work, study, and lovemaking. Duluoz may satirize this routine (and Gatsby, Alger, and Franklin along with it) by having Cody work at petty thieving, make love to a retarded maid, and study the encyclopedia, but Duluoz believes in it and envies it, too. Duluoz's Cody is an updated, skid-row version of the American child-man who is imagined to exist on the margin of society and preserves our quintessential American identity. He is unshaped by society though also at times its victim, and his ability to resist "that strange American iron" that attempts "to straighten and quell the long wavering spermy disorderliness of the boy" (VC, 48–49) authenticates him as more truly American than the society that attempts to suppress him.

Although Duluoz's Cody is active in the real world, he shares with Duluoz the traits that make sketching possible.

Cody is "pure-souled" (VC, 57), "a great idealist" (VC, 56).
He is intensely imaginative. As a child, he fixes "his eyes on
the mosaic of the tiles of the barbershop floor" and imagines
that

> each little square could be peeled back endlessly, tiny
> leaf by tiny leaf, revealing in little microcosmic en-
> cyclopedia the complete history of every person that
> ever lived as far back as the beginning, the whole thing
> a blinding sight when he raised his eyes from one tile
> and saw all the others like the dazzling crazy huge in-
> finity of the world swimming. (VC, 53)

And Cody is alert to every implication of what he encounters. In "the great American poolhall night" when
Cody "at a very early age" makes his "appearance" on the
"stage" of "the lonely poolroom scene,"

> the intricate and almost metaphysical click and play of
> billiard balls became the background for his thoughts;
> till later the sight of a beautifully reverse-Englished
> cueball leaping back in the air, after a cannonading
> shot at another ball belted straight in, bam, when it
> takes three soft bounces and settles back on the green,
> became more than just the background for daylong
> daydreams, plans and schemes but the unutterable
> realization of the great interior joyful knowledge of the
> world that he was beginning to discover in his
> soul . . . Cody knew, he knew everything like mad,
> sitting as though he wasn't noticing anything and not
> thinking anything on the hard onlooker's bench and yet
> noticing the special excellence of any good shot within
> the aura of his eyeball and not only that, the
> peculiarities and pitiful typehood of every player
> whether some overflamboyant kid . . . or some old
> potbellied rotation wizard who's left his lonely wife in

a varnished studio room above a *Rooms* sign in the dark of Pearl Street, he knew it all. (VC, 49)

And even though the poolroom stage "has been trampled smooth in a number of crowded decades," Cody does not "pose" or play a role. He is not limited by identity or anxious for it. His face has a "happy prim self-belief" (VC, 48).

Duluoz's Cody is a wish fulfillment, a transcendent individual who seemingly experiences no conflict between inner and outer worlds. Cody is a transparent eye who retains his awareness of self, his I. Instead of the cold serenity of an Emerson or the paranoia of a Poe, Cody has the optimism of a Whitman, the frontier vitality of a Twain. And yet Duluoz is only partly convinced by the Cody he projects. When Duluoz views Cody close-up and by himself, he senses Cody's completeness. This Cody is self-authenticating, independent, and ultimately mythic in his absolute Americanness. But when Duluoz views Cody from a distance, against the backdrop of his surroundings, he senses Cody's insignificance and vulnerability. Imagining Cody's father, Cody, and Bull Balloon on their flyswatter selling venture, Duluoz writes:

> Huge prairie clouds massed and marched above the indescribable anxiety of the earth's surface where men lived as their car belittled itself in immensity, crawled eastward like a potato bug over roads that led to nothing. One bottle of whiskey, just one bottle of whiskey was all they needed; whereas little Cody who sat in the rattly back seat counting the lonely pole-by-pole throb of telegraph lines spanning sad America only wanted bread that you buy in a grocery store all fresh in a happy red wrapper that reminded him speechlessly of happy Saturday mornings with his mother long dead—bread like that and butter, that's all. (VC, 54)

Cody's mortality epitomizes his humanity and suggests Duluoz's fear that transcendental individualism, though heroic in its own terms, may be tragic (or simply pathetic) when placed against the larger view of the human condition.

When Duluoz imagines Cody mythically, Cody is large enough and comprehensive enough to overcome any conflict, but Cody is then also so much larger than life that he represents a solution unavailable to Duluoz. When Duluoz projects a more human Cody, he creates a figure vulnerable to his own problems. In a sense, even though Duluoz projects Cody as active and decisive, once Duluoz begins to imagine narrative, imagines Cody acting in the world rather than seeing Cody primarily as an image, he begins a process that leads back into the conflict between inner and outer rather than beyond it. As an image, Cody can exist on many levels, but Cody as a figure in a series of actions implies that one level is primary and other levels secondary. Sequence and causality take precedence, and Cody's possible "truth" from other levels, other perspectives, must be suppressed. Because of this, Kerouac is able to project a Cody who is mythically whole and also of the world only when he is first setting the "stage" at the beginning of the second section. As soon as this opening "vision" leads out to imagined action, the vision's internal contradictions become manifest, and Duluoz's wish fulfillment begins to self-destruct.

The conflict between Cody as narrative and as image in the second section is by no means explicit. Kerouac's style and Cody's actions are so forceful on the surface that it is only as one scrutinizes Duluoz's stake in the action that the full significance of the narrative of Cody's youth becomes apparent. And scrutinizing Duluoz's role in the second section shows that the reader, in effect, must deal with two narratives. One is the narrative of Cody's youth that Duluoz projects in a series of performances just as he projects the sketches of the first section, and the other is the narrative of Duluoz's struggle to balance the causality of narrative and the freedom of image, which is another form of the struggle of Duluoz in the first section to balance the needs of his imagination and the demands of the world. As in the first section, this second narrative is the product of the construction of the individual performances and shows up in the way shifts in style parallel the stages of the first narrative of Cody. In this way, the second section, in spite of a different tone and its seeming openness, is fundamentally similar to the first section. Performance reveals the vitality of the imagination, and construction suggests the struggle of the self in the actual world.

In spite of the turmoil Duluoz relates to his narrative of Cody, the narrative itself follows a simple and obvious line. Duluoz presents Cody on his poolroom stage and then uses this tableau as a kind of image-object for the narrative that follows. The narrative itself moves from Cody's childhood through his adolescence to early manhood. In each phrase, Cody is imaginatively self-sufficient and yet troubled by a sense of isolation which propels him to the next phase. Cody the child can create a world out of whatever he encounters, the tile floors of the barbershop or a newspaper comic strip. He spends "hours" with Major Hoople and

> the whole pitiful interesting world in back of it [the comic strip] including maybe a faint cloud in the distance, or a bird dreamed in single wavy line over the board fence, and the eternal mystery of the dialog balloon taking up whole sections of the visible world for speech. . . . (VC, 52)

But Cody still feels the "disappointment" when his wino father and father's friends celebrate their "wild joy" and ignore him. Cody wants to belong and doesn't realize that their "agony" is their own attempt to belong and return to "piteous memories" of "fleecy cradle days." Nevertheless, Cody resolves to avoid his father's fate through his regimen.

Cody's adolescence is associated with the poolhall. Cody sees it as a place he can belong, an entry to the brotherhood denied him by the winos. Cody's entry into this pool hall world is represented primarily through the alliance he creates with Tom Watson, the young crippled pool shark that Cody elects as a mentor. Cody proposes that Watson be his "big brother" and he, Cody, Watson's helper with such vehement and unintentionally comic energy that Watson clothes Cody, feeds him, and introduces him to the crowd that becomes Cody's "gang." Watson is "the great American Image of beautiful sadness" (VC, 59), and Cody watching him is the "American boy for the first time perceiving the existence of an American poet" (VC, 58). When Watson unfolds "sculptured fingers" to cue his stick, it is a "gesture so sophisticated in America that boys see it in their dreams as soon as they've seen it once" (VC, 58). To Cody, his new status is "a vision," but his choice of mentor suggests that his "vision," like Duluoz's image of Cody at the beginning of the section, is inherently problematic and difficult to act on. The "poet" is marginal in every sense. It is the source of his grace. He competes with no one and so sees all. He is transparent:

> melancholy Tom Watson, the habitue . . . dreaming at his upright cue-stick as naturally as the sentry with his spear or the hull-bump of a destroyer that you see on the horizon with its spindly ghost of a foremast, a figure so familiar in the brownness of the room that after awhile you didn't see him any more like certain drinkers disappear the moment they put their foot on the brass rail. . . . (VC, 58)

Cody can coexist with this comrade because Watson has no ego. Cody can expand to his full vitality with no conflict but

203

also without contact. The gang, though, is another matter. There, Cody must compete and be either leader or member. If Cody is to be the hero, the transcendent individual, he must be the leader, but as the leader he is alone again. Duluoz imagines Cody's mastery of the gang as a spontaneous football game between Cody and the current leader as Cody, Watson, and the gang are on their way to the rendezvous at the whistle-stop.

Cody's adolescent "penetration" of the pool hall expands his field of action but resolves little. It sets the "stage" for the next stage—Cody's entrance to adulthood, which apparently takes place at the whistle-stop with Cody demonstrating his mastery of men, the "gang," and of women. For Cody, it is a short step from adolescence to being an adult. Cody's mastery of the gang in the football contest is immediately followed by an episode where he demonstrates or discovers his mastery of women. But Kerouac declines to present this rite of passage. He implies it by talking of Cody as a boy before and as a man after it, as if Cody's entry into the status of adult is too volatile and ambiguous to approach directly. Instead, Kerouac juxtaposes Cody's football exploits with the miscarriage in the empty lot and then veers to Duluoz's fantasy of Times Square and Ruth's gray breast. The significance of Cody's sexual initiation is framed by the image of "girls" who "are frightening when you see them under these circumstances" of being "confronted by a miscarried whatnot" (VC, 71), and the "nameless but revealing nipple" and "its secret girlish shame, which is best of all what we want" (VC, 76). Neither of these images suggest union. One is either "frightened" or one controls, and this represents "a loneliness" unmatched by the child's exclusion from the father's world or the longing of the adolescent for comrade and gang (VC, 79). After the trip to the whistle stop, Cody possesses "a suit and topcoat" and a new "adult gesture" (VC, 78), but he possesses these things at the cost of recognizing that the union he seeks is partial and must be paid for with the recognition of an ultimate futility that offers in return a joy that is real but only fleeting.

In effect, Duluoz's narrative of Cody shows the child longing to belong, the adolescent acting to belong, and the young adult discovering the cost. Duluoz imagines Cody's attempt to recognize the outcome of his growth through Cody's encounter with "the redbrick wall behind red neons, waiting" (VC, 80). The image of red brick and neon also marks Duluoz's recognition that the Cody he projects is as unable as Duluoz himself to overcome the gulf between self and other, self and world. It is also worth recalling that Kerouac when writing the red-brick material early in 1952 cites it in his letter to Solomon as the point where he discovers that his writing about Cassady is really about himself. Duluoz and the Cody he imagines associate the red brick with the world of the city, particularly the "backplaces of what we call downtown" (VC, 78). And the red neon is associated with "our frontward noticeable desperately advertised life" and hides, or at least colors, the "sooty" reality of the city (VC, 79). Sensing the red brick wall behind the red neon is like the loneliness that comes to Cody as an adult. It evokes the contrast between Cody's experiences as a child of the "smoky exciting dumps of Saturday morning,"

and standing in the middle of the winter night on a sidewalk that is not your home beneath cold red neons glowing as softly as if it was still summer but now on a redbrick wall which eschews a humid and perforated iciness of its own, corrupted, dank with winter, not the place to lean a lonely back and in spite of all this grimness inherent in it suggesting more than it ever could suggest in the summer and with infinite greater adult excitement than the dump a joy, but a joy so much stronger than the joy of the dump that it was like the man's need for whiskey supplanting the boy thirst for orange soda and took as much trouble and years to develop, the joy of the downtown city night. (VC, 79)

Red brick and neon as a combination is "an aura of invitation calling men to come and make their mothlike approach" (VC, 81) to some ultimate mystery at the "center of Saturday night" that leaves one "haunted by sorrows" (VC, 57), perhaps because the ultimate mystery is in this vision ambiguous, a life force and a perversion of life, a death force. And it, "the vision," is "what you get, what there is" (VC, 80);

> that thing twelve, thirteen feet over his head, that spot haunted red wall, what it is that makes the approaching night so exciting, so shivering, so all-fired what-where, so deep. It was years later before he found the answer in the little nameless second when, after meeting Joanna in a sodafountain and taking her to the Ouray Hotel, Tremont corner fifth floor room, and turning from his pants on the chair to go on with what he was saying to her his future wife as she spread her thighs experimentally on the faded pink bedcover, a beauteous creature of the first order with long ringlets and curls and only incidentally fifteen at this time he saw in the act of swinging his eyes from chair to bed a nameless red tint fading and flashing on the redbrick wall just outside the window, saw this in a fraction through the little dirty thin muslin curtain that billowed in the drafts of steam from the silver radiator which was also slightly roseate from the neon, the dirty sooty sill also almost rusty lit from the glow, a scrap of paper one hundred feet off the snowy ground suddenly swirling past in the January nightwind, the whole big flat window rattling, the neon coming and

going on the brick, the poor hidden brick of America,
the actual place that you must go if you must bang
your head to bang it at all, the center of the grief and
what Cody now saw and realized from all that time the
center of the ecstasy. (VC, 86–87)

This vision may well be the controlling image for the
book as a whole, as Kerouac tries to evoke in a single passage
the unity of his own concerns and Cody's, and the relationship of his private and single consciousness to that larger imaginative and actual enterprise "America." And at the
"center" of them all is an unreconcilable, unresolvable
duality of "grief" and "ecstasy." The vision of red brick and
neon ends the search that has been behind all of Duluoz's
actions, imagined, imaginative, and actual. And it ends his
narrative of Cody. The fictional projection has led not to
solution but final conflict. Other "visions" may, and do,
follow but without the sense of a meaningful personal
history that Duluoz attempts in the second section.

The vision of red brick and neon does not end the second
section, though. The vision may be one of conflict with no
hope of resolution and that may effectively disrupt Duluoz's
fictional projections, but there is still the problem of
Duluoz's response to the outcome of his narrative of Cody.
In a sense, in the segment of red brick and neon, he has
already defined his alternatives. He can "bang [his] head,"
or he can back off and shine "a white unloading light" on
the brick instead of red neon. If Duluoz does this, accepts
the world of the rational, of daylight and society, the brick
wall becomes simply "any old brickwall of a factory" and
"as forlorn as brown snow" (VC, 80). Duluoz does both in
the remainder of the second section which is series of sketches, journal entries, and dreams. He laments "America,"
whose promise of imaginative and individual fulfillment
covers over an oppressive social reality and thereby

enmeshes grief and ecstasy with confusion and evil:

> America, the word, the sound is the sound of my
> unhappiness, the pronunciation of my beat and stupid
> grief—my happiness has no such name as America. it
> has a more personal smaller more tittering secret
> name—America is being wanted by the police, pur-
> sued across Kentucky and Ohio, sleeping with the
> stockyard rats and howling tin shingles of gloomy
> hideaway silos, is the picture of an axe in *True Detec-
> tive Magazine*, is the impersonal nighttime at crossings
> and junctions where everybody looks both ways, four
> ways, nobody cares—America is where you're not even
> allowed to cry for yourself—it's where Greeks try hard
> to be accepted and sometimes they're Maltese or from
> Cyprus . . . America (TEENAGE DOPE SEX CAR
> RING!!) is also the red neon and the thighs in the
> cheap motel—it's where at night the staggering drunks
> began to appear like cockroaches when the bars
> close—It is where people, people, people are weeping
> and chewing their lips in bars as well as lone beds and
> masturbating in a million ways in every hiding hole
> you can find in the dark—It has evil roads behind gas
> tanks where murderous dogs snarl from behind wire
> fences and cruisers suddenly leap out like getaway cars
> but from a crime more secret, more baneful than
> words can tell—(VC, 90)

And Duluoz also resolves to satisfy himself with the real
world of "Brown halls of men" (VC, 98). He will join Cody,
who he now imagines to be a simple and good working
man: "in the rainy dawn I walk rapidly on the balls of my
feet like a Cody heading for work . . ." (VC, 97).

The second section concludes with journal entries that
present Duluoz's trip west to Cody. These function in a
similar manner to the letter that closes the first section.

They locate Duluoz in a physically and socially realistic setting that clarifies what precedes, and anticipates what follows. They show Duluoz caught between his allegiance to a life of the imagination and a life of productivity in the "brown world" of working men, and caught as well between beliefs that the imagination has relevance only to the self, and that it has relevance to the world of men. Duluoz must, in other words, decide whether to write or work; and furthermore, whether he will write about his "soul" which he claims to have "discovered" with sketching on "October 25" (VC, 93), or write fiction, "create a great universe" (VC, 93). His confused but optimistic response is that he will do all three. He will work, and he resolves

> I must write down *books*, too, story-novels, and communicate to people instead of just appeasing my lone soul with a record of it—but this record is my joy. (VC, 107)

From his perspective preparing to join Cody, Duluoz's excited oversimplification of matters is easily understood. But the actual struggle to sketch that the first section reveals, and the struggles to write "story-novels" in the second suggest that the Kerouac of *Visions of Cody* does not believe his earlier social self, does not believe the writing and work can be so easily compartmentalized, nor that the writing itself can be separated into two different impulses, one directed toward the self and the other toward the world. If he did, it is unlikely that he would allow the narrative of the second section to exist as it does.

In fact, the section represents five distinct phases of composition. The earliest material, Cody's childhood, seems to come largely from early summer of 1951 when Kerouac worked on inserts about Dean's past for *On the Road.* Cody's pool hall propositioning of Watson apparently comes from work early in 1951 after *Pic* and before *On the Road.*[23]

The next segment, the empty lot and Times Square passages, are sketches from the fall of 1951. The red brick and neon passage come from early 1952 just before Kerouac's conception of *Visions of Cody* crystallized, and the journal material comes from late December 1951. Kerouac in no way expects his reader to date the material, but he does call attention to its disparate nature and his manipulation of it. And Kerouac does mean for his reader, at least in retrospect, to see the way each segment of the section involves a distinct and different trade-off between narrative and image, vertical and horizontal, ranging from the almost totally narrative segment of Cody conning Watson to the almost totally imagistic segment of Cody's discovery of red brick and neon. In the section, narrative derives from image and leads to image. And both reveal the self more than they do the world.

In a sense, the Kerouac who constructs the book realizes that his true allegiance is to the "soul" and sketching, but he also realizes that this commitment is only meaningful if it admits its relevance to others and if it admits the world in its full intransigence. The sketching of the first section tends to veer toward the private and purely imaginative world of dream. It functions initially as redemption but becomes obsession. It releases the "I" from the bondage of viewing writing as the making of objects. It frees the "I" to see writing as process, as the recording of things and states in transformation; but it leads to a reduction of experience and the world that leaves nothing to transform. The sketching experiment, though itself only partially successful for the "I" in solving conflicts over himself and his writing, does lead to a further experiment, and the narrative of the second section shows the "I" striving to admit the world more as an existence apart from the self and yet retain that sense of writing as process, as discovery and unfolding. But this too is only partly successful. Narrative can be treated as performance, and Duluoz does focus on an imagined other and not himself, but this imaginative admission of the demands of the world is overcome by the transformation into image in the same way that physical objects are overcome in the first section. Duluoz's narrative of Cody turns out to be Duluoz's exploration of his own obsessive concerns with America, identity, sexuality, and death. It becomes a new way of viewing the old but not a way of moving outward and recognizing new experience, further experience. What the "I" discovers is that his imaginative act reveals itself more than the world, and it raises the question of whether the imagination can ever be free enough of its own impulses to present the world and action. The first section frees the "I" from a sense of fiction as a mirror of the world, but once Duluoz begins writing for the sake of his "soul," he discovers that fiction is a mirror of the self and that he must still find a way to recover the outside world. And this recovery must not allow the reader or writer to pass the real off mistakenly as "fiction"—that is, something real but less so than actual experience. Since Kerouac suggests that experience is only real as it is assimilated and expressed as "truth" in all its "myriad profusion," Duluoz and Kerouac must be "a great rememberer redeeming life from darkness" (VC, 103); and that means overcoming any tendency to divide writing as a public and private act into two schizophrenic activities.

Kerouac's motives in the writing and his sense of the reader are quite complex. He mistrusts his own motives, and he mistrusts the motives of the reader. At the same time, his sense of writing as process and discovery implies that he must trust his own impulses, and his sense of democracy as an idealistic community means he must believe in his reader, believe in the reader's existence and the reader's own spontaneous and imaginative energy. Like Whitman on the Brooklyn ferry redeeming the reader who follows, and in turn being redeemed by the reader he has just willed into existence, Kerouac perceives his relationship with the reader as a transaction, and if at time he treats this transaction in an oblique and tortured manner, it is largely because his sense of self, sense of other and sense of history all suggest that the transaction is impossible. The activity is redemption and ecstasy, but the most likely outcome is damnation and grief.

The need to reestablish connection with the outside world and get beyond his own distorted sense of self and the reader's distorting sense of writing as a debased reality are all involved with Kerouac's decision in the third section of *Visions of Cody* to relate Duluoz's encounter with Cody through transcribed tape recordings. The appeal of the tape recorder is the same as the appeal of the movie camera. Both, as Magny says of the camera, are "mechanical means of reproduction" that tempt the artist with the possibility of "becom[ing] more objective than nature itself," a possibility for a "Hyperreality."[24] Ginsberg has characterized the tapes as a kind of cinema verité, a "slice of life." The tapes are "(like Warhol's *Empire State Movie*) (watching Empire State eight hours all nite all day with one Camera eye)" that Kerouac "placed . . . in the center of his book as an actual sample of the Reality he was otherwise Rhapsodizing."[25] And the tapes do have a documentary function, though of a more complex sort than Ginsberg seems to credit.

In the tapes, the recorder takes the place of both the sketcher's eye and the narrative voice. It is the speaker in the section. Impersonal, with no rhetorical bias of its own, the machine passively records whatever is in the range of its microphone. The breadth and self-interest of a human speaker is replaced by the narrower accuracy of the machine that is the product of what amounts to a two-fold reduction of what occurs. The machine filters actual conversation first through the microphone and then through the typewriter. The microphone removes most traces of the physical and temporal setting, everything but physical sound, and the typewriter reduces this record to its abstract equivalent in written characters. The effect of this processing is to merge the act of perception and expression by removing the intermediate stage of understanding and interpretation which may enrich but which also distorts. Ironically, this diminution of the human presence by the tape is what allows Kerouac to present the human issues and social situation of the book. The machine puts the reader in the position of overhearing conversation, and the microphone and machines reduce the friends to their identities; to reveal, that is, the foolish, enthusiastic, banal surface that might appear to a stranger rather than the created reality of selves that exists between friends or the imaginative, thematically controlled projections of intensified human character created by the artist. The transcripts assert Jack Duluoz's identity as a writer and his concern with perceiving Cody. They also reveal a Cody considerably less decisive and visionary than Duluoz's images of him, and a Duluoz less passive and transparent than he has imagined himself to be. The two have quite ordinary fears of aging, of being misunderstood, of being unable to express themselves. These realities do not negate the earlier images, but they do reaffirm that the book's action is in the process of Kerouac's and Duluoz's meditation and not in the book's quite limited physical action. In a sense, the recorder attenuates the energy of performance by reducing it to an object, and this makes the role of construction in the book correspondingly more available for the reader by allowing a view of the constructor—Duluoz, Kerouac—temporarily unobscured by his own fascination with himself.

Aside from their function as a realistic and documentary counter to the imaginative material that precedes and follows, the tapes have thematic and structural significance in themselves. Even though they give a view of the self that the self cannot reveal on its own, their "hyperreality," their

213

objectivity, does not preclude their being manipulated for other purposes at the same time. Some manipulation is, of course, inevitable. Someone has to be behind the camera as well as someone or something in front of it. Someone has to start the machine, change reels, and transcribe the tapes, and Kerouac largely handles these matters straightforwardly. He designates each speaker with a bold face entry— "CODY," "JACK,"—and his editorial comments are few and essentially parenthetical descriptions: "(laughing)," "(whispering)," and "(REEL ENDS) (MACHINE BEGINS)." In addition, Kerouac breaks the transcripts into basic time units such as "first day," "second day," and "later on." But even this minimal apparatus reveals order and intention, reveals the Kerouac who chooses to use the transcripts in the book and the Duluoz who chooses to experiment with the machine. Duluoz is admittedly a writer, but his purposes in using the recorder do not come from any sense on his part that he will use them in a book. Duluoz sees the tape recorder as a device to study Cody in order to distinguish between the Cody of his fantasy and Cody himself. Kerouac, in turn, is able to study the results of Duluoz's experiments not only for what they say about Duluoz and Cody but in terms of what the experiment suggests about the proper role of imagination and interpretation as a mediating screen between perception and expression. Kerouac's decision to use them in the text for their documentary value is, in effect, only the third and final gesture revealed in the tapes.

The tape transcripts of the first night ramble. There is little sense of control, and the direction that exists comes from Duluoz's attempt to fish out of Cody the story of his stay in Texas with Bull Hubbard, Irwin Garden, and Huck. Duluoz and Cody are both high, and this contributes to the disjointed nature of the dialogue. But there is also Cody's difficulty in remembering what would interest Duluoz about his experiences. Cody says, but man, what I'd tell you is, I didn't know that I'd appreciate remembering these things more, so therefore when I was there I didn't pay much attention to any of this, I was hung up on something else, you know, so I can't remember, say, like for example, I can remember NOW for example, but now that I CAN remember it doesn't do any good, because . . . man . . . I can't get it down. (VC, 123)

And Cody is not sure that he wants to remember. "But I'm not digging any of this so much, I'm on other things somewhere . . ." (VC, 126). The marijuana has heightened Cody's awareness of himself and gives him a sense of vulnerability, perhaps intensified by his awareness of the recorder and a feeling that Duluoz's questioning may be an attempt to manipulate and not an attempt to share an experience. Cody's attempt to bring the conversation around to his self-consciousness and their present situation brings an end to the first session of taping:

CODY. Yeah. Well I'll tell you, man, the interesting thing about this stuff is I think the both of us are going around containing ourselves, you know what I mean, what I'm saying is, ah, we're still aware of ourselves, even when we're high.
JACK. Well I feel like an old fool
CODY. Is that it? Yeah . . . yeah. That's very good . . . I feel, ah, man, what do I feel? I . . . yeah I feel very foolish
JACK. Hee hee feel foolish . . . but you still feel like a YOUNG fool
CODY. Well . . . I've been an old man, Jack, in Watsonville, and my eyes going bad, and my . . . yeah . . . Well I feel like a middleaged fool
JACK. You do?
CODY. Yeah. But I know I'm very young

kid—type—in fact sometimes it might even occur to me to worry about it—but I haven't ever yet. You know. Man, I kinda dig you as a young kid type too you know
JACK. What?
CODY. I kinda dig you as a young kid type, like myself. But anybody else digging us thinks we're young kids but not you so much 'cause you're dark but I'm light complexioned so I look like a young kid all the time. But I never thought of that as—anything to worry about . . . (pause). Well I'll tell you this, I don't feel very intelligent . . . any more, at times, for a long time . . . When I get high I feel—* * * I can't write it, I can't say, I can't, ah, you know, I mean, I'm—I can't get anything personally done like that. (VC, 128–29)

By the second night, Jack makes his strategy apparent. Between the first and second nights, he has prepared a typescript of the initial session. When he shows it to Cody, Cody tells him,

See . . . I know you got the recorder on, if I . . . ah, even if I . . . (*laughing*) damn him
JACK. Huh?
CODY. No, that's awright, man, that makes it alright, I just didn't want to have you under any false impressions, you know, YOU know what I'm saying, you know because like if I acted as if I didn't know it was on, why then, there'd be an ambiguity of . . . of, ah, ulterial motives, drooning, you know, 'cause you'd be in the process of getting me around under the machine and I'd be in the process of, ah, saying, like for example, the reading of the manuscript, see, wal, hmm, wait a minute—I lost it (*laughing*) (VC, 131–32)

Duluoz then interrogates Cody about the transcript while

the machine records the proceedings which in turn may be processed, studied, and serve as the text for a further encounter.

JACK. Then I remembered this, "demurely downward look"
CODY. I seem to remember that myself
JACK. Although it wasn't really
CODY. No
JACK. It was *my* idea
CODY. Yeah
JACK. About the look you had
CODY. Well yeah . . . it was kind of a—
JACK. But it apparently wasn't . . . what you were really doing . . .
CODY. That's what it really amounts to, though
JACK. Why, because lookit . . . the talk is far way from demure . . .
CODY. Well, the reason for the *demure* is . . .any approach to the words like, as I remember like what I said . . . here, ah, "I can't get it down," for example, you know, "I can't get it down"—Well, I approached that very terribly * * * you know, and even as I say it it sounds awful, then also it sounds like struggling to get it down, and also sounds like whatever approach a young kid would, ah, approach with definite talk of getting it down, or in other words it might be an idealist who is no longer idealistic, and so he no longer wants to talk about ideals, y'know, and he doesn't want to, you understand what I'm *sayin'* though don't you . . . And, so—that's what I say when I say "I can't get it down," and then . . . "two minutes"—but you picked up on that, of all the different things I was sayin, and so you said, "But you don't *have* to get it down," you know, that's what you said . . . and so the demure downward look . . . was simply in the same

217

tone and the same fashion . . . as my reaction and feeling was when I said the words "but you can't get it down" you know * * *

JACK. I thought you were being demure because when I said "You don't have to get it down" . . .

CODY. Yah?

JACK. . . . you thought it meant, ah, that I was saying . . . ah, you don't have to write, see, *I'll* write. You looked away demurely, guy's saying "I got bigger muscles than you have"

CODY. Yeah yeah, that's right, yeah. Well it wasn't— and I didn't dig it personally, I dug it, as a, like I say . . . ah, a remembrance of my own past, my own, you understand—it was all an inward thing—not outward, you understand . . . So when I looked down demurely it was the same way as . . . ah—in my own self . . . I approached a word, just like when you hear a bad word, or see a poor word, or dislike some particular phrase . . . like some guys are hungup on disliking phrases . . . you know, like for example I can remember, the Okies, in this country, especially out here in California when they say something, like instead of saying it's either one or the other, or something like that, they'll say "Man (*cough*) I was either gonna shoot that guy, or beat him up, *one!*" See, they use the word "one," one or the other they mean, see, I was either gonna do this or that * * * Well I'm sayin, like when you come to dislike that phrase, the same way here, I come to dislike any concern about talking with the facts of "I can't get it down"—meaning . . . generally, writing . . . or, whatever it is the object that—* * * I'm talking about something I no longer want to approach, or am approaching properly . . . or, what I'm, saying is, you know . . . you have certain things inside you mind . . . when you catch yourself talking some other way from . . . what the way you

want to be . . . caught talking
JACK. Yeah yeah yeah! (VC, 133–34)

The questioning, association, and further questioning is somewhat similar to analysis, with Cody on the couch and the probing Duluoz at the ready with electronic notebook.

Duluoz uses the tape recorder in hopes of uncovering and verifying the true Cody. The machine tempts Duluoz with a reality beyond the distorting concerns of his own self, but it delivers something else. The machine confronts Duluoz with its own limitations and distortions. Duluoz's experiment shows a naive faith in science. His apparatus yields data, but the data are necessarily abstract and of little use. Duluoz's question has to do with human character and human value, something the machine can not recognize and which must be supplied by the human act of interpretation. The machine can record but not reveal. Perception and understanding are not the same. And reality must be enacted and constructed even at the cost of the distortions introduced by the self. Reality is partly willed, partly creation, and the "I" cannot be dispensed with. And finally, even the "scientific" data of the tapes is compromised and ambiguous. The machine distorts by its presence. Cody and Duluoz behave differently because of it even on the first night. And Duluoz must interpret the machine even to create the partial record of the transcript.

Ironically, Cody and Duluoz are most humanly present for each other and for the reader as they mutually interpret the tape. Their interpretation quite possibly distorts, but the transcript provides a context for an exchange between them that makes the concerns of each available for the other. Duluoz, in short, possesses Cody at the moment he begins functioning with him, creating with him; at the moment, that is, when he begins to respond to Cody as a process, something emerging, and not as a state, a fixed quantity. Cody indicates his awareness of the way friends

fabricate a context for their communication when he tells
Duluoz

> now the understanding that Irwin and I had was not
> any—coming back to understanding about anything,
> but we were just—we'd been high together all of three
> days, see we'd been together and we both were still
> young enough that we would talk and talk and talk
> every minute see and naturally it builds up a big lot of
> structure that's private that you build on the way
> down, and is just an interchange of different feelings
> but not about concretely or anything, but just, you
> understand what the person means 'cause he said that
> before or something—something like he'll say "Like
> what I'm sayin so and so what I really mean is *this*"
> and so the guy'll understand either because you tell
> him or either because he picks up on the way that what
> you meant about—something when you tell it *before*
> like that something-or-other, why, he'll keep building
> up so then (laughing) around a pyramid . . . (VC,
> 139–40)

This suggests why Cody has more difficulty relating his
Texas experiences to Duluoz than in revealing the more
private and complicated set of feelings tied to
"demureness." To relate the Texas experience, Cody must
establish a "pyramid" with Duluoz and then discover a new
language appropriate to the new relationship if he is to con-
vey the old experience as anything more than abstraction.
With "demureness," though, the "pyramid" already exists.
Even though Cody and Duluoz are talking about their
uneasiness with each other and locating that uneasiness in
an abstract and arbitrary term, they are both wrestling with
it and each other in the present, and this suggests the
possibility that image, even though seemingly static, may be
more successful in catching the nature of process than nar-

rative which is seemingly dynamic. If this is the case, it may
be a factor in Kerouac's sense of finally locating the action
of his fiction in the process of recording and speculating
about images, locating it finally in "the world of raging action and folly and also of gentle sweetness seen through the
keyhole of [Ti Jean's] eye."[26]

In effect, recalling and relating an experience outside of
context, outside of present human process and concern,
abstracts it in the same way the machine abstracts voice.
Cody tells Duluoz,

> what it actually was, was a recalling right now on my
> part, a recalling of me having either told about or
> thought about the bed concretely before, see, so
> therefore I, all I did now was re—go back to that
> memory and bring up a little rehash of, ah, pertinent
> things, as far as I can remember, in little structure line,
> a skeletonized thing of the—what I thought earlier,
> and that's what one does you know, you know when
> you go back and remember about a thing that you
> clearly thought out and went around before, you know
> what I'm sayin, the second or third or fourth time you
> tell about it or say anything like that why it comes out
> different and it becomes more and more modified . . .
> (VC, 145)

And yet Duluoz's fascination with memory is clear in the
sketches. Duluoz and Cody are fascinated with memory but
mistrust simple repetition. Rather, the memory must be
recreated, performed. It must be shaped to its present audience, its present context. Duluoz may be more aware of this
distinction than Cody. Certainly Kerouac seems to be. As
the taping continues over a period of days, Duluoz and
Cody gradually build up their own "pyramid" of understanding, their own "structure." And by the end of the
process, they actually begin performing their pasts for each

other with something like the excitement in *On the Road* when Sal and Dean share "IT" as they recount childhood fantasies in the travel bureau car on their way from San Francisco to Denver. And whenever Cody seems to be losing his sense of flow and context, Duluoz is ready to reaffirm and revitalize Cody's sense of "understandings."

> CODY. . . . we would sit there and drink beer—you know that little bar the Marion Inn—
> JACK. Marion Street
> CODY. Yeah Marion, that's right, the little bar up there at Park, Seventeenth and Marion, Park Avenue also, it's a three-way intersection
> JACK. I know that bar
> CODY. Yeah, and, so we sat—well that bar also has a lot of other happenings and meanings to me which I won't go into now, I mean 'cause they're more a-ah, different type of thing, but at any rate—
> JACK. I got unconnectedly drunk in there one time (*a lie*)
> CODY. Yeah. Well I did too—I got so drunk in there that . . . Val would have to go home and I'd lay in the grass, beside the bar there, and * * * (VC, 217–18)

Duluoz's "lie" is in a completely different spirit than his earlier manipulative questioning. And even when Cody breaks off his narrative altogether out of fear that he is rehashing,

> I told this story before but I mean, it's what I'm talking about when you tell the same thing over then you just, ah, say the words as they come to your mind that you've already thought about before and so there's nothing—you're not pleased by it, no one else is, but the fact is, there's no, ah, spontaneity, or anything, there's no, ah, pleasure, you see, because you're-

—you're just rehashing old subjects see? (VC, 232)

The momentum of performance is strong enough that a whispered comment from Cody's wife is sufficient to restart the narrative.

Reading the tapes, particularly the earliest section, it is easy to lose patience with them. If at times the first two sections of *Visions of Cody* seem almost too dense, the tapes seem slack. But the more one grasps their design, the more the turnings and pauses reveal. They are not a total success, and the strategy is not one Kerouac bothered to repeat. However, the tapes do have a function. They slow the pace but also build the "pyramid" between reader and writer. They demonstrate to Duluoz that the creative and interpretive force of the imagination cannot be subjugated by an objective reality. And the tapes show that Duluoz's belief in the self as an object, a thing, or essence must be modified by his recognition that the self is more properly an activity, a becoming which may be governed by a constant shaping logic but a logic knowable only in action since it exists only through action.

Duluoz's discovery that the self is not static, not an object, may be the most important feature of the tapes. Character is no longer something the writer represents but something he enacts, something dynamic and in flux. This means there is no absolute and final Cody for Duluoz to know. There is only Cody as he functions in a given "pyramid" of connections and actions that includes Duluoz. There is only Cody as Duluoz is able to "vision" him, and this Cody may itself be multiple, be visions of Cody that involve both glimpses and imaginative projections of Cody. Also, if character does not exist, Kerouac is ultimately relieved of his anxiety about assuming the role of narrator since he too is in flux, knowable only in terms of what he becomes and continues to become. He can talk of himself without the silly melodrama that is apparent in the book

Duluoz claims to be writing and which he reads to Cody at one point.

> JACK. First sentence of the book (*reads*) I TAKE MY FRIENDS TOO SERIOUSLY
> CODY. Great, great, great * * *
> JACK. (flutes) Awright. Second sentence (*reads*) EITHER THAT OR I DON'T LIKE LIFE ANY MORE * * *
> CODY. Man . . . that's the way to write
> JACK. (*reading*) I MEAN *MY* LIFE OF COURSE
> CODY. That's right. That's your third sentence
> JACK. Third sentence (*flutes*) IT'S TOO GUILTY NOW TO HAVE FUN . . . (*waits, flutes, no reaction*) IF I HAVE TO MAKE A MATURE ADJUSTMENT TO A FUNLESS LIFE I THINK I'D RATHER COMMIT SUICIDE
> CODY. Jesus Christ, whoo! (VC, 151–52)

It means Duluoz need not struggle to avoid admitting to the role of narrator as in the first section, nor struggle to maintain it as he does in the second. He can drop these ploys and openly admit the actions of the eye and the imagination. He can admit that he, like Cody, is more than a single self, a single vision.

Kerouac nowhere in the book claims this freedom explicitly, but he enacts it in the fourth section, the "Imitation of the Tape." In this section, he adopts a "voice" that does not imply the "authority" of a narrator or the static identity of a character, but implies instead a self-creating (selves-creating?) and performing "I" balanced between inner and outer worlds. And the ending of "The Tape" anticipates this "voice" of the fourth section. The last voice of the tape transcripts is neither Jack nor Cody. The editor simply notes that Duluoz is "*gone*," and after a "*long silence*," the machine records a "COLORED REVIVAL MEETING ON

RADIO" (VC, 246). This voice is both singular and plural. The call and response of preacher, individuals in the congregation, and the congregation as a whole transform the various voices into a collective voice just as the group's celebration creates a communal identity. For the duration of the "MEETING," the congregation is able to express itself with the logic of a single performance while still admitting its multiplicity. It is, in a sense, self-contained and self-sustaining but open to the outside world. The congregation is able to project the inner world onto the outer and acknowledge the outer world because it is both performer and audience in a single entity. The transcript of the revival meeting suggests that the "I" of the Spontaneous Prose writer can express himself with the logic of a single performance while at the same time admitting and preserving his multiplicity and freedom to evolve. The transcript also suggests that the spontaneous writer can overcome his separation from the reader by recognizing his, the writer's status as both performer and audience. The writer's selves can enact a collective identity, a congregation of selves, which includes from the start the "pyramid" of connections necessary to make the "visions" available in a way that is neither arbitrarily and restrictively private, reductively real, nor an escapist fantasy. The revival preacher repeats the phrase "I HEARD," over and over in the passage, and Duluoz seems to hear as well and sense a rebirth of his own creative energy and faith in himself. Duluoz, along with preacher and congregation, seems suddenly to believe "A MAN MAY DO WORKS" (VC, 246) and rejoice in his "SURANCE!" (VC, 247)

The call and response quality of the revival meeting is apparent from the beginning of the "Imitation of the Tape."

COMPOSITION . . . . . . by Jackie Duluoz 6-B
"Now up yonder in Suskahooty," said Dead Eye
Dick—no, I exaggerate, his name was Black Dan—"up

yonder in Saskahoty," said Dead Eye Dick Black Dan, "we used to catch suckers every day on Main Street down by the bank, you know the one with the red bricks, that I was standin in front of when—but you introduced (ain't that right?) me to them two suckers from Edmonton or somethin—yeh, that's right (just when you said that you reminded me—"This was in Muscadoodle, Wyo., many years ago, had a circus there, we was makin the line from around Ogallala, Nebraska, clear to the Willamette Valley—my old lady got sawdust on her dress in Ohio that year—shucks and *god-damn*, I'm gonna go to Charleston, West Virginia Saturday night, or jump in the river, *one*." But no, wait in here, don't you know I'm serious? you think I'm?—damn you, you made, you make, the most, m—I guess—but now wait a minute, till I l—but no I'll jump on in, I meant to say, w— . . . Too, there was a movie house (what? house?) around the (wah? corner?) of the Strand Theater not to be confused with hair strand, in my dreams: this perfect little B- or C-movie full of Sunday afternoon children—a dream! See? Never no hassles there, (they had a toilet. I go down to it in the dream and hang around the drink rotgut when I get too old to enjoy the picture), nothing, no hassles, I love my sweet dreams, they sustain me, I see—I see—what! Wake up to reality my boy! Howk? Signed, for today, for now—no we'll continued right along the monologo. (VC, 249–50)

This passage suggests Kerouac's sense of the stylistic implications of his tape experiment. Both revival meeting and the conversation of Jack and Cody show how much meaning can actually be carried by movement rather than by statement. And in the "Imitation," Kerouac assumes the freedom to stop and start, shift form of address, and follow out digressions while leaving what seems the primary syntactic unit dangling and uncompleted. Kerouac, here, also uses two other strategies implied by the transcripts. He poses; he assumes roles. And he plays with diction as a way of characterizing roles. Like the preacher or like Cody and Jack imitating W. C. Fields and Bull Balloon, the speaker of the "Imitation" senses that true freedom and visibility may come from a willingness to assume roles and yet treat the pose provisionally, as one of an almost infinite series of roles. And the speaker of the "Imitation" knows how much can be suggested about these poses by even the simplest verbal formula, such as the use of *"one"* as an intensifier in the passage above that echoes Cody's observation in the tapes about "Okies" in California.

In the "Imitation of the Tape," Kerouac is free to confess, mock himself, lose himself in fantasy, and indulge in puns and elaborate plays with sound. The implications of this freedom are apparent in the way the fourth section develops. Even though the jumps from confession to dream to reportage to play seem to give the section an arbitrary, fragmented quality, these jumps are part of a single performance, and the various fragments are finally connected to the whole in the same way the interjected fragments of members of the congregation are connected to the whole of the revival meeting. Here, though, instead of enacting the congregation, Duluoz or Kerouac enacts the self by bringing his various voices together into a single, though at root still multiple, presence. He recreates himself by blending his own past with the materials of his present, and the structure of the "Imitation" reflects the successive stages of this recreation. The adventurous fantasies of the child lead to a dream "movie house" that combines the "golden light" of dream, the "deeply shaded brown" of memory, and the "misty gray" of the actual world and where children "all squeezed together" are diggin the perfect cowboy B-movie" (VC, 251). This is replaced by the older child's sense of separation from his parents:

> AT THIS POINT IN HIS DREAM DULUOZ WOKE
> UP . . . recalled that he hadn't seen his father for the
> longest of times and that possibly he must be dead just
> as real as death. "Well then," he thought, leaning on
> the boxcar down the edges of which ran the stain of his
> sperm . . . I hung myself up. (VC, 253)

This in turn is replaced by the excitement and failure of college and then the romanticized frustration of the young
writer in a passage that nostalgically refers back to *The
Town and the City*. And finally, there is the adult's fear of
the "swamp":

> but now wait, I'm not supposed to enter into this but I
> guess I might as well, now the thing that we're gonna
> talk about now is not limited to anything really specific
> and generally antecephilic, that word I looked up in
> Web—but making—it's just like Hemingway says, in
> the swamp the fishing would be more tragic . . . (VC,
> 267)

Kerouac sees the "Imitation" as a

> running consciousness stream that can be used as the
> progressing lightning chapters of a great essay about
> the wonders of the world as it continually flashes up in
> retrospect; as, for example, this night I ran cold water
> into a glass at the sink while everybody was high and
> immediately was reminded completely and perfectly of
> the cool exact waters of Pine Brook on a summer after-
> noon. (VC, 258)

And the way this "stream" expresses itself through a self
who tells us he is "speaking from a pulpit" (VC, 274) give
Kerouac a stylistic range and freedom analogous to what he
perceives in Miles Davis. Late in the fourth section while

momentarily playing the role of Cody, Duluoz comments,

Old Witchdoctor Remus Khayyam Duluoz, he just sits
and lets go another blast at the government. "War is
the health of the State." "War is Obsolete." "War is
Existentialist." "War is Nowhere." Well blow, baby,
blow! blow, world, blow! go! Yaah—shee—it!-
—Sh'cago, that's *no* town—it's th'apple, man, it's
th'apple, it's scrapple from the apple, it's *down*. And
meanwhile Miles Davis, like the sun; or the sun, like
Miles Davis, blows on with his raw little horn; the
prettiest trumpet tone since Hackett and McPartland
and at the same time, to flesh some of its fine raw
sound, some wild abstract new ideas developed around
a growing theme that started off like a tree and became
a structure of iron on which tremendous phrases can be
strung and hung and long pauses goofed, kicked along,
whaled, touched with hidden and active meanings; to
come in, then, like a sweet tenor and blow the super-
finest, is mowd enow. I love Miles Davis because, send
in your penny postcard. "Goof the people," Little Zagg
used to say, serious as a hill, "just go along and upset
the people," hills bills . . . (VC, 323–24)

This same flexibility is apparent in the way Kerouac mixes
materials in his reinvention of the self and also in the way he
inserts two seemingly self-contained set pieces into his
"imitation" of the tape. "Joan Rawshanks in the Fog" and
the "Visions of Cody" are not part of the "imitation" itself,
but they are preceded and followed by material from the
"imitation," and they represent specific roles or voices that
emerge from and return to the substratum of the "imitation" of the tape, the "consciousness stream" of dialogue
among selves.

"Joan Rawshanks in the Fog" and the "Visions of Cody"
show Kerouac's sense of how the discontinuous surface of

"Imitation of the Tape," itself inspired by the fluctuating voice of the tapes, allows a sense of performance where the performer is aware of his place in the final construction. The voice can be both a "performing self" and a "constructing self." Once the imaginative self is enacted in the initial segment, Kerouac can then use his new sense of voice to annex new material. He can move from the "imitation" where the inner world dominates, to "Joan Rawshanks in the Fog" where the outer world dominates, to the "visions" where inner and outer intersect; and this intersection defines Cody's symbolic significance, allowing Duluoz to repossess his experiences of Cody "on the road" which leads, in the fifth section, to a "telling of the voyages again . . . each in one breath" (VC, 337). This new awareness by the performer in the fourth section helps bridge the gap between reader and writer found earlier in the book where, in the first section, the private self of the "eye" cannot admit the existence of the reader and where, in the second section, the narrator cannot admit to the reader his private stake in what he narrates. Here in the "Imitation of the Tape," "Joan Rawshanks in the Fog," and the "Visions of Cody," the voice can alternate freely between exposition and direct discussions of a thematic or personal nature without being pompous, self-conscious, or maudlin. In the congregation of selves, each voice is independent and private at the same time that it defines and is defined by the collectivity, and the "preacher," likewise, is not a narrator in the traditional sense but a private self acting out the duties of an office which derives its authority not from the self's identity, but from the collectivity that "elects" him or a divine energy beyond either self or collectivity.

The collective voice that emerges from the "imitation" of the tape enables Kerouac for the first time to record his experiences in the actual or outside world while simultaneously addressing their effect on the inner world. In "Joan Rawshanks in the Fog," Duluoz is scriptwriter, director, technician, bit player, star, audience, and critic, and his awareness of the process of film as a metaphor for writing provides the key for structuring performances into a single text. The significance of the collective voice is particularly apparent when the "Visions of Cody" are compared to *On the Road*. In the "Preamble" to the "Visions," Duluoz explains that Cody's significance for him dates from "the summer of 1949" when Duluoz decides to leave Denver and join Cody in San Francisco. Kerouac then relates the same scenes used earlier in *On the Road* where Duluoz, like Sal, wanders about Denver romanticizing the ghetto life of "soft sweet old Denver" to explain and justify his loneliness. But in *Visions of Cody*, Kerouac is able to suggest the sentimentality of this response without being sentimental in his expression of it. He can admit the sentimental naiveté, value it, undercut it, and place it in context:

> I had just suddenly realized (I had just seen a very successful young American off on a plane, an executive he was) that nothing in the world matters; not even success in America but just void and emptiness awaits the career of the soul of a man. I walked across a giant plain from the airfield, of course all Denver's a plain; I was a sad red speck on the face of the earth; I was also a beat hitch-hiker that nobody was giving rides to except one poor Negro soldier who tried to be nice to me when I asked him hep questions about Five Points and Denver niggertown and he didn't know, not being involved in a white man's preoccupations about what colored life must be. I came to the streets of Denver in their infinitely soft, sweet and delightful August evening; dusk it was, I say, purple, with shacks in soft alleys, and many lawns . . . (VC, 292)

For Duluoz, Denver marks the realization that his image of the adult and outside world is unsupportable fantasy, and this calls into question the vitality associated with the child and the imagination. Duluoz's recognition of the falseness of the child's narcissistic sense of self-sufficiency, and Duluoz's feeling that the "general brownness" of the world of the productive adult must become his "salvation," turn his thoughts to Cody because Duluoz has perceived Cody as proof that the child can survive into the world of the adult. For Duluoz, Cody's childlike purity and imaginative energy is signified by his status of "angel" and Duluoz's "lost brother," and Cody's adult assurance and stability is signified by his skill as a workman and his willing assumption of the role of father. Cody also represents for Duluoz "America, all of America as it has been conceptualized in my brain" (VC, 297).

Duluoz's fascination with the image of Cody is clearest in the vision of Cody and the Three Stooges. Here Duluoz projects an image of child and adult, play and work, isolation and shared experience that can only be American in its use of "Democratic" materials and its freedom from convention. As Duluoz and Cody are on their way to "the railyards where we worked," they begin talking of the Three Stooges:

> Nothing, only bright California gloom and propriety . . . whiteness and everything busy, official, let's say Californian, no spitting, no grabbing your balls, you're at the carven arches of a great white temple of commercial travel in America, if you're going to blank your cigar do it on the sly up your asshole or in the sand behind the vine . . . but really—when it came into Cody's head to imitate the stagger of the Stooges, and he did it wild, crazy, yelling in the sidewalk right there by the arches and by hurrying executives, I had a vision of him which at first (manifold as it is!) was swamped by the idea that this was one hell of a wild unexpected twist in my suppositions about how he might now in his later years feel . . . I saw his (again) rosy flushing

face exuding heat and joy, his eyes popping in the hard exercise of staggering . . . I saw his whole life . . . .

Supposing the Three Stooges were real? (and so I saw them spring into being at the side of Cody in the street right there front of the Station, Curly, Moe, and Larry . . . Moe the leader, mopish, mowbry, mope-mouthed, mealy, mad, hanking, making the others quake . . . they do muckle and moan and pull and mop about like I told you in an underground hell of their own invention, they are involved and alive, they go haggling down the street at each other's hair, socking remonstrating, falling, getting up, flailing, as the red sun sails—So supposing the Three Stooges were real and like Cody and me were going to work, only they forget about that, and tragically mistaken and inter-allied, begin pasting and cuffing each other at the employment office desk as clerks stare; supposing in real gray day and not the gray day of movies and all those afternoons we spent looking at them in hooky or officially on Sundays . . . by now they've learned not only how to master the style of the blows but the sym-bol and acceptance of them also, as though inured in their souls and of course long ago in their bodies, to buffetings and crashings in the rixy gloom of Thirties movies and B short subjects . . . and seriously Cody talking about them, telling me, at the creamy Station, under palms or suggestions thereof, his huge rosy face bent over the time and the thing like a sun, in the great day—So then I knew that long ago when the mist was raw Cody saw the Three Stooges, maybe he just stood outside a pawnshop, or hardware store, or in that perennial poolhall door but maybe more likely on the pavings of the city under tragic rainy telephone poles, and thought of the Three Stooges, suddenly realiz-ing—that life is strange and the Three Stooges exist—(VC, 303–6)

The Three Stooges, like Cody, remain childlike as they function in the adult world. Like Cody, they are comic, a source of vitality; and like Cody, tragic, an image of the cost of maintaining the perspective of the child. Cody's willingness to act out his "goofs" keeps the child alive even though it may do little to resolve the conflict between the child's creative impulse and the structuring force of adult society.

"Supposing" and spontaneous celebration may have much to be said for them if the alternative is despair, however. Duluoz underscores this by following the vision of Cody and the Stooges with a quote from T.S. Eliot. Eliot's statement is implicitly a criticism of the vision, and Kerouac presents it in order to refute it.

"Obviously, an image which is immediately and unintentionally ridiculous is merely a fancy."—T.S. Eliot *Selected Essays, 1917–1932*, Harcourt, Brace and Company, 383 Madison Avenue, New York 17, New York, Fifth Printing, June 1942, when little Cody Pomeray was sixteen, and was just beginning to learn the things that would eventually lead him through the mazes of the mind growing to all kinds of realizations that when a thing is ridiculous it is subject to laughter and reprisal, and may be cast away like an old turd in front of the pearly old pigs of the sty, a thing gone dead. There were no images springing up in the brain of Cody Pomeray that were repugnant to him at their outset. They were all beautiful. There was a clarity and pureness in his mind. Someday he would realize that it was necessary to go back and get it . . . But there was nothing ridiculous, there were no images immediately and sensationally ridiculous; it was just a matter of believing in his own soul; it's just a matter of loving your own life, loving the story of your own life, loving the dreams in your sleep as parts of your life, as

little children do and Cody did, loving the soul of man
. . . (VC, 306–7)

In a sense, Cody himself is a "ridiculous" image, but ridiculous in the same way as a Great Gatsby, and Kerouac here
insists on his prerogative to invest Cody with a significance
Cody might not have objectively in the same way that Cody
invests the Stooges with significance. Cody enacted by
Duluoz and the Stooges enacted by Cody both take on
qualities and importance they do not have objectively.

Duluoz's conviction that the Stooges "exist," that the vision is real, is a rebirth of the imagination and the world of
the child that died in Denver, but it is also a death. This
renewed sense of vision admits not only the real joy of vision, but the real suffering and failure of those who choose
to live on the margins of society to preserve freedom of action and imagination. Duluoz's double sense of the positive
reality of vision and the negative reality of its cost is behind
the conflicting views of Cody in the section of "visions."
Cody is both the redemptive image Duluoz projects, a
figure that contains the split between inner and outer, child
and adult; and a figure who exists in time, victimized by the
very conflict Duluoz imagines him to overcome.

Duluoz's "Visions of Cody" provide him with a key to
understanding his fascination with Cody. They counter his
firsthand experience of Cody at the time of the tapes to
enable him to recognize clearly the distinction between the
actual and the symbolic Cody, and they reveal that his
allegiance to the symbolic Cody is tied to the implied unity
of inner and outer worlds. This recognition provides the impulse for the narrative of the final section. It shows Duluoz
that all of his experiences with Cody and their travels
together have been motivated by Duluoz's paradoxical sense
of Cody, and this, in effect, shows these experiences to
Duluoz from a new angle and allows him "spontaneously"
to reperform and rediscover them. The energy this

discovery releases is itself a kind of rebirth, but the discovery is also a kind of death in that it reveals the failure of the trips ever to resolve the conflicts that motivated them and implies as well that these conflicts cannot be resolved. Kerouac evokes this simultaneously positive and negative quality of the "visions" and their relation to the narrative of the trips in the image that closes the fourth section:

> Things have a deceiving look of peacefulness, the beast is actually ready to leap—lookout— . . . The thing to do is put the quietus on the road . . . God, please direct me in this—The telling of the voyages again, for the very beginning; that is, immediately after this. The Voyages are told each in one breath, as is your own, to foreshadow that or this rearshadows *that, one*! (VC, 336–37)

The "beast about to jump" and putting the "quietus on the road" suggest a positive breaking out of the conflicts of the "visions" in search of resolution, but the source of the image of "the beast" in Henry James's "The Beast in the Jungle" gives the passage an insidious undertone. In the James story, the protagonist steadfastly refuses "experience" in order to remain ready for the encounter that will distinguish his life from other lives, only to discover at the end that he is the butt of his own unintended joke. His distinction is to be the man who has not lived, and the leap of the beast in his imagination is his recognition of his own death within life.

Implicitly at least, the major issues of *Visions of Cody* are all established and explored by the end of the fourth section. The "Imitation of the Tape" delineates an approach to voice that resolves the earlier experiments and questions. "Joan Rawshanks in the Fog" puts this voice to work and establishes a model for the construction of the text, while further clarifying the relationship of the writer's imaginative act to the text and to his experience. And the "Visions of Cody" establish the symbolic significance of Cody and the relationship of the Cody that Duluoz creates to the Cody he encounters in his actual experience. The final narrative section simply puts these elements together and into motion. It reinforces and focuses what the rest of the novel has developed in a more digressive and fragmentary manner, and the effect of this is to verify to Duluoz the unity of his experience, to justify to Kerouac his exploration of the means of fiction, and to define for the reader the unity and direction of the novel as a whole.

The narrative of the final section repeats many of the details and most of the incidents from parts two, three, four, and five of *On the Road*, but the effect is markedly different. Sal tells his story. In *Visions of Cody*, Duluoz meditates on his story, and the difference is precisely that between traditional fiction as Kerouac understood it and Spontaneous Prose as he shows it developing in the process of composing *Visions of Cody*. Sal is a narrator who is also a character in the book. He relates his story from a perspective where the nature and boundaries of the fictional world are known and fixed from the outset. Duluoz is a voice, in effect a writer discovering the coherence of his experience as he unfolds it. Sal is, as Cody might put it, "rehashing," while Duluoz is writing "from jewel center of interest in subject of image at *moment* of writing,"[27] as he has located it in his "Visions of Cody."

In *Visions of Cody*, Duluoz often seems to be rushing through the events of the trips as if making a quick survey of his data, his footage, in order to locate the key images which can then be explored at length. Even though a story is being told, the real action occurs in the sketching of the key images. The descriptions of Duluoz's first encounter with Cody discussed earlier is a case in point. When Sal describes Dean, he moves through the details relatively quickly in

237

order to go on and explain what happened that first night. Duluoz, though, only vaguely remembers what happened. Instead, he treats the impression Cody made on him as the real event, as the experience to be recovered and interpreted. Duluoz's sense that the incidents of the trips are subordinate to the images that derive from them grows stronger as the section progresses. When Duluoz recounts Cody's surprise Christmas visit to North Carolina, where Duluoz is spending the holiday with relatives, he centers on the way Cody assumes control of Duluoz's records and record player:

> There was something frantic in the air anyway Christmas 1948—I had "The Hunt" Dexter Gordon and Wardell Gray cutting each other with tenors, I had four of the sides blowing them good and loud in the little white house in the country when Cody drew up . . . he immediately played my record, but louder than I had ever dared . . . Cody wanted his jazz powerful, simple, like the early swing of Coleman Hawkins and Chu Berry; my mother, sister, others, great troops of somber relatives of the South with the great faces of Civil War generals and frontier (matriarchs)—Oh goddam—(making the mistake of following a bum story line already written)—(VC, 346-47)

Kerouac's complaint is not with anything he has written in *On the Road* or elsewhere, but with the "story line" acted out by Cody, himself, and the others in the experience itself, and the way his sense of following it interferes with his ability to "digress freely" to the more significant "truth" of the scene contained in the image of how Cody listens to jazz.

Less than ten pages after the scene in North Carolina, Duluoz has reached a point where he seems to want to find out just how much of a digression from the action he can, in

238

fact, get away with, without having things break down altogether. Ostensibly, Duluoz is relating Cody's response to the meddling of the wife of a former poolroom buddy. Cody complains that Helen Johnson's "nose is too long," just as Dean did with Dorothy Johnson:

> "trouble with Helen," Cody said out of the corner of his mouth, rasping like those Texas Okie farmboys but now big old farmbulls with tufty beards and booze on the floor of the car, having just snuck from their chores to go brawl in drinking fields, loose disconnected necks hanging surly heads into the black of a boozy old Oklahoma Buick made crack and matter dust by forlorn interminable storms and drought clouds searing the harvest the souls of juicy men, hunglipped, booze shining on their *gueles*, their mugs, pugs, mouths, like gleaming starlight in the rainy night, "Which way is it to Houston?" the driver's asking me, having just forced me to the side of the road in the rainblind to ask this counsel, this direction, and Cody and Joanna asleep in the backseat; just at the last minute I swung the Hudson over as the head-on lights showed they weren't simply on the wrong side of the road but head-on; "Which way to Houston?"; the tremendous rainy darkness splattering all Texas around, the dim view of just edges of muddy plowed fields, gulches, sand bars, bushes, whistling thin trees hidden in a solidwall right over, the wilderness enow of all tragic present rain, drenching; swung the car, luckily onto sand level, got out, woke Cody, Joanna handled the wheel, we pushed our backs to bumper with hair in our eye, and mud in our teeth; took all morning to dry and drove on. Just like that, Cody rasped it, "her *nose* is too long." (VC, 354)

The digression is actually an account of an incident from

Duluoz's and Cody's travels that is related in *On the Road*, but the event is used here with no regard for its chronology. It is simply a way to illustrate Cody's pose and the texture of his voice even to the point of obscuring Cody's complaint about Helen Johnson. By the time Duluoz and Cody reach Denver on their second trip together, the action has come to take place almost entirely in the imagery, and the incidents themselves are reduced to brief, nearly parenthetical comments:

Between Salt Lake and Denver lies the mystery of the soul of Cody. Here he was born, there he was raised; the apex of the raw wild space between that nameless place with an eagle on a shrouded mineshaft pole, in the northwest corner, in raw pines, the thing there first was about Colorado, Utah territory, the great grayday of the wild West, the grim reminder like Russia, the powerful rugged earth and souls of Colorado, that land; . . . the Dillinger voids of crosscountry . . . the mighty mountain wall Berthoud stood black and bleak in a Gibraltarean shroud in the clouds; a Gate. Uprushed that, we did; rolled on in, tongued a pass, dropped pines on our left (a mile) and scared clay on our right from protuberant roadcliffs, like the ones children draw in cartoons; the Rocky Mountains of Cody's birth consequence and youthful girl-parties in hot cars in the bye and bye. It was suddenly hot Denver again, flat pancake in the sea-floor plain. His growing up town, the Chicago of his despairs, in this town he made neons twinkle on themselves like they belonged to Toledo, he rendered Denver, he was the wildhaired Cody Pomeray of his own city—hurrying along the wall there, with a strange key in his hand and a girl waiting for him in a car.

This was when Cody stole those cars and raised Cain with dust and idiots, that—

We got hungup in Denver and had to move on for
various reasons . . . (VC, 364)

This and a few more details replace what is one of the
longer sequences of On the Road.

In On the Road there is also, finally, a split between the
world of image and the world of action. Sal comes to
distinguish between Dean as a symbol of America and Dean
as he actually exists with his confusions and sufferings. But
in Visions of Cody, Duluoz comes to understand this split
more fully, and this allows him to deal with the final trip to
Mexico in a way that Sal can not. In On the Road, Sal comes
to understand the split between image and action as a split
between the unity of the culture as it exists symbolically,
and the individual's actual fragmentary and contradictory
experience of the culture. For Sal, the climactic recognition
of this occurs in the Detroit movie house at the point when
the idealized marriage of comrades is disintegrating under
the double stress of physical exhaustion and the comrades'
increasing awareness of the actual limits of American space.
The trip to Mexico allows Sal to grasp more fully the distinction between Dean as a symbol of the culture and an ordinary person within it; but, even though the trip is billed as
the final and ultimate trip, it does not significantly extend
the issues beyond what has already been established in
Detroit. Dean's seeming awareness of his own mythic implications and his inability to enact them in the gesture of
giving away his watch to the Indian girls adds for Sal a
tragic dimension to Dean he would not otherwise have, and
triggers the elegiac passage that closes the book, but the effect of the Mexico trip and closing elegy, in spite of their
beauty and energy, is to move On the Road perilously close
to anticlimax. At the least, the Mexico trip blurs and
obscures Sal's confrontation in the Detroit movie house with
the myth of the East, the myth of the West, and his dream
of the womb of rubbish.

In effect, in *On the Road* Sal must free himself from the illusory comfort of existing within the false unity of the symbolic realm, and accept the conflict of living in the actual world. Sal's recognition of the existence of conflicting myths, of East versus West and dark versus light, points the way for him finally to free himself of his naive and shallow optimism. In *Visions of Cody*, though, the situation is reversed. In coming to perceive the dichotomy of actual experience in the outer world and imagined experience in the inner world, Duluoz also comes to perceive that the symbolic projections of the imagination can themselves involve and contain conflict. Duluoz's "visions" of Cody embody the conflict between child and adult, between controlling time and being controlled by it, and Duluoz can face up to implications of the "visions" or attempt to ignore them in the same way he can face up to or gloss over the nature of the actual Cody. In fact, for Duluoz to ignore his "visions of Cody" and deal only with the Cody of the actual world would be in *Visions of Cody* the unacceptable and illusory simplification. Duluoz cannot avoid his "visions" if he is to account adequately for behavior such as Cody's spontaneous imitation of the Stooges. The imagination must project the depth of the inner world to encompass such a gesture or the gesture must be ignored. For Duluoz, the challenge is to recognize and accept the way the perspective of the child and adult complicate each other.

In *Visions of Cody*, Duluoz's consideration of the trip to Mexico is the occasion for the final integration of the conflict between the redeeming genius of the child and the death-bound experience of the adult that overlays all of *Visions of Cody* and the work on *On the Road*. Duluoz's ability to reunite the worlds of image and action is visible in the emergence of his sense that these two realms involve two fundamentally different experiences of time. From the perspective of the outer world, time is experienced as sequence, as the process that leads through the limiting experiences of causes and effects to the final limitation of death. From the perspective of the inner world, time is experienced as permanence, as the imagination's ability to take the images of its experiences and turn them into constructs that exist on their own terms freed from the sense of flux. Retrospectively, in terms of his Mexico experiences with Cody, Duluoz recognizes that these two aspects of time are interdependent, and this recognition finally allows Duluoz to attain the paradoxical goal that has been behind his studies of Cody: he is able both to free himself from his fascination with Cody, and to experience a sense of union with Cody.

The importance of time to Cody and Duluoz's concern with him is indicated in the first of the "visions" in the fourth section. Cody talks about "Time . . . all the time" (VC, 296). And Duluoz in his "vision" sees Cody as a "strange angel from the other side . . . of Time" (VC, 296). Duluoz can only approach this Cody in a manner "like bop, . . . getting to it indirectly and too late but completely from every angle except the angle we all don't know . . ." (VC, 296). Kerouac does not state what this last angle is, but the implication is that it too is "Time." In this "vision," Duluoz sees Cody as someone able to ignore or transcend time, and this is also the case in Duluoz's narration of his first two trips with Cody. The young Cody acts without regard for time or cost while Duluoz is oppressed by it. Narrating his early experiences with Cody makes Duluoz sense how quickly so much has passed. He is troubled by the way "time flies" and cuts him off from his past, even though his sense of the experiences as they happened involved a sense of time as slow and empty rather than fast and fleeting. He complains that "events do drag" (VC, 347), and then breaks off in exasperation and attempts to put the matter of time aside by admitting the obvious and then dismissing it: . . . "but time passed—I won't even mention time again" (VC, 347). Duluoz, though, cannot ignore the matter this easily. On the next page, he talks about the trip east with Cody as "the unrolling of a mighty thread of accomplished moments" (VC, 348), almost as a jazz player might talk of filling the moments that the melody presents to him. And it is a short step from this sense of time as significant moments to a sense of time as a space to be inhabited. As Duluoz and Cody listen to "Frisco jazz," Duluoz suddenly realizes what Cody has meant in his attempt to explain "IT," and Duluoz exclaims about himself, the horn player, and audience, "all realize they've got *it*, *IT*, they're in time and alive together and everything's alright, don't worry about nothing, *I love you*, whooee—" VC, 352). Duluoz's sense of "being alive in time and alive together" is a glimpse of how time exists for Cody in his ability to ignore the consequences of its passage, but the ecstasy of "IT" is momentary for Duluoz. The next day he sees Cody "standing like a ghost in the tenement doorway" as he waits for Duluoz and the others "to make up our minds about TIME . . ." (VC, 357). Cody's attempt to ignore time makes him a source of renewal to those around him, "the SAINT" (VC, 356), but also a "wild example and purgation for us to learn and not have to go through . . ." (VC, 357).

Cody attempts to "know time" and escape it by ignoring it. This is a source of his power and aura, but Duluoz recognizes that Cody's escape is futile. Sal's perception of this point about Dean in *On the Road* is what leads Sal to give in to time and to accept the world of the adult as primary, but in *Visions of Cody* Duluoz discovers that Cody's battle with time is based on a misperception about its nature and one's relation to it. In recalling the progress of the Mexico trip and how Cody's eventual defeat grows more and more obvious, Duluoz realizes, "It was in Mexico that I think—he couldn't go much further, nobody could, find an answer, the time pressed in— . . ." (VC, 387). And the pressure leads Cody to decide to return to his wife, attempt to adjust to marriage, and accept the passage of time. When

The Redeeming Eye

Duluoz next sees Cody some months later in New York, the comrades are no longer "on speaking terms" but are "old buddies of the night grown sad, just like once exuberant basketball quintets meeting in sad maturity hotel lobbies with their shamefaced wives (in Worcester)" (VC, 395). Duluoz recognizes Cody's surrender to time in Mexico even more clearly in retrospect, and with it Duluoz recognizes as well the law of sequence and the passage of time that can lead only to death. But in retrospect Duluoz also recognizes that the trip continues to have a kind of permanence in his memory and even a kind of life in his imagination, and these actions of the inner world impart value to the fragmentary experience of the outer world. In other words, Duluoz discovers that the imagination, rather than simply providing an escape from time as sequence, has its own sense of time that moves freely without regard to actual chronology, and in the process fixes and discovers the relationships that create meaning. In this sense, Duluoz's recognition retrospectively of Cody's submission to time as sequence and Duluoz's own acceptance of it is simultaneously Duluoz's transcendence of time. It is, as with the image of the beast about to jump, a death into time and a simultaneous faith in one's freedom from time.

Duluoz's paradoxical renewal through the recognition of his death is apparent in the explanation for "writing this book" that Kerouac interpolates into the narrative:

> I'm writing this book because we're all going to die—in the loneliness of my life, my father dead, my brother dead, my mother faraway, my sister and my wife far away, nothing here but my own tragic hands that once were guarded by a world, a sweet attention, that now are left to guide and disappear their own way into the common dark of all our death, sleeping in me raw bed, alone and stupid: with just this one pride and consolation: my heart broke in the general despair and

opened up inwards to the Lord, I made a supplication
in this dream. (VC, 368)

And as Duluoz details the Mexico trip, the nature of the
heart's rebirth becomes clearer and clearer:

we all stumbled out into raggedy American realities
from the dream of jazz: all our truths are at night, are
to be found in the night, on land or sea. Pray for the
safety of the mind; find a justification for yourself in
the past only; romanticize yourself into nights. What is
the truth? You can't communicate with any other being, forever. Cody is so lost in his private—being—if I
were God I'd have the word, Cody is my friend and he
is doomed as I am doomed. (VC, 373)

Duluoz is by no means overly optimistic here, but he
realizes what one can create out of the past and one's own
despair, out of the recognition that "Time" is both "the
purest and cheapest form of doom" (VC, 374).

Duluoz's recognition of death and the redeeming vitality
of the imagination leads him to a sense of a principle of
vitality in the world itself that seems to offer itself in com-
pensation for his own individual mortality. Freed from his
concern over self and concern for the nature of Cody,
Duluoz is able to see the road as an image of "promise" and
"power."

THE MAD ROAD, lonely, leading around the bend
into openings of space towards the horizon Wasatch
snows promised us in the vision of the West, spine
heights at the world's end, coast of blue Pacific starry
night . . . The raw cut, the drag, the butte, the star,
the draw, the sunflower in the grass-orangebutted west
lands of Arcadia, forlorn sands of the isolate earth,
dewy exposures to infinity in black space, home of the

rattlesnake and the gopher . . . the level of the world, low and flat: the charging restless mute unvoiced road keening in a seizure of tarpaulin power into the route . . . Pencil traceries of our faintest wish in the travel of the horizon merged . . . "dotting immensity" the crazed voyager of the lone automobile presses forth his eager insignificance in noseplates and licenses into the vast promise of life . . . (VC, 391)

This sense of power in the world at large sweeping everything up into a whole that transcends the individual's concern with pleasure and pain and replacing it with a sense of wonder is perhaps even clearer in this sentence that Kerouac cited as the best in the book:

Lester [Young] is just like the river, the river starts in near Butte, Montana in frozen snow caps (Three Forks) and meanders on down across states and entire territorial areas of dun bleak land with hawthorn crackling in the sleet, picks up rivers at Bismarck, Omaha and St. Louis just north, another at Kay-ro, another in Arkansas, Tennessee, comes deluging on New Orleans with muddy news from the land and a roar of subterranean excitement that is like the vibration of the entire land sucked of its gut in mad midnight, fevered, hot, the big mudhole rank clawpole old frogular pawed-soul titanic Mississippi from the North, full of wires, cold wood and horn. (VC, 392)

By the end of *Visions of Cody*, Duluoz realizes that the "road is over" for him and Cody, but Duluoz's compensating sense of a life beyond any personal endings is suggested clearly in the Whitman-like imagery of grass in the penultimate sketch:

A BLADE OF GRASS waves in the sunny Frisco after-

noon, it grows out through the greasy rocks of the
railroad track of Cody; tars smell, are warm, railroad
executives who once were vain young clerks with
slicked hair and pressed pants now roll themselves bag-
gily along Track 66 . . . Someone yells and wakes me
up from an afternoon dream . . . Geometric visual
perspective vanishments of double rails into crowded
sooty distance with backs of boxcars reposant by vague
"storage" signs on meaningful buildings—figures crossing the general raily layout in a flat void of activity—afternoons: unused cabooses waiting for the
evening shapeup so they can go be backbroken and
jawboned and rattle-headed in a mountain brake—
rickety orange baggage cars sitting in sun-glints soft-
ened by smoke—those track-grasses waving like hair
here, making green carpets there for the rails' flow to
points unseen—Smoke works up from over by the
roundhouses and general Out Our Way toolshops
where at evening overalls all greased are hung up on
nails by lockers in brown sad light . . . the light of
Cody, work, night, fatherhood, gloom . . . at these
final rails that deadhead hump of greeneries, the holy
Coast is done, the holy road is over.
Tonight the stars'll be out. (VC, 396–97)

In these descriptions, Duluoz discovers a life and
significance not located in Cody, either the actual Cody or
the Cody of Duluoz's "visions."

Ironically, this sense of separation from Cody both in the
actual experience of Mexico and the renewed life of the
imagination leads in Visions of Cody's final passage to the
merging with Cody that Duluoz has sought throughout the
book.

YET, AND YES, THERE'S CODY POMERAY . . .
cuttin to work. A new day is dawning in the blue

lagoon east over Oakland there, a silent sad Coast Line truck trailer sits by a skeletal shed in the soft dawn of all America marching to this last land, this receiving California . . . the dew is on the road again . . . I'm a fool, the new day rises on the world and on my foolish life: I'm a fool, I loved the blue dawns over racetracks and made a bet Ioway was sweet like its name, my heart went out to lonely sounds in the misty springtime night of wild sweet America in her powers, the wetness on the wire fence bugled me to belief, I stood on sand-piles with an open soul, I not only accept loss forever, I am made of loss—I am made of Cody too— . . . .

Adios, you who watched the sun go down, at the rail, by my side, smiling—

Adios, King. (VC, 397–98)

One can only know another self imaginatively, and if the imagination is not seen as real and able to contain the conflicts of life, then one cannot know another self and may not be real oneself. Again, the comparison to *On the Road* is helpful. *Visions of Cody* ends with a lament for Cody just as *On the Road* ends with a lament for Dean, but the relationship of this final passage to the book as a whole is quite different in the two. In *On the Road*, Sal laments his loss of Dean and Dean's falling away from his earlier heroic stature. In *Visions of Cody*, Duluoz's lament is also a celebration. In recognizing Cody's human frailty and accepting his own, Duluoz makes possible the union of comrades. It may only exist in the imagination and in retrospect, but it still yields a sense of renewal which, in spite of being imaginary and inner, makes life in the outer world continue to be possible. In his final "adios," Duluoz's acceptance of loss means giving up the child's false sense of omnipotence, but his faith in the creative act means that he can admit the reality of adult experience without being trapped totally by the inevitability of time as sequence.

249

Two final matters need comment. First, Duluoz's discovery of the imagination as a sustaining counterpoint to the cost of living is achieved at a certain cost. It functions only retrospectively. To turn the imagination on the future is to escape into fantasy. Rather than recovering the aspect of the child relevant to the adult, this kind of fantasy is a tempting but destructive regression. Duluoz must accept a future of loss and losses in the real world as the price for the compensating gesture of romanticizing his past, of synthesizing the whole world that exists but is graspable only in the inner world. And this means that Duluoz must also forsake his hope for identity. The world of the adult offers only a final dissolution of identity, and the inner world cannot be restricted to a single identity if it is to perform its redemption. Identity is static. Instead, Duluoz must content himself with a sense of the self as multiple and ever changing. He must adapt himself to projecting a series of selves, each doomed to destruction in the experience of the adult and each recreated and located in the past by the child. This is what happens in *Visions of Cody*, and in this view, the self is defined by the intersection of the images one holds of oneself in the past and the as yet unknown and yet shaping dissolutions to come. In this view, the self remains finally in part unknowable, an experience of uncertainty, but Duluoz and Kerouac come to accept this as the necessary price of the inner world's vitality.

This problem of self leads to the second matter. If the self is finally seen as ever changing, there can be no final style that will express it. Kerouac's sense of how to imitate the discontinuous surface of the tape in the final sections of *Visions of Cody* seems at least in part a reflection of this. The voice discovers itself as it proceeds and that discovery need not be a single, continuous process. It can even be willful and solipsistic: "I CAN GOOF if I want to, that's the name of this chapter; but far from talking, but to con—The thing I couldn't get over then was the magnificence of the actual car trip . . ." (VC, 348). But this approach can lead finally to such randomness that style ceases to function altogether. Kerouac's sense of how to solve this problem while retaining his freedom to follow the inspiration of performance can be seen in "Essentials of Spontaneous Prose" and any of the passages in *Visions of Cody* that derive from sketching, including the "Imitation of the Tape." In order to write with the freedom that comes from utilizing the discontinuous nature of speech as the tape reveals it, the language itself must have an impulsion, a forward moving energy phrase to phrase, that creates a sense of momentum and the illusion that a story is being managed. In "Essentials of Spontaneous Prose," Kerouac places great emphasis on the need for a phrasing that is jazzlike, rhythmic, and *"runs in time* and to laws of *time."*

Perhaps partly because of the public misperception of Kerouac and *On the Road* in the fifties, perhaps because *On the Road* is less fully developed in its sense of the relation of style to voice to self, and perhaps partly because Kerouac is so successful in creating a momentum to his language, readers have not generally noticed his complex sense of the function of the conversational twists and turns of voice. Kerouac's style initially seems easily imitated in its colloquial nature and sense of liberty with normal syntax, and one suspects that the style of much of the so-called New Journalism as it has developed from Tom Wolfe may take a simplistic sense of Kerouac's "confessional" voice as its stylistic model. However, nothing in Wolfe matches the intensity and precision of the best passages in *Visions of Cody*. It should also be noted that nothing in *On the Road* is as successful as the best of *Visions of Cody* either.

One wonders whether, if *Visions of Cody* had been published before *On the Road* and followed by the book Kerouac wrote next, *Doctor Sax*, rather by the much later and much shallower *Dharma Bums*, Kerouac might not have been regarded much more seriously than he has been.

251

Perhaps he might be considered more often as an important experimenter. Perhaps *Visions of Cody* might be considered along with Burroughs's *Naked Lunch*, a book partly modeled on *Visions of Cody*. At the least, Kerouac would no longer be the "King of the Beatniks," and Kerouac's better books, *Doctor Sax*, *The Subterraneans*, and *Desolation Angels* might have received some of the attention they, along with *Visions of Cody*, greatly deserve. Books like *The Subterraneans* do not show the same extreme degree of having been constructed from separate pieces, nor the extreme self-consciousness about the nature of language and the imagination as *Visions of Cody*, but they assume the possibilities that Kerouac won for himself in *Visions of Cody*. They develop from the same interplay of performance and construction, and they explore the interaction of the inner and outer worlds and the problems of isolation and ecstasy that Kerouac sensed in some way to be the conflicting heritage of his America, an America to which he stood witness in some twenty books and which he has expressed with more intensity and force of linguistic invention than any other of our novelists who have emerged since the Second World War. Perhaps the time has come to recognize this talent and this achievement. A book like *Visions of Cody* has flaws, certainly, but perhaps the time will come when we recognize that such flaws of excess, of extreme emotional and aesthetic risk taking, have often marked the important and vital writers in the American tradition.

Notes

Introduction

1. John Clellon Holmes, *Nothing More to Declare* (New York: E. P. Dutton & Co., 1967), p. 68.

2. Kerouac's biographers particularly have tended to treat *On the Road* as simplistically autobiographical. Norman Podhoretz's "The Know-Nothing Bohemians" is typical, though more vehement, in its sense of *On the Road* as popular culture in a reductive sense. It is reprinted both in *A Casebook on the Beat*, ed. Thomas Parkinson (New York: Thomas Y. Crowell Company, 1961), and in Jack Kerouac, *On the Road*, ed. Scott Donaldson (New York: Penguin Books, 1979). Allen Ginsberg's various comments on Kerouac and *On the Road* and Gilbert Millstein's review of *On the Road*, 5 September 1957 in the *New York Times* are a fair representation of those who see Kerouac almost more as a religious figure than as a writer.

Chapter One

1. Kerouac to Ginsberg, May 1952. This letter and most of Kerouac's letters to Ginsberg are located in the Ginsberg Archive of Columbia University's Butler Library. Subsequent references to material from this collection will be noted in the text by the names of the author and recipient, the date, and the abbreviation "GA."

2. Jack Kerouac, *Excerpts from Visions of Cody* (New York: New Directions, 1960), p. 5.

253

3. Jack Kerouac, *On the Road* (New York: The Viking Press, 1957), p. 3. Subsequent references to *On the Road* will be noted in the text by the abbreviation "OR" and page number.

4. Henry Murray, introduction to *Pierre or, The Ambiguities*, by Herman Melville (New York: Hendricks House, 1949), p. xx.

5. Carole Gottleib Vopat, "Jack Kerouac's *On the Road*: A Reevaluation," *Midwest Quarterly*, summer 1973, reprinted in *On the Road*, ed. Donaldson, pp. 437–38.

6. Kerouac's tendency to look at people in terms of literary classifications is suggested in the interviews with Kerouac's friends collected as *Jack's Book*. In one, Allan Temko, portrayed as Roland Major in *On the Road*, says, "I could never understand the fascination these people held for Kerouac, except that he thought they were America, and they are. He always thought that Neal [Cassady] was Huck Finn and Bob Burford [portrayed as Ray Rawlins in *On the Road*] was smart-aleck Tom Sawyer." Barry Gifford and Lawrence Lee, *Jack's Book: An Oral Biography of Jack Kerouac* (New York: St. Martin's Press, 1978), p. 64.

7. The dream of the "Shrouded Traveler" is shared by Kerouac and Allen Ginsburg. It appears in Ginsberg's "The Shrouded Stranger," in *Empty Mirrors: Early Poems* (New York: Totem/Corinth Books, 1961), pp. 60–62. The figure of the Shrouded Traveler is also incorporated into the figure of Doctor Sax in Kerouac's *Doctor Sax*. Whether the dream originated with Ginsberg or with Kerouac is unclear, but it seems to have passed back and forth between them as a collective possession as they shared and analyzed each other's dreams and writings in these years.

8. Greil Marcus, *Mystery Train: Images of America in Rock 'n' Roll Music* (New York: E. P. Dutton & Co., 1976), pp. 15–16.

9. Kerouac to Holmes, 24 June 1949, in *The Beat Diary*, ed. Arthur and Kit Knight (California, Pa.: TUVOTI, 1977), p. 128.

10. See John Tytell, *Naked Angels: The Lives and Literature of the Beat Generation* (New York: McGraw-Hill Book Co., 1976); idem, "Revisions of Kerouac," *Partisan Review* 40, no. 2 (1973); Aaron Latham, *New York Times Book Review*, (28 January 1973; 7); Leslie Fiedler, "The Eye of Innocence," in *The Collected Essays of Leslie Fiedler*, vol. 1 (New York: Stein and Day, 1971); and John P. Sisk, "Beatniks and Tradition," reprinted in *A Casebook on the Beat*, ed. Parkinson.

11. Fiedler, "The Eye of Innocence," pp. 491–92.

12. Herman Melville, *Moby Dick*, ed. Harrison Hayford and Hershell Parker (New York: W. W. Norton & Co., 1967), p. 165.

13. Kerouac, *On the Road*, Viking Compass edition (New York: The Viking Press, 1959), back cover.

14. F. Scott Fitzgerald, *The Great Gatsby* (New York: Charles Scribner's Sons, 1925), p. 182.

15. Richard Brautigan, *Trout Fishing in America* (New York: Dell Publishing Co., 1972), p. 116.

16. Kerouac to Holmes, 11–12 July 1950, letter held by Holmes.

Chapter Two

1. Kerouac to Holmes, 14 July 1951. This letter is held by Holmes and partly reproduced in his *Nothing More to Declare*, p. 80.

2. Ann Charters, *A Bibliography of Works by Jack Kerouac* (New York: The Phoenix Book Shop, 1967) p. 4.

3. John Clellon Holmes, *Nothing More to Declare* (New York: E. P. Dutton and Co., 1967) p. 77.

4. Quoted in Ann Charters, *Kerouac: A Biography* (San Francisco: Straight Arrow Books, 1973), p. 61.

5. Jack Kerouac, *The Vanity of Duluoz* (New York: Coward-McCann, 1968), p. 273.

6. Kerouac, *Vanity of Duluoz*, p. 278.

7. Quoted in Charters, *Kerouac: A Biography*, p. 66.

8. Ted Berrigan, "The Art of Fiction XLI: Jack Kerouac," in *Writers at Work: The Paris Review Interviews, Fourth Series*, ed. George Plimpton (New York: The Viking Press, 1976), reprinted in Jack Kerouac, *On the Road*, ed. Scott Donaldson (New York: Penguin Books, 1979), p. 555.

9. Charters, *Bibliography*, p. 3.

10. Charters, *Kerouac: A Biography*, p. 67.

11. Holmes to author, 19 September 1973. See also Barry Gifford and Lawrence Lee, *Jack's Book: An Oral Biography of Jack Kerouac* (New York: St. Martin's Press, 1978), pp. 76–77.

12. Kerouac's essay, "Lewis and Dreiser: Two Visions of American Life" is held by Elbert Lenrow, Kerouac's instructor in the course.

13. Jack Kerouac, "Journal during first stages of 'On the Road,'November 29, 1948–April 23, 1949." The journal is held by the Humanities Research Center of the University of Texas, Austin. The quotation is from opening entry, 29 November 1948, and is also reproduced in *A Creative Century* (Austin: Humanities Research Center, The University of Texas, 1964), pp. 35–36. Subsequent references to the journal are noted in the text by the abbreviation "WJ" and the date of entry; subsequent references to material from the Humanities Research Center are noted in the text by the abbreviation "H.R.C."

14. Charters, *Kerouac: A Biography*, p. 101.

15. Charters, *Bibliography*, p. 27, and OR, pp. 171–72.

16. Kerouac's 28 June 1949 letter to Lenrow and Kerouac's 5 July 1949 letter to Ginsberg both contain the excerpt from the work in progress. The letter to Ginsberg is in the Ginsberg Archive, and Lenrow holds the letter addressed to him.

17. Holmes to the author in conversation, July 1976.

18. Kerouac to Lucey, 14 January 1950, manuscript collection, Butler Library, Columbia University.

19. Holmes to the author, 19 September 1973.

20. Jack Kerouac, *Pic* (New York: Grove Press, 1971), p. 110. Subseuent references to *Pic* will be noted in the text by *"Pic"* and the page number.

21. Gifford and Lee, *Jack's Book*, p. 159.

22. Charters, *Bibliography*, p. 6.

23. A copy of Kerouac's Guggenheim application statement from 1951 is held by Elbert Lenrow.

24. Holmes, *Nothing More to Declare*, p. 78.

25. Holmes to author, 19 September 1973.

26. Charters, *Bibliography*, pp. 13–14.

27. WJ, 29 November 1948, and in *A Creative Century*, pp. 35–36.

28. Kerouac to Holmes, 17 or 15 or 21 June 1952, in *The Beat Diary*, ed. Arthur and Kit Knight (California, Pa.: TUVOTI, 1977), p. 137.

29. Holmes to author, 19 September 1973.

30. Holmes, *Nothing More to Declare*, p. 78.

31. Charters, *Bibliography*, pp. 5–6.

32. Charters, *Kerouac: A Biography*, pp. 133–34.

33. Ibid., p. 130.

34. Cassady to Kerouac, 30 December 1950, H.R.C. Also, Charters, *Kerouac: A Biography*, pp. 128–29.

35. Holmes to author, 19 September 1973.

36. Holmes, *Nothing More to Declare*, p. 78.

37. Holmes to Kerouac, 27 December 1950, *The Beat Diary*, ed. Arthur and Kit Knight, pp. 121–23.

38. Charters, *Kerouac: A Biography*, p. 134.

39. Holmes in conversation with author, 19 May 1975; and also "John Clellon Holmes: Interview," in *The Beat Journey*, ed. Arthur and Kit Knight (California, Pa.: TUVOTI, 1978), pp. 151–52

40. Ginsberg to Cassady, 7 May 1951, in *As Ever: The Collected Correspondence of Allen Ginsberg and Neal Cassady* (Berkeley, Calif.: Creative Arts Book Company, 1977), pp. 106–07.

41. Charters, *Kerouac: A Biography*, pp. 134–35.

42. Kerouac to Holmes, 14 July 1951. The letter is held by Holmes.

43. Holmes, *Nothing More to Declare*, p. 80.

44. Holmes to author, 19 September 1973.

45. Jack Kerouac, *Excerpts from Visions of Cody* (New York: New Directions, 1960), p. 5.

46. Kerouac to Holmes, 3 June 1952. This letter is held by Holmes and partly reproduced in *Nothing More to Declare*, p. 81.

47. Holmes, *Nothing More to Declare*, p. 81.

48. Jack Kerouac, "Essentials of Spontaneous Prose," *Evergreen Review*, 2, no. 5 (summer 1958). reprinted in *A Casebook on the Beat*, ed. Thomas Parkinson (New York: Thomas Y. Crowell, 1961), p. 65, and in idem, *On the Road*, ed. Scott Donaldson (New York: Penguin Books, 1979), p. 531.

49. Kerouac, "Essentials of Spontaneous Prose," p. 531.

50. Jack Kerouac, *Visions of Cody* (New York: McGraw-Hill Book Company, 1972), p. 338. Subsequent references to *Visions of Cody* will be noted in the text by the abbreviation "VC" and the page number.

51. Kerouac, "Essentials of Spontaneous Prose," pp. 531–32.

52. Ibid., p. 532.

53. Thomas Clark, "The Allen Ginsberg Interview," *The Paris Review*, no. 37 (winter 1967): 24, reprinted in *Writers at Work: The Paris Review Interviews, Third Series*, ed. George Plimpton (New York: Penguin Books, 1967).

54. Clark, "The Ginsberg Interview," pp. 27–28.

55. *A Creative Century*, p. 36.

56. Kerouac, *Excerpts from Visions of Cody*, p. 5.

57. Allen Ginsberg, "Cezanne's Comedy," Ginsberg Archive, Columbia University. This is a rough draft of a paper that may or may not have been completed.

58. Burroughs to Kerouac, 18 September 1950, manuscript collection, Butler Library, Columbia University.

59. Allen Ginsberg, *The Visions of the Great Rememberer* (Amherst, Mass.: Mulch Press, 1974), p. 10.

60. Burroughs to Kerouac, 12 February 1955, manuscript collection, Butler Library, Columbia University.

61. Kerouac to Holmes, 12 March 1952, letter held by Holmes.

62. Kerouac to Holmes, 3 June 1952. This letter is held by Holmes.

63. See John Tytell, *Naked Angels: The Lives and Literature of the*

Beat Generation (New York: McGraw-Hill Book Co., 1976), p. 69; idem, "Revisions of Kerouac," *Partisan Review*, 40, no. 2 (1973): 302; Aaron Latham, *New York Times Book Review*, 28 January 1973, p. 42; and Charters, *Kerouac: A Biography*, chapter 13.

64. Ginsberg to Cassady, 3 July 1952, *As Ever*, p. 130.

65. Jack Kerouac, "The Origins of the Beat Generation," *Playboy* 6, no. 6 (June 1959), reprinted in *A Casebook on the Beat*, p. 74.

66. Kerouac to Lenrow, 13 January 1958, letter held by Lenrow.

67. Holmes to author in conversation, July 1976.

Chapter Three

1. Ted Berrigan, "The Art of Fiction XLI: Jack Kerouac," in *Writers at Work: The Paris Review Interviews, Fourth Series*, ed. George Plimpton (New York: Viking Press, 1976), p. 555.

2. Kerouac's fascination with sound as a key to character is readily apparent in his letter of 24 June 1949 to Holmes. This letter is reproduced in *The Beat Diary*, ed. Arthur and Kit Knight (California, Pa.: TUVOTI, 1977), pp. 131–33.

3. I would like to thank Max A. Zimmer for a chance to read his essay on Jack Kerouac's "October in the Railroad Earth," which he drafted while a graduate student at the University of Utah.

4. Warren Tallman, "Kerouac's Sound," *The Tamarack Review* (spring 1959), reprinted in *On the Road*, ed. Scott Donaldson (New York: Penguin Books, 1979), and in *A Casebook on the Beat*, ed. Thomas Parkinson (New York: Thomas Y. Crowell Company, 1961).

5. John Clellon Holmes, "An Interview by John Tytell," in *The Beat Book*, ed. Arthur and Glee Knight (California, Pa.: TUVOTI, 1974), p. 41. My sense of this issue is supplemented by conversations with Holmes, July 1976.

6. Kerouac to Holmes, 3 June 1952. This letter held by Holmes.

7. Kerouac to Holmes, 17 or 15 or 21 June, 1952, in *The Beat Diary*, p. 138.

8. Conversations with Robert Creeley, fall 1974.

9. John Clellon Holmes, *Nothing More to Declare*, (New York: E. P. Dutton and Co., 1967), p. 102.

10. Claude-Edmonde Magny, *The Age of the American Novel: The Film Aesthetic of Fiction Between the Two Wars*, trans. Eleanor Hockman (New York: Frederick Ungar Publishing Co., 1972), p. 37.

11. Ibid., 29–30.

12. Ibid., pp. 92 and 22.

13. Ibid., p. 92.

14. Jack Kerouac, *Excerpts from Visions of Cody* (New York: New Directions, 1960), p. 5.

15. Magny, *The Age*, p. 73.

16. Ibid., p. 69.

17. Kerouac, *Excerpts from Visions of Cody*, p. 5.

18. Ezra Pound, quoted by Daniel Pearlman, *The Barb of Time* (New York: Oxford University Press, 1969), p. 20.

19. Jack Kerouac, "Manhattan Sketches," In *The Moderns*, ed. LeRoi Jones (New York: Corinth Books, 1963), pp. 266–77.

20. Ralph Waldo Emerson, "Nature," in *Selections from Ralph Waldo Emerson*, ed. Stephen E. Whicher (Boston: Houghton Mifflin Co., The Riverside Press, 1957), p. 24.

21. Ibid., p. 24.

22. Jacques Derrida, "Structure, Sign, and Play in the Discourse of the Human Sciences," in *The Structuralist Controversy*, ed. Richard Macksey and Eugenio Donato (Baltimore: The Johns Hopkins Press, 1972), p. 248. Readers familiar with Derrida will notice that the terms of my argument as a whole do not reflect Derrida's terms. My use of "presence" marks me as needlessly retrograde, but I am using it here, I think, in a way that does not violate Derrida's observations about the possibilities of structure defined not by a "center" but by the tension created by the interplay of the various elements of the structure. My use of Derrida here as a way of distinguishing between *On the Road* and *Visions of Cody* parallels the distinction Roland Barthes makes between "work" and "text." Barthes writes in "From Work to Text," (in his *Image—Music—Text* [New York: Hill and Wang, 1977], pp. 158–59):

> The Text can be approached, experienced, in reaction to the sign. The work closes on a signified . . . . the work itself functions as a general sign and it is normal that it should represent an institutional category of the civilization of the Sign. The Text, on the contrary, practices the infinite deferment of the signified, is dilatory; its field is that of the signifier and the signifier must not be conceived of as 'the first stage of meaning', its material vestibule, but, in complete opposition to this, as its deferred action. . . . The logic regulating the Text is not comprehensive (define 'what the work means') but metonymic; the activity of associations, contiguities, carryings-over coincides with a liberation of symbolic energy (lacking it, man would die); the work—in the best of cases—is *moderately* symbolic (its symbolic runs out, comes to a halt); the Text is *radically* symbolic: *a work conceived, perceived and received in its integrally*

symbolic nature is a text. Thus is the Text restored to language; like language, it is structured but off-centered, without closure. . . .

"Essentials of Spontaneous Prose" is, in this sense of Barthes's, a polemic on behalf of writing as a praxis, as a text, and one which emerges, significantly I would think, out of Kerouac's working as a writer and not out of any particular reading of Western metaphysics except insofar as his experience of the inadequacy of the language of the work for his own moment participated in the struggle to manage books of wild form.

23. Conversations with Holmes, July 1976. See also Holmes, "An Interview."

24. Magny, *The Age*, p. 73.

25. Allen Ginsberg, "The Great Rememberer," in Jack Kerouac, *Visions of Cody* (New York: McGraw-Hill Book Company, 1972), p. viii. See also idem, *The Visions of the Great Rememberer* (Amherst, Mass.: Mulch Press, 1974), pp. 13–14.

26. Jack Kerouac, *Excerpts from Visions of Cody*, p. 5.

27. Jack Kerouac, "Essentials of Spontaneous Prose," *Evergreen Review* 2, no. 5 (summer 1958): p. 532.

Index

Action Painting, xviii, 144–47

Barthes, Roland, 259–60
Beat Generation, the, xvi, 90
Blake, William, 116
Bunyan, John, *Pilgrim's Progress*, 89–90
Burford, Bob, 254
Burroughs, William, 83–84, 129, 132–33, 139, 148; *Junkie*, 119, 134; *Naked Lunch*, 134, 252

Cassady, LuAnne (Mrs. Neal Cassady), 5
Cassady, Neal: as character in Kerouac's fiction, 87, 91, 108, 116–18, 120; Denver youth of, 136–37; *The First Third*, 109, 137; Ginsberg and, 83; Joan Anderson letter, 108–9; Kerouac and, 97–98, 135, 138–39, 254
Celine, Louis-Ferdinand, 166
Charters, Ann, *Kerouac*, 81, 86, 98, 104, 106, 108–9, 112
Columbia University, Kerouac at, 78–79
Crawford, Joan, 157
Creeley, Robert, xviii, 154

Derrida, Jacques, 188
Dreiser, Theodore, 83–85
Duncan, Robert, xviii

Eliot, T. S., 234
Emerson, Ralph Waldo, 46, 49, 184–85, 200
Everitt, Rae, 115–17

Factualism (Kerouac), 85–86. *See*

also Burroughs, William
Fiedler, Leslie, 52–54
Film, 47–51, 155–66, 212
Fitzgerald, F. Scott, xvi; *The Great Gatsby*, 8–10, 73, 235
Frank, Robert, 107
Freud, Sigmund, 133

Ginsberg, Allen, 84, 86, 254; *The Gates of Wrath*, 133; *Howl and Other Poems*, 133; interest in Cezanne, 130–33, 183; Kerouac and, 83, 119, 133, 134; views on *On the Road*, 114–16, 253; views on *Visions of Cody*, 139–40, 212
Giroux, Robert, 112, 113, 114, 115
Goodman, Benny, 110–11

Hawkins, Coleman, 146
Hemingway, Ernest, 172; *The Sun Also Rises*, 114
Holmes, John Clellon: *The Horn*, 106–7, 114; Kerouac and, 108, 114, 140, 141–42; on composition of *On the Road*, 83, 99, 105, 110, 113, 122; on composition of *Visions of Cody*, 147; on Kerouac, xv, 8, 78, 96; the scroll experiment and, 111–12

James, Henry, "The Beast in the Jungle," 236
Jazz, 146, 160, 176, 185, 189, 244
Joyce, James, 166; *Ulysses*, 168

Kazin, Alfred, 95
Kerouac, Gabrielle Mémêre Levesque (Kerouac's mother), 101, 113, 115, 120

261